Advance Praise for
UP FROM WALL STREET
and Thomas Croft

"The recent, absurd boom and bust in alternatives has exposed the destruction—for investors and society alike—wrought by short-term speculative investment and high-flying financial engineering. *Up from Wall Street* is a good new field guide that offers a path towards, and real life examples of, investments in private equity and real estate that create value for investors by producing sustainable wealth for businesses, their employees, and communities alike. It offers a vision of what alternative investments in well-functioning markets are meant to support."

—**David Wood**, Director, The Institute for Responsible Investment, Boston College Center for Corporate Citizenship, and co-author, *Handbook on Responsible Investment Across Asset Classes*, 2008

"This study captures a rising wave of progressive investment activity that will define the 'prudent investor' standard for all investors in the future. Croft demonstrates that investments that make a difference have a place in every investment portfolio; they produce solid returns and measurable outcomes for the environment, job creation, community and economic development. The book's examples are worth looking at today and will undoubtedly spark the creation of new investment opportunities over the coming months and years."

—**Kirsten Snow Spalding**, Ceres' California Director (formerly pension fund lawyer, labor leader and State of California Deputy Treasurer)

D0815794

"In light of the current financial crisis gripping the financial world, *Up from Wall Street* is a must read for anyone who wants to understand the linkages between the financial world and the real economy! Tom Croft provides an insightful critique of the current financial crisis and the toxic combination of greed and arrogance that has put the pensions and assets of ordinary people at risk. But this book doesn't stop there. It offers real investment alternatives that connect our hard-earned savings to investments that strengthen jobs, increase environmental sustainability, develop liveable cities, and create affordable housing. This volume provides a necessary review on how these investments are doing both in terms of their financial impacts and their ancillary benefits. Those with an interest in making sure their savings are put to work in a manner that strengthens our economy must read this volume."

—**Dr. Tessa Hebb,** author *No Small Change: Pension Funds and Corporate Engagement*, co-editor of Working Capital, and Director, Carlton Centre for Community Innovation, Carleton University, Ottawa

UP FROM WALL STREET

The Responsible
Investment Alternative

Thomas Croft

Foreword by Richard L. Trumka

COSiMO

NEW YORK

Up from Wall Street: The Responsible Investment Alternative

Copyright © 2009 by Thomas Croft

For information, address:
Cosimo, Inc.
P.O. Box 416, Old Chelsea Station
New York, NY 10011

or visit our website at:
www.cosimobooks.com

Ordering Information:

Cosimo publications are available at online bookstores. They may also be purchased for educational, business or promotional use:
- Bulk orders: special discounts are available on bulk orders for reading groups, organizations, businesses, and others. For details contact Cosimo Special Sales at the address above or at info@cosimobooks.com.
- Custom-label orders: we can prepare selected books with your cover or logo of choice. For more information, please contact Cosimo at info@cosimobooks.com.

Cover design by Lana Abrams, Nine Design
Interior design by Pamela Rice

ISBN: 978-1-60520-925-8

Cosimo aims to publish books that inspire, inform and engage readers around the world. We strive to align our editorial mission with our book production process: our books are made available through on-demand printing, an innovative new technology that enables books to be available, anywhere, anytime regardless of the size of their audiences. Cosimo, by using this on-demand technology, eliminates an artificial scarcity of publications and empowers authors to make their books widely available in the most efficient and environmentally sustainable manner.

Furthermore, we endeavor to work with printers using paper made by companies that practice and encourage sustainable forest management, while advancing best practices within the book and paper industries. We print our books on paper certified by the FSC, SFI and PEFC, whenever possible.

Table of Contents

PART TWO A FIELD GUIDE TO RESPONSIBLE CAPITAL

Acknowledgments

The author, Thomas Croft, Executive Director, Heartland Network Office of the Steel Valley Authority, thanks Teresa Ghilarducci, Irene and Bernard L. Schwartz Professor of Economic Policy Analysis and Director of the Schwartz Center for Economics Policy Analysis for her tremendous contributions as consultant and collaborator. I also want to acknowledge the able production assistance from Cindy Doolittle, Office Manager of the Steel Valley Authority and the help of Anne Zakas and Karen Manier, assistants to Dr. Ghilarducci while she was at Notre Dame University.

We are especially grateful for the generous financial support and encouragement from the Heinz Endowments and their Economic Innovation Program.

Big thanks also to Dr. Tessa Hebb, Professor David Woods, Monte Tarbox, Paul Quirk, Dr. Andrew Williams, Daniel Pedrotty, David Blitstein, John Adler and Patrick O'Meara for their huge contributions as readers. And especially to David Mackenzie, who provided able and invaluable copy editing assistance. And thanks to SVA Vice Chairman Tom Michlovic and Deputy Director Bob Value (and the SVA itself), and friends who assisted with timely ideas. Credit also goes to Amanda Procter, Project Officer, Global Union Committee on Workers' Capital (CWC), for additional thematic ideas. We also want to acknowledge Rochelle Lefkowitz and her able staff at Pro-Media Communications, Lana Abrams at NineDesign (for the cover art), and Alexander Dake, Publisher, and his team at Cosimo, Inc.

Finally, thanks for the hours of time and encouragement provided by the investment fund managers and other investment principals and friends who helped us gather our data. Through their diligent and intelligent investment work, they are providing hope and inspiration to us all, and building a better future.

Foreword

By Richard L. Trumka
President, AFL-CIO

In 1995, while serving as President of the United Mine Workers, I was invited by Leo Gerard and Tom Croft to attend a meeting at the international offices of the Steelworkers in Pittsburgh. Leo, then Secretary-Treasurer of USW, asked me to join a group that he called his "grievance committee," formed to better understand how pension fund investments affect the real economy. This "Heartland Working Group" brought together a remarkable assembly of trade unionists, economists, academics, regional development activists, and investment and political leaders from across the U.S. and Canada. Many of us were concerned about the dynamics behind continuing industrial job losses. At the time, our economy, and especially towns and cities in the industrial heartland, were still struggling from the effects of the recession.

We asked a couple of simple questions: Why is it that pension funds are obsessed with short-term profits instead of long-term strategic investments (investments that are aligned with the interests of pension beneficiaries)? And, does Wall Street operate the financial markets—using our pension funds—in ways that undermine the very workers whose savings they deploy?

The first Heartland Labor/Capital Forum came out of those grievance meetings. As the keynote speaker, I drew a line in the sand, declaring, "There is no more important challenge for the labor movement today than to stop the use of our own money from cutting our own throats." At this moment, that challenge is more important than ever.

In the last fifteen years, we've made great strides in the labor movement to enhance long-term shareholder returns through active ownership. I became the Secretary-Treasurer of the AFL-CIO during this time, and one of my first tasks was to launch the Federation's Capital Stewardship program, which organizes worker capital into an effective voice for corporate accountability and retirement security. Heartland's second great conference, which we co-sponsored, resulted in *Working Capital: The Power of Labor's Pensions*, published by Cornell University Press. This book was a product of four years of intense discussion and research and became, arguably, the most popular textbook for labor and other concerned trustees across North America. I've greatly admired the efforts of Leo and Tom and the many visionary labor leaders to re-claim workers' capital, the immense sums of money that represent the deferred wages of millions of workers across this country.

Tom's new book, *Up from Wall Street: The Responsible Investment Alternative*, picks up from *Working Capital* and catalogues many of the investment lessons learned over the last four decades in the workers' capital field in the U.S. and Canada. This book is a good "field guide" as to how it all works and presents important case studies of investments in such diverse areas as advanced manufacturing, affordable and workforce housing, renewable energy, efficient transportation, and other critical sectors of the economy.

As an alternative to Wall Street excesses, the "worker-friendly" investment funds highlighted by this book have made entrepreneurial investments in companies and real estate projects where workers were treated with respect and have the choice of joining a union. This book focuses on these innovative investment programs inaugurated by union and public pension funds, and tracks the performance of the investors.

Up from Wall Street argues that investing in "economically-targeted investments," undertaken within the guiding ethos of responsible investment, allows capital stewards to truly serve beneficiaries and their communities over the long run. Moreover, Tom demonstrates that Economically-Targeted Investments (ETIs) offer pension and other trust funds and endowments an opportunity to join the burgeoning responsible capital movement, investing in environmentally-friendly firms, buildings, products, and processes, while strengthening portfolio diversification. These investors also encourage employees to become true stakeholders, owning part of the company or participating in the long-term governance of the corporation.

The book then shines a torch on some of the dreadful mistakes and damaging mis-investments made by Wall Street, which cost us dearly. It offers some valuable lessons as to how not to repeat those financial blunders.

Leo and many other imaginative leaders have now branched into new terrains with their notable advocacy work in "blue-green" alliances-coalitions among union, environmental, and community activists to push for renewable energy and green jobs. Tom's book suggests a path as to how to invest in those jobs, sometimes in partnerships with other private and public investors. In other words, he provides a field guide on how to get there.

The book concludes by looking to the future and to what has been called the third wave of responsible investment. This third wave approach, pioneered by the leaders of our own construction trusts, combines enterprise and real estate strategies to drive real economic revitalization efforts in our communities. It suggests that capital stewards explore new opportunities such as co-investing, cross-border investing, new government partnerships, and green projects. If we pool our investments, we can achieve results on a larger scale.

I am hoping that many of my friends, and many of the people who pushed for change in Washington, D.C. and across North America, will read this book. It is a helpful and hopeful manual that shows we have the capacity to rebuild our economy and infrastructure, reinvigorate our cities, and create those highly-anticipated green jobs of the future.

PART ONE

Pensions and Institutional Trust Funds and the Long-Term Investment Landscape

Introduction

The last of the Civil War widows, a young woman who in the 1920s married an elderly veteran of the war, received a pension into the early part of the 21st century.[1] No other anecdote can make it clearer that pensions are promises to people that involve long periods of time—in this case, a time period that spanned three centuries. Yet, as the business-led Conference Board and many economists and other policy leaders have warned, the pension fund investments that back those promises have grown increasingly short-term.[2] Too often, the managers of retirement trusts advised the funds to adopt investment strategies based on a short-term perspective and speculative projections.[3] Unfortunately, such short-sighted advice is unlikely to lead to the long-term returns on which pensions beneficiaries depend.

The market crash of 2008 has shaken many of the investment and savings trusts and institutions that we, as a society, rely on as "guaranteed." Trillions of dollars vanished due to reckless, over-levered loans and imbecilic short-term bets that failed. As working people and retirees awoke from the aftermath of the crash, they asked: Is there an alternative to the massive bets on the risky, ephemeral, and all-too-often fraudulent investment schemes—often using our savings and retirement assets—that triggered the financial market crash?

As a new administration in Washington, D.C. tries to maneuver the troubled economic landscape left behind from the Wall Street meltdown, it is asking the same question and others: Where will the money come from to rebuild our economy and infrastructure, re-invest in our cities, and create the highly anticipated green jobs of the future? How can we re-grow the economy?

The savings and assets of teachers, steelworkers, students, church members, insurance holders, and everyday people—our institutional trusts—should be managed responsibly and on a long-term foundation, guaranteeing the benefits that were promised. And they should be used in a way that doesn't harm the greater society. For instance, since pension funds are, by definition, the deferred wages of workers, there is increasing recognition that pension investments should reflect the intrinsic interests of its "owners"—working people and retirees. They should not only yield competitive financial returns but also contribute to the long-term vitality of societies, economies, and environments (and even social standards). The trustees of pensions and similar funds should know that the investments made today affect jobs and quality of life for their beneficiaries, not just because of the monetary return, but also in the quality of economic development and community livability.

This book will hopefully point the way to some promising answers to these questions. Before we get to those answers, though, America owes the rest of the world a lasting commitment to clean up our boom-and-bust addiction. We need to reconstruct the protections put in place after the 1929 crash, so arrogantly abandoned in the last quarter century. That Canada's finance systems generally avoided the kind of wipeout that hit Wall Street speaks to this country's closer adherence to finance regulation and conservative banking principles. Finally, the immense investment complex that manages our money—people's savings and assets—must be re-aligned around trust principles, capital preservation, and the sustainable growth of capital, and not subjected to un-regulated foolery. Our elected leaders and watchdogs should prosecute high-finance bank robbers (and "shadow bank" thieves) before it's too late—not after they've stolen our treasure and made billions.

Up from Wall Street: The Responsible Investment Alternative will show how *our* money can be one of the building blocks to turn the economy around. This field guide to responsible capital will also depict how people's capital has already been providing many of the crucial long-term investments that we need—in all parts of the economy—across the U.S. and Canada. And the book will show that most of these responsible capital strategies also yielded great returns on investment. Here's some of the good news in the book about what our money has accomplished:

- Creating and retaining hundreds of thousands of jobs, providing living wages and good benefits;
- Constructing thousands of affordable homes and new and renovated multi-family dwellings and commercial buildings;
- Turning around and modernizing strategic industries;
- Launching new and sustainable energy and transportation enterprises; and,
- Growing and retrofitting green buildings and, in some cases, green communities.

Our money—the assets in retirement accounts and mutual funds, insurance companies, endowments, college savings funds, etc.—actually owns a lion's share of the economy. This share has increased since 1980, and this capital literally drives markets. How much money? In the U.S., institutional investors own $24 trillion and control $11 trillion in equities, and pension funds own $9.4 trillion.[4] These trusts invest globally and are part of the giant pools of capital and institutional investments flowing to markets.

The sheer size of global pension and institutional assets, and therefore the potential role that these funds can play in influencing investment at a global level, provides a basis for greater participation by their owners in "capital stewardship." At the same time, other global trends (corporate malfeasance, soaring executive compensation, etc.) requires "active" owners to be more proactive and diligent in how and where their capital is being invested and to ensure responsible management in order to build long-term investment value.[5]

Of these assets, "workers' capital"—primarily the assets accumulated in collectively funded pools to provide retirement security—has grown tremendously, according to the Organization for Economic Cooperation and Development (OECD, Global Pension Statistics). These include workers' pension funds, retirement savings, and funds held by trade unions. In a global survey of the eleven largest workplace pensions systems in 2007, pension assets doubled in value since 1997 to more than $25 trillion. Defined benefit (DB) assets were 56% of the total, defined contribution (DC) assets the balance (for the seven largest member countries). On average, these funds owned 56% equities, 28% bonds, and 16% other assets, including those in the "alternative asset" class. The report said that pension funds were still increasing their investment in alternatives.[6]

Investing in the Wrong Alternatives

Allocating part of a pension (and similar) fund to alternative investments— such as private equity, venture capital, real estate, and hedge funds; investments that are not publicly-traded stocks and bonds—is a strategy meant to bring investments back in line with the long-term nature of the liabilities.

As we finished writing this at the end of 2008, however, many alternative investment vehicles set off alarms for their potential roles in the mortgage crisis, the financial market crash, and the new global recession, the worst since the Great Depression. The economies of the U.S. and Canada are now in a major slump, less than a decade after the last recession, the dot-com implosion, and the corporate accounting scandals. Together, those prior events severely challenged the funded levels of retirement systems in the U.S. and Canada. This new crisis has, as well.

Not long after the dot-com bubble deflated, there were dire warnings by progressive economists like Dean Baker about the dangers of new bubbles in the housing markets, and by others about the over-weighted pension investments in unregulated financial instruments. Warren Buffett, the so-called "Oracle of Omaha," expressed concerns in 2005 about the real estate bubble. And about the destabilizing effect of hedge funds on the financial markets, he said:

> There are more people [like hedge-fund managers] that go to bed at night with a hair trigger than ever before. It's an electronic herd, they can give vent to decisions that move billions and billions of dollars with the click of a key. We will have some exogenous event…There will be some kind of stampede by that herd.[7]

Other "oracles" included Nouriel Rubini, an economist at New York University, who sounded the alarm about the housing bubble and coming crash on September 7, 2006. Rubini said that:

> ...the United States was likely to face a once-in-a-lifetime housing bust, an oil shock, sharply declining consumer confidence and, ultimately, a deep recession. He laid out a bleak sequence of events: homeowners defaulting on mortgages, trillions of dollars of mortgage-backed securities unraveling worldwide and the global financial system shuddering to a halt. These developments, he went on, could cripple or destroy hedge funds, investment banks and other major financial institutions like Fannie Mae...[8]

The Trade Union Advisory Committee (TUAC) of the Organization for Economic Co-operation and Development (OECD) had long urged caution about the damages by hedge and mega-buyout funds to global markets and corporations and their drag on growth and innovation in the economy. TUAC issued this statement on the financial bailouts:

> The light regulatory approach that has prevailed in the past decade has nurtured a culture of excessive leveraging among financial institutions. This was favored by lightly regulated entities such as hedge funds and private equity, but also by main street investment banking groups which are not subject to the same prudential rules than deposit banks. The toxic effect of leveraging was amplified by the financial "innovation" of the originate-and-distribute model of securitization of debt: bad debt was traded under the guise of "structured products."[9]

As we witnessed the catastrophic events of the fall of 2008, it became clear that the worst-case scenarios came true. And those hair-trigger hedge managers invested—and lost—huge sums of people's capital and retirement trusts in the process. But how did these "lightly regulated" entities become so prevalent and powerful? How can we stop the mega-LBO funds on Wall Street from using our capital to buy up good companies and then destabilize them with too much debt? And how is it that so many of these suspect vehicles served as a greased transmission belt for pension and institutional investors?

Up from Wall Street makes the case that there is a more prudent investment path than the "short-term" speculation practices that have shaken the financial markets. The purpose of this guide is to illustrate, through investment fund profiles and case studies, how the responsible investment (RI) of retirement and savings assets can be targeted to generate specific social, economic, and environmental benefits, along with financial returns. Such an "asset targeting" approach (a complement to asset managing or asset screening) is also referred to as economically-targeted investments (ETIs, Chapter 3).

This book tells the story of a group of responsible enterprise and real estate investors who are profitably investing pension and similar assets in good jobs, affordable housing, and a green future. The book shows how workers' capital, endowments, and other institutional investors, through responsible investment principles, can do well and do good at the same time. This guide profiles, in Part II, thirteen investment managers in the U.S. and Canada with over $30 billion in assets. The reported findings are very hopeful. As the drivers of an emerging "third wave" of innovative pension capital strategies (highlighted in Chapter 6), these funds are:

- Investing in advanced manufacturing and industrial enterprises, affordable and workforce housing and commercial real estate, and also in renewable energy, green construction, and other sustainable products and processes; and,
- Re-investing in urban cities, crafting planned communities and multi-use complexes that are smartly anchored by housing, commercial workplaces, public facilities, and jobs-producing firms, and connected to new energy, transportation and infrastructure hubs.

This guide offers a unique window into the work of these innovative investors, describing their organizations and investment track records, and providing investment case studies. The guide also provides a glimpse of their operating philosophies, which has often run counter to the market. In 2006, for instance, Michael Psaros of KPS Capital Partners, one of the profiled enterprise funds, was baffled by the huge ramp-up in levered mergers and acquisitions: "That leverage was being supplied by hedge funds...more interested in clocking carried interest...than recovering their capital back. So we perceived this mania, primarily in New York, in which people had basically lost their minds."[10] In 2007, one of the veteran real estate managers in this book expressed dismay at the return of the "market cowboys" to Wall Street.

Up from Wall Street is the first such public record of the progress made in this particular field, and it follows a considerable body of new literature on the advances in responsible investment inspired by the United Nations. Despite the overpowering rush by many institutional investment managers to "chase yield," these responsible fund managers chose to invest prudently in more durable enterprises, projects, and outcomes, and have done so, as it turns out, in a manner that usually yielded competitive returns. In so doing, they abided by the cardinal rule of pension stewardship: fiduciary responsibility.

This book only hints at the extent of their portfolios. In hundreds of "best practice" cases, pension funds are investing profitably in at-scale firms and projects—not only in North America, but around the world. We want to share our findings and illustrate the great promise being realized by responsible investors, and the potential to help re-shape and re-build cities and communities. We hope that the strategies and tools we've found will be useful to the professional and layperson alike.

This guide comes at a crucial moment, as there is an urgent need to rebuild the economy and the infrastructure, re-invest in cities, and find a way to capitalize new clean-tech industries and green buildings. In the midst of such economic turmoil, it is these capital stewards who may have breached a new frontier—investing in a responsible future and in a vision of the economy that's more humane and sustainable.

But before we get to the good news, we are obliged to revisit the "irresponsible" investment schemes and vehicles that fueled the recent financial crisis and prompted severe losses in the retirement and savings systems of working families and retirees.

The Uber-Financiers

In the last few years, a fleet of mega-buyout and hedge funds took the world by storm, acquiring long-established, highly regarded corporations.[11] Excessively leveraged and initially hatched on Wall Street, their conquests included prominent corporations that traditionally prioritized long-term value and good labor relations. Then, in too many cases, the mega-investors began "stripping and flipping" these firms, and/or they loaded the firms with extraordinary debt levels. Too often, the result was business failure, job loss, the loss of labor collectivity, and other negative community effects.

During this same period, large blue-chip financial houses and hedge funds gambled hundreds of billions of dollars on the housing bubble and inflated mortgage-backed securities, obscure derivatives, and instruments that re-packaged sub-prime loans. These bets were "tranched" and re-sold so many times that financial experts confessed they didn't know the extent of the colossal amount of "toxic debt" hidden in the packages.

When the party ended, a series of desperate de-leveraging events caused, literally, many runs on many banks. In the U.S., several national banks and three of our five blue-chip financial houses failed. Hedge funds, structured products, and offshore entities, thought to be the profit engines behind many of the investment houses, instead became a down elevator to rapid losses. After the world's financial system nearly seized up, the cheap and hefty debt behind the mega-buyout funds began drying up due to the resulting credit crunch. The financial collapse drained retirement funds worldwide by $4 trillion by early November 2008, according to the OECD.

Many of these Uber-Financiers, or "the New Masters of the Universe" as they were called—the incredibly wealthy investment barons of mainly New York City and Greenwich, Connecticut—were considered brilliant financial engineers and prominent community leaders. Managers and caretakers of pension and institutional funds flocked to their doorstep. But as we said earlier, their "financial engineering" models (and the resulting "financialization" of the economy) were questioned in some circles. The warnings were unheeded.

The low-interest rate seduction that led to the real estate and sub-prime boom—compounded by the spread and depth of re-packaged securities, etc.—has been more extensively documented, so this book will not focus on that part of the crisis.[12]

We instead examine the evidence of systemic risk and corporate instability in the meltdown that point directly to those "lightly regulated entities," the mega-hedge and LBO funds. As a *New York Times* chronology reminds, the first shoe to drop was the collapse in June 2007 of two Bear Stearns-owned hedge funds that had invested heavily in the subprime mortgage market. But there are many other disturbing correlations between these players and the market collapse (partly covered in Chapter Four).

The trustees of trillions of dollars in funds that are meant to care for working people need to consider the long-term interests of their beneficiaries, which, again, include the interests of their communities. While pension and other funds invariably invest in alternative pension investments to diversify their asset allocation portfolio, more often heavily weighted in stocks and bonds, there has been a disturbing tendency to "grow" risk in these sub-classes (such as hedge funds) beyond normal means.

Some observers have pinned the debacle of 2008 on these new bosses of finance capitalism (see Chapter Four). In our earlier book, *Working Capital: The Power of Labor's Pensions*, we termed this negligent and speculative investment regime, when it involved pension funds, "collateral damage" investments. What will we do if this assault on retirement security continues?

Will pension fund leaders today be able to ensure that retirees (or survivors) living into the 22nd century can trust the promise of the pension provision?

Meet the New Boss?

Behind these disturbing trends has been a new shift in corporate ownership, too often capitalized by institutional trusts, which could have huge ramifications for beneficiaries, workers, and communities. Global corporate ownership may be going through a new stage: the growth of the mega-buyout, which started with LBO funds but has continued with hedge funds. In Chapter One, we describe how the employees of six of the ten largest U.S. employers have new "bosses" as a result of this stunning new ownership shift.

It is troubling, then, that the new corporate owners—the mega-buyout and hedge funds—have been bankrolled by pension funds and institutional assets without an assessment of the long-term impact. Indeed, too many pension funds invested in these complex, fast-moving, hot-money arenas without adequate fiduciary responsibility, due diligence, or sensible safeguards against bad buyouts and privatization plots, and extreme real estate speculation.

Working families and retirees who live in the real economy have endured one speculative bubble after another. Hundreds of millions of people have suffered unnecessarily from over-exposure to systemic risk by these same unregulated finance tools and derivative schemes that were called "weapons of mass destruction" by Warren Buffett. How many institutional investment managers truly understood "quant" analysis and algo trading techniques,[13] CDOs and credit swaps, black box trading technologies?[14] Business journalists only recently began exposing the so-called "shadow banking system."[15]

When this crisis has run its course, the capital markets will most likely brew another. But, it is high time that policy leaders and the stewards and managers of our retirement and investment institutions take another look at responsible capital stewardship and other measures of prudent investment.

While there will be volumes written about the crash, this report is not about the larger question of the public equity markets, which lost an estimated $8 trillion in shareholder wealth by end November 2008. Instead, it will focus on institutional investments in the private investment world, though numerous investment instruments are now intertwined in both, like two bird's nests that are joined. So, this book will cover a small but decisive field in capital stewardship: alternative investments, the asset class in which, before the crisis, institutional investors dramatically increased their allocations.

Responsible Capital and the Right Alternatives

There is a much better way. A few astute global leaders have long urged responsible approaches to the stewardship of people's capital. They have called on investors to take into account the broader environmental, social, and governance consequences of their investment decisions (sometimes abbreviated as ESG). This investment ethic is actually a movement, launched by the United Nations, and it has been built around the UN Principles for Responsible Investment (UN-PRI). The UN-PRI campaign now counts among its adherents pension funds, labor unions, foundations, corporations, and financial institutions with over $19 trillion in assets.

One of the ways that pension funds can invest responsibly is through what are called ETIs, or Economically-Targeted Investments. ETIs seek competitive rates of return on investments that also provide "collateral benefits." These strategies are highlighted in Chapter Three/Four.

Along those lines, this book recognizes that not all alternative investments are alike. Indeed, many high-powered, market-disciplined, and competitive alternative investment funds support the conviction that well-trained workers and environmentally-sustainable technology, to take just two examples, can aid economic growth and, in the long-run, bring high risk-adjusted rates of return. However, this form of long-term investment—"responsible capital"—is marginalized in a world where investors, consultants, and managers focus on quarterly returns and too-quickly dismiss the analysis of "non-financial" factors like good jobs, affordable housing, and environmental impacts as beyond the scope of their work.[16]

This manual is different and shows that responsible investing can be profitable. *Up from Wall Street* shines a light on a baker's dozen of responsible private equity, venture capital, and real estate funds that are capitalizing on a new, longer-term vision of the economy, a vision that respects working people and prioritizes community-friendly, environmentally sustainable investments. How? The responsible funds are investing in growth strategies, not measures to solely extract value. They've invested in firms, industries, and real estate projects where workers are treated as stakeholders and offered livable wages, benefits, and training; and they are increasingly investing in green products and processes. Furthermore, as of the survey period, these investors were tracking and often beating their respective investment indexes. Their investment fields include:

- Affordable and workforce housing, commercial development, hotels, hospitals, and community facilities;
- Green buildings—new and retro-fit construction—and transit-oriented development;
- Advanced manufacturing, transportation and distribution, medical and high-tech industries;
- Renewable energy, efficient vehicles and fuels, and other clean-tech industries;
- Urban revitalization, brown-field redevelopment, and land conservation.

The funds' investment managers are innovative professionals who have designed well-developed business plans and who specifically identify themselves as having "long term" and "responsible" goals. We have found these individuals to be solid entrepreneurs with track records that sometimes stretch back almost four decades. Their fund profiles describe their investment philosophies and provide some notable examples of their investment successes. This guide will help pension trustees and other capital stewards make strong arguments that consultants and fund managers must seriously consider this rising cadre of responsible alternative investment managers.

INVESTMENT FUNDS PROFILED IN THE FIELD GUIDE

Responsible Private Equity Funds	Highlighted Case
GESD Capital Partners (San Francisco)	Golden County Foods
KPS Capital Partners, LP (New York)	Blue Ridge Paper
Landmark GCP (Boston)	Cascade Helmets
Solidarity Fund (Montreal)	Glydyne Slate
Growth Works (Vancouver)	Xantrex
The Yucaipa Companies (Los Angeles)	Pathmark

Responsible Real Estate Funds	Highlighted Case
AFL-CIO HIT/AFL-CIO BIT (Washington, DC)	Gulf Recovery Project
Amalgamated Bank, LongView ULTRA (D.C.)	The Wharf At Rivertown
The BUILD Fund (Troy, MI)	Riviera Dunes
Concert Properties (Vancouver)	Collingwood Village
The Erect Fund (Pittsburgh)	Armstrong Cork Building
MEPT Fund (Washington, DC)	The Octagon
Union Labor Life J for Jobs (Washington, DC)	Smithsonian Observatory

Why Institutional Investors Need This Book

This book includes our "A Field Guide to Responsible Capital," a survey of self-avowed "responsible" investment firms that aims to assist trustees, managers, and public and environmental policy designers in fulfilling their duties as fiduciaries of pension, endowments, and other institutional funds in the U.S. and Canada.

People who control other people's money (fiduciaries) must make decisions using commonplace, traditional financial principles. But they must also be mindful that they do not have commonplace responsibilities. High-performing fiduciaries need to know how their actions affect the interests of the owners of the funds and the stakeholders who depend on the funds. These include:

- Workers, retirees, and their families;
- Insurance holders, students, foundation stakeholders;
- Taxpayers, in the case of public sector pension funds, and consumers, in the case of private sector funds;
- And other employers who contribute to the funds—companies, governments, universities, and not-for-profit organizations.

Currently, when the trustees and managers of pensions and endowments, etc., want to find investments that will achieve long-term and sustainable returns, they often have to hire specialized consultants to get even the most basic information. Sometimes, consultants' costs are viewed as too expensive, especially for smaller trust funds. This guide will help trustees and investors by reducing the cost of obtaining information about "responsible funds," those funds that claim to maximize risk-adjusted rates of return while achieving sustainable economic development.

Managers of responsible funds have more information than is available to most investors when they make their decisions. They take into account the quality of labor relations, the impact of investment on environmental quality and sustainability, and the impact on communities; these are all clues to potential risk and profit. They aim to earn large and sustainable returns by considering factors that are missing from conventional analysis, factors that other investors ignore.

While these responsible investment managers have historically responded to longstanding market gaps to make investments in affordable housing and manufacturing enterprises, they are now paying close attention to investment opportunities in "clean-tech" industries and "green" buildings. The growing clean technology industry had become an economic driver in North America, growing to the third largest category of venture capital investment prior to the credit crunch of 2008-2009 (which may reduce capitalization sources).[17]

Up from Wall Street profiles a small cluster of responsible investment funds, reviews their habitat, range, successful investment habits, and other distinguishing characteristics. It will not do the same for the much larger universe of irresponsible mega-funds and vehicles. They have already received substantial publicity in recent months.

The Outline of this Book

Part One of this book orients the trustee in the world of alternative investments and in the burgeoning "responsible" investment field.

The first chapter describes the importance of pension fund and other institutional investors to financial markets in general, and to alternative investments in particular. It describes both the framework for pension asset allocation and the portfolios of the largest pension funds.

The second chapter reviews the strategies of "responsible" investment vehicles, especially with regard to private equity, venture capital, and real estate. It summarizes responsible investment "best practices" and surveys the growing international movements and institutions that are pioneering in this field.

The third chapter provides a primer on Economically-Targeted Investments, a tried-and-true methodology for investing pension funds responsibly, and provides legal justification as well as examples of various types of ETIs.

The fourth chapter comments more fully on the explosion of mega-buyout and hedge funds in the past few years, and registers serious concerns about these practices from corporate, governmental, and labor leaders.

The fifth chapter addresses the trustees' dilemma—how do trustees talk to the experts they hire? Capital stewards must always ask tough questions about pension and institutional funds' investment practices. They should always examine alternative investment "favorites." In other words, this chapter explains how to "talk back" to the consultants and the many other investment professionals whose purpose is to protect your investments. It's a "hands-on" guide for trustees and fiduciaries who need to be more involved in their fund's "alternative investments."

The sixth chapter describes the lessons learned from analyzing the responsible investors featured in this guide and highlights some of the most important developments and potential for future partnerships and collaborations.

Part Two then provides the "meat" of this book, "A Field Guide to Responsible Capital," our survey of over a dozen responsible private equity, venture capital, real estate and real estate-oriented fixed income funds, divided into two chapters, seven and eight. The performance information for the funds spans the 2007 to mid-2008 period.

The appendix provides a longer catalogue of investment cases and a methodology for the guide, as well as a glossary.

Caveats and a Field Alert

The thirteen investment funds profiled in our field guide represent but a handful of the responsible fund managers in the field (in the U.S and Canada). This is a growing arena, and while we have tried to provide a solid overview of a particular group of responsible investors—those capitalized in whole or part with pension assets—it was impossible to capture all of the talent and activity currently deployed.

The field of pension fund investment and alternative investments is fraught with risk. The profiles in this guide focus on largely successful investment managers. But, historically, some pension fund principals and fund managers also experienced notable failures. While success often goes unheralded, failures are broadcast widely. A few years ago, this book might have included in its profiles a large profitable private equity fund in the U.S. and a smaller, once-successful Labour-Sponsored Investment Fund in Canada. Both funds suffered significant losses; today, they are either in receivership or no longer actively investing. Another investment vehicle, a large multi-union insurance fund, experienced a disaster with one of its investment vehicles, though the larger insurance program survived. While the principals of these funds made a number of positive investments that benefitted workers over the years, in the end, investment failures came home to roost.

In a more general sense, the vintage year of an investment fund can be a strong indicator of success, and funds launched prior to a major downturn can face a stiff wind. As we know, in the case of everyday private investments, economic and market conditions (and prices and demand) can change quickly, and firms and industries that were once profitable can lose money in the blink of an eye. Real estate developers can suffer a similar fate and also be impacted by changes in interest rates and other financial shifts. Portfolio firms and projects can be mismanaged. And investment bubbles can form suddenly. There is far less transparency in the private investment universe (though extreme secrecy is now being challenged), so investment monitoring is more complicated. It can be very difficult to detect fraud (just ask the investors in Bernie Madoff's "hedge fund," a criminal Ponzi scheme).

Though there has been a slow erosion of retirement security, historically pension funds have been remarkably stable, especially since the establishment of ERISA (The Employee Retirement Income Security Act of 1974). ERISA and other laws provided more protection for beneficiaries from broken promises by employers, chronic underfunding, a few infamous instances of pension fraud and self-dealing scandals, etc. But even as this book was going to print, a new "pay-to-play" scandal had spread to several state public pension plans (allegedly involving mega-funds). In addition, a number of large state pension funds were found to have wildly over-invested in hedge funds—and paid a price—seemingly ignoring not just common sense but gravity itself. So, institutional investment boards and staff must be constantly vigilant, and

PRIVATE EQUITY/VENTURE CAPITAL FUNDS,

continues on facing page

FUND NAME DATE FOUNDED	HABITAT AND RANGE	FUND TYPE
GESD Capital Partners 1998	San Francisco Invests primarily in US	Private capital growth and buyout fund
GrowthWorks 1991	Vancouver, Toronto. Funds invest in B.C., Ontario and other provinces in Canada	Venture and private capital funds
KPS Capital Partners, LLP 1997	New York City. Invests primarily in U.S., but also in Canada, Europe.	Private equity fund focused on "special situations"
Landmark Growth Capital Partners 2002	Simsbury (CT), Boston. LGCP invested primarily in U.S.	Private equity fund growth fund
Solidarity Fund 1983	Montreal, with regional fund offices in Quebec. Invests primarily in Quebec, but can also invest in North America, etc., through subsidiaries	Venture and private capital funds
The Yucaipa Companies 1986	Los Angeles. Invests primarily in US, Canada.	Private capital growth and buy-out funds

FUND NAME DATE FOUNDED	FUND STRUCTURE	CAPITAL PARTNERS	ASSETS
GESD Capital Partners 1998	Limited Partnerships	Pension, institutional investors, private investors	Over $250 million
GrowthWorks 1991	"Retail" VC/PE Labour-Sponsored In-vestment Funds (LSIFs)	Individual investors capitalize the fund through a tax-credit savings program	C$ 900 million
KPS Capital Partners, LLP 1997	Limited Partnerships	Private investors, pension and institutional investors	$1.8 billion
Landmark Growth Capital Partners 2002	Limited Partnership	Mainly multi-employer pension funds	$78.2 million
Solidarity Fund 1983	"Retail" VC/PE Labour-Sponsored Investment Funds (LSIFs)	Individual investors capitalize the fund through a tax-credit savings program	C$7.4 billion
The Yucaipa Companies 1986	Limited Partnerships	Institutional and private investors, multi-employer and public pensions	$6 billion

FUND NAME, FOUNDED	HABITAT AND RANGE	FUND TYPE
AFL-CIO Housing Investment Trust 1965	Washington, D.C. Invests primarily in U.S.	Fixed-income fund specializing in real estate
AFL-CIO Building Investment Trust 1988	Washington, D.C. Invests primarily in U.S.	Real estate equity fund
Amalgamated Bank, Long View ULTRA 1998	Washington, D.C. Invests in U.S.	Fixed-income fund focused on real estate
The BUILD Fund of America 1999	Troy (MI). Invests primarily in the U.S. in secondary and tertiary markets	Open-end com-mingled real estate funds
Concert Properties 1983	Vancouver, Toronto and Edmonton. Invests primarily in British Columbia, Ontario and Alberta	Tax-exempt real estate investment trust
ERECT Funds 1983	Pittsburgh. Invests primarily in Western Pennsylvania, Eastern Ohio and West Virginia	Commingled real estate funds
Multi-Employer Property Trust 1982	Washington, D.C. Invests primarily in U.S.	Open-end commingled real estate equity fund
Union Labor Life Insurance Company 1977	Washington DC Invests primarily in U.S.	Open-ended commingled fixed in-come insurance company separate account

FUND NAME, FOUNDED	FUND STRUCTURE	CAPITAL PARTNERS	ASSETS
AFL-CIO Housing Investment Trust 1965	Open-end mutual fund, internally managed	Pension funds, institutional investors	$3.7 billion
AFL-CIO Building Investment Trust 1988	Bank Collective Trust, with PNC Bank as Fund Trustee and PNC Realty Investors, Inc. investment advisor	Pension funds, institutional investors	$3 billion
Amalgamated Bank, Long View ULTRA 1998	Commingled Trust (managed by Amalgamated Bank)	Pension funds, institutional investors	$1.1 billion
The BUILD Fund of America 1999	Specialty Bank Collective Trust; Investment Advisor-Labor-Mgt. Fund Ad-visors, Fund Trustee- Ameriserv Bank	Primarily multi-employer pension funds	$278.6 million
Concert Properties 1983	Tax-exempt real estate investment corporation	Canadian multi-employer and management pension funds	C$1.3 billion
ERECT Funds 1983	Specialty Bank Collective Trust; Portfolio Manager: Pen Trust Real Estate Advisory Services, Inc.; Trust agent: Ameriserv Bank	Primarily multi-employer and public pension funds	$200 million
Multi-Employer Property Trust 1982	Bank Collective Trust, with Portfolio Man-agers: Trustee- NewTower Trust Company, Invest-ment Advisor-Kennedy Associates, Investor Relations Landon Butler & Company LP	Pension funds, institutional investors	$7.29 billion
Union Labor Life Insurance Company 1977	Separate account of an insurance Company	Primarily multi-employer and public pension funds	$3.2 billion

insist on continual independent auditing. And, the mantra of responsible investment should be embraced as an integral part of fiduciary duty.

As pension experts note, even though there are some barriers to investing pensions in a manner that incorporates ESG and ETI concerns, pension fund stewards have, for decades, made prudent and durable investments in responsible alternative asset classes. Downstream investment managers have capitalized well-managed firms and projects that yielded good returns and sustainable outcomes. With proper policy frameworks, legal grounding, and due diligence, pension trustees and investment stewards can do the right thing.

While the book could describe a wide range of institutional investment strategies, it will utilize the more muscular foundation of alternative pension fund investments as the proxy for the larger arena. There is more case law and applied field work in this field. And we admit to a bias in preferring defined benefit pension plans to defined contribution programs in terms of long-term returns, protecting the beneficiary, and providing an additional societal benefit.

While the story-line of this guide continued well into the end of 2008, the profiles in Part II essentially cover the years 2007 to mid-2008 (unless noted), prior to the financial markets crash of 2008 (or, B.C., Before the Crash). We do not, in this book, track their progress after the crash (A.C.), though undoubtedly there will be funds that suffer the effects of the recession. The primary thrust of this book was to gauge their financial performance in a more stable environment and test their success at achieving positive collateral benefits (ESG, etc.) for beneficiaries and the population-at-large.

CHAPTER ONE

How Pension Funds Affect the Economy

The Exceptional Role of Large Pension and Endowment Funds

The modern corporation in the United States has experienced three stages of ownership and control. For many decades around the turn of the last century, the original owner-founders and a small group of shareowners ran the corporations. Beginning in the 1920s and '30s, a major shift occurred. As the original owner-founders passed on, a larger group of individual shareholders gained control of corporations. They hired professional managers who didn't have significant ownership to manage the businesses, resulting in a separation of ownership and control. Termed "managerial capitalism," this form of corporate ownership was prevalent from the 1920s to the 1970s.

By the 1960s, however, concurrent with the phenomenal growth of pension funds and other institutional investors, a third pattern of corporate ownership emerged. As late as 1970, individuals still owned almost 80% of corporate equity; a few years later, they had been swamped by the new wave of institutional owners.[1]

This concentration of share ownership is consolidated in large institutions, especially retirement and mutual funds, which hold trillions of dollars of beneficiary assets. In particular, public and private pension funds now hold a sizeable portion of the outstanding equity (23 percent) and bonds (5 percent) of the largest U.S. firms.[2] These trusts had grown to almost $10 trillion in assets by the first quarter of 2007.[3]

The 2007 Conference Board Report on Institutional Investment reported that pensions funds grew from 33% of all institutional investment assets in 1980 to 39% in 2005 (and mutual funds grew even faster), while U.S. banks and trust companies have declined from 39% of total assets in 1980 to 11% in 2005.[4] Thus, the retirement trusts of working people and retirees make up the single largest component of U.S. institutional investment. Similar patterns also exist in Canada, where the assets of defined benefit pension funds surpassed $800 billion in 2007.[5]

In recent years, corporate ownership may have entered a fourth, new stage that has been materializing rapidly: mega-buyouts by gigantic private equity and hedge funds that have purchased large, long-established corporations—both public and private. Just since 2004, acquisitions have included the Chrysler Corporation, Toys "R" Us, the Hertz Corporation, Metro-Goldwyn-Mayer, SunGard, Equity Office Properties, HCA, the Hilton Corporation, Burger King, Alliance Boots, and TXU. Whether or not the mega-buyouts will continue at the same pace after the 2008 market crash and credit crunch is resolved is unknown.

Nonetheless, these new corporate owners have already become very large—KKR and Blackstone Partners are among the largest employers in the U.S., according to White House advisor Lawrence Summers in an article in Financial Times (7/29/07) and other observers. The Service Employees International Union (SEIU) estimates that six million people work for companies owned by private equity firms. Further, if the number of employees at each operating company were added together, private equity groups would control six out of the ten largest employers in America.[6] And workers' pensions and other institutional funds are often used for the buyouts.

What do these conflicting trends mean for the workers and stakeholders of those companies? For the owners of pensions and other funds? While pension funds constitute a large sum of corporate wealth, workers still have little to say about how it's managed. Economic policy journalist William Greider argued that this mismatch between ownership and control needs to change:

> Given the vast wealth of the country, the financial system forms a rather narrow funnel through which tens of trillions of dollars are continuously poured. Yes, the transactions are

dizzyingly diverse and complex, involving thousands of large and small financial firms, but the work itself is actually done by a fairly small number of people. With a few important exceptions, the agents of capital operate with dedicated blindness to capital's collateral consequences, an indifference to the future of society even as they search for the future's returns. The great contradiction—and the reason reform is possible—is that Wall Street works with other people's money, mainly the retirement savings of ordinary Americans whose values it ignores, whose common interests are often trampled.[7]

The Challenge of Long-Term Investing

Because of the separation between the "owners" of investment funds (the savers and retirees) and the "agents," or fund managers, the owners generally have little impact on the practices of external investment managers or operators in the capital markets. That the investment fund owners (the sources of capital) have such little impact on the investments is a rather recent phenomenon.[8]

In the past, an investor who depended on long-term growth could monitor a company or project for its ability to garner long-term returns, more easily identifying and assessing the risks involved. For many reasons related to short-termism and "financialization" (see "What Is Financialization?" in Chapter 4), pension investors have increasingly moved to accelerate returns. While the preponderance of pension funds still rely on the "80-20 rule"— 80% stocks and bonds, and 20% alternative investments—fund managers are ratcheting up their investments in short-term stock trades, alternatives, and "opportunistic" investments.[9] This overall jump in the pursuit of shorter-term investment strategies can unfortunately lead to "churning," defined as "the procedure of excessive trading in the asset portfolio in an attempt to generate superior short-term returns."[10]

But short-termism, churning, and the corollary—chasing yield—are not going unchallenged. For instance, pension funds, as fiduciary institutions, have large and diverse investment portfolios, and long-term time horizons—not least because of their obligations to beneficiaries. It doesn't make sense to focus solely on maximizing the short-term price of the company's shares. A small shareholder might benefit from encouraging a company to pursue risky strategies that put the company at risk and harm bondholders; pension funds that hold stocks and bonds cannot.

As finance professors Hawley and Williams have written, large institutional funds "own the economy as a whole."[11] As a result, a pension fund may actually harm its beneficiaries if it focuses on maximizing share value on a firm-by-firm basis. For example, the fund's equity portfolio may decline in aggregate value when the companies it holds work to increase their profits by imposing external costs on and withholding external benefits from each other. Such short-term strategies hurt a "universal shareowner" such as a large public pension fund that holds equity in thousands of firms, owns bonds and real estate, and whose beneficiaries have interests not only as indirect stockholders but also as "stakeholders"—employees, consumers, and citizens.

Wall Street professionals offer sophisticated techniques finely tuned to maximize value. They depend on complex networks of people and institutions and elaborate layers of information. Processing the information requires a great deal of judgment and knowledge of history and technical prowess. But no one can foresee the future. So there's always a risk of being wrong. But if they have to be wrong, Wall Street professionals want to be wrong for the same reasons as everyone else. They don't want to be seen as "wacky." This means their behavior has a number of specific biases. In selecting investments, in a very general sense, larger enterprises are preferred to small; geographical areas with growth and momentum are preferred to areas where growth is slow; and information coming from mainstream sources is trusted more than other sources of information. Profits are often competitively high in small enterprises in stable communities, but for the Wall Street or Bay Street professional, the reputation price of being wrong about such "atypical" investments is higher than the price of being wrong in more conventional areas.

Such judgments and practices may make sense, especially when judged as individual investments, but they all add up to the formation of "capital gaps,"[12] that is, when worthy investments with strong growth potential can't get finance capital at competitive rates. Many entities, including pension funds, can sometimes take advantage of these gaps and arbitrage an extra return. Finding such gaps and profiting from them is the goal of an investor who is uniquely positioned to take the long-term view. And long-term can be really long-term—just consider those Civil War veterans' widows!

But taking the long view isn't happening nearly often enough. There are growing fears on the part of pension plan beneficiaries that the managers of workers' and taxpayers' savings are not simply "red-lining" certain investment markets, they are sometimes investing in ways that destroy workers' livelihoods.[13] An example would be the taxpayer (and pension holder) in Pennsylvania who might be living in the shadows of shut-down factories— and in a neighborhood with many underemployed neighbors—while the state's pension funds are building shopping malls halfway around the globe in areas that, in a short period of time, may have too many shopping malls.

A significant investment movement is responding to those fears and questioning the irresponsible investment practices of the pension-finance complex. Broadly described in a report by the United Nations as "responsible investment," this movement is inspiring investors around the globe to think more long-term. Responsible investment—understood as the incorporation of environmental, social, and governance analysis (ESG) into investment decision-making—is a growing discipline that offers opportunities for long-term value creation both for investors and society as a whole.[14]

The bottom line is that pension, endowments, and other funds operating under conventional prudent financial rules can defeat their own purposes by encouraging companies to pursue strategies that increase short-term returns at the expense of investments in research and development, employment and training, good labor relations, or energy conservation, for instance. Pension funds and other institutional owners cannot truly benefit their beneficiaries as shareholders if they unduly harm their beneficiaries as employees, consumers, and citizens. Therefore, institutional investors should, logically, seek ways to earn high risk-adjusted rates of return and reward corporate practices that advance the interests of their participants.[15]

The Largest Pension Funds and Asset Allocation

For pension funds, "asset allocation" is the starting point for prudent and responsible alternative investment. Asset allocation is the strategy whereby an investor selects investments among various investment classes (e.g., stocks and bonds, etc.).

ASSET ALLOCATION

A well-diversified portfolio is made up of a spectrum of asset classes as a means of spreading risk across classes. A fund's asset allocation policy is the targeted percentage of funds to be invested in an asset class as a percentage of total assets, and is assessed by the actual investment mix.[16]

The largest U.S. pension fund, CalPERS (California Public Employees Retirement System), near its peak before the crash, had an asset mix composed of 53% equities, 29% global fixed income assets, 8.7% private equity, and 8% real estate.[17] The second largest pension fund in the U.S., the Federal Retirement Thrift, which covers federal employees and uniformed services,[18] is a participant-directed fund; it mainly invests in U.S. Treasury Securities. Among the largest state pension funds, the average asset allocation was as follows: 44% U.S. equities, 14% non-U.S. equities, 6% real estate, 6% private equity, 29% global bonds; and 1 percent cash.[19]

The asset mix for the top 1,000 pension funds was similarly invested in public equities, fixed income, international equities/bonds, with about 14% in alternative investments and others.[20] Holdings in private equity and hedge funds are the fastest growing asset class in pension fund portfolios, and real estate has been a constant choice. Moreover, the fastest growing source of funds for hedge funds and private equity these past few years has been pension funds, according to the *Financial Times* (June 1, 2007).

Some experts believe the enthusiasm pension funds have for alternative investments can be problematic due to a lack of basic information about their returns and risk. Consider the following view from Brett Hammond, manager of TIAA-CREF (New York) in 2007: "Collectively, these are assets we don't know as much about as stocks and bonds...There is an 80-year time series with stocks and bonds...We're not really quite as certain that new alternatives behave consistently... It's not just investment risk. It's plain uncertainty."[21]

On the next page is a chart of the asset mix for the top 1,000 defined benefit (DB) pension funds, and on the following page is a list of the 10 largest pension funds in the U.S. In terms of the largest pension funds, they each had diversified portfolios, and they were increasing their allocations to "alternative" investments, as they are termed. Investments in alternative investment classes vary widely, however. It is in this class that institutional fund managers can target long-term investments in housing, clean-tech investments, and the overall growth economy, but managers too often made risky short-term wagers (such as an over-exposure to hedge funds).

Pension Funds and Private Equity Markets

It is well known that workers' retirement savings—pension funds—have become the largest single source of financing for the public equity markets. What is less known is their role in private equity markets. The sources of investments in these markets have changed over the past 20 years; now the largest source is pension funds.[22] In the early 1970s, the U.S. Department of Labor, citing data on diversified venture capital (VC) portfolios, became convinced that, under ERISA, VC investments were prudent investments. After endowment funds led investments in the field, many pension funds followed suit and also increased their allocations to private equity.

What is private equity? As explained in the recently published *Handbook on Responsible Investment*, private equity consists of investments in companies that are not listed on public stock exchanges; these range from venture capital investments in start-ups, to mezzanine financing for established companies, to buyouts of public companies. Other categories of private equity investment include leveraged buyouts, growth capital, angel investing, etc.[23] Pension funds and other institutional funds can invest in private equity funds as an asset class. Private equity funds typically control

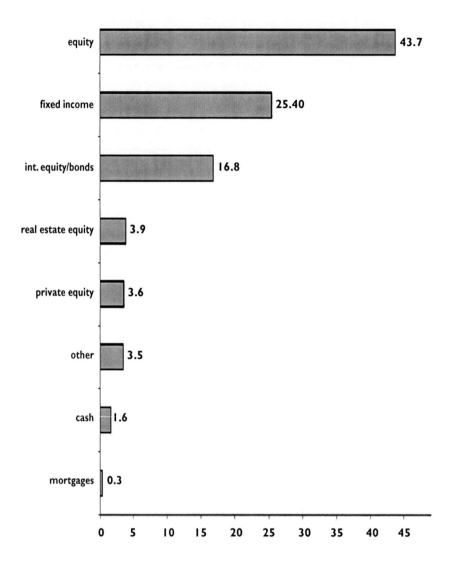

ASSET MIX FOR TOP 1000 US DB PENSION PLANS

equity	43.7
fixed income	25.40
int. equity/bonds	16.8
real estate equity	3.9
private equity	3.6
other	3.5
cash	1.6
mortgages	0.3

Source: Flow of Funds Accounts of the Federal Reserve Board, 2007

TOP 10 PENSION FUNDS/SPONSORS
(RANKED BY TOTAL ASSETS, IN US MILLIONS)

Rank	Sponsor (2006 rank)	Assets	Total DB	Total DC	DB stocks	DB bonds	DB cash	DB other
1	California Public Employees	$254,627	$253,551	$1,076	58.4%	26.0%	0.8%	14.8%
2	Federal Retirement	$223,338		$223,338				
3	California State Teachers	$176,270	$176,098	$172	60.9%	21.4%	0.2%	17.5%
4	New York State Common	$164,363	$164,363		58.4%	22.2%	4.8%	14.6%
5	Florida State Board	$142,519	$138,439	$4,080	58.9%	27.1%	0.9%	13.1%
6	General Motors	$133,835	$110,237	$23,598				
7	New York City Retirement	$127,945	$112,132	$15,813	68.0%	26.0%	1.0%	5.0%
8	AT&T	$117,537	$75,973	$41,564				
9	Texas Teachers	$114,878	$114,878		64.2%	24.7%	0.9%	10.2%
10	NY State Teachers	$106,042	$106,042		67.5%	17.8%	2.2%	12.5%

Source: Pensions and Investments, January 2008 (snapshot of September 30, 2007)

the management of the companies in which they invest and often bring in new management teams that focus on making the company more productive and profitable.

To summarize, the most common private equity investment categories are:

- *Venture capital,* which funds start-ups or small emerging companies. Venture capital is generally invested in companies whose products are still developing. These "seed" and early-stage investments often involve companies that are either developing unproven technologies and/or targeting unproven markets, often in high-tech, communications, or bioscience fields.
- *Private capital,* which traditionally invests in existing companies seeking expansion, adding new products, etc. Private capital funds generally make sizable, privately placed debt and equity capital investments in small-middle market firms, spanning manufacturing, transportation, distribution, communications, the technology industry, and other sections. Existing firms (and industries) are easier to evaluate for profits and productivity than venture markets.
- *Buyout and turnaround funds,* which acquire a large and often controlling stake in both profitable and troubled—but potentially profitable—companies. Buyout funds specialize in helping more mature companies expand through capital investments and reorganizations. Historically, the leveraged-buyout funds (LBOs) of the 1980s were reliant on debt financing.

A subset of buyout and turnaround funds are "special situations" funds that target financially distressed firms, even those in bankruptcy. These funds generally seek to restructure the underlying business in order to return it to profitability, stabilize employment, and build long-term value.

Of the categories of alternative private equity investment, venture and growth capital are important sources of financial entrepreneurial development. And during downturns or slow recoveries, access to private equity is critical for existing companies that need to recapitalize, restructure, grow, find new investors, or sell (especially in owner transition situations, where firms try to find a successor to an aging owner).[24]

TYPES OF PRIVATE EQUITY
- Venture capital funds start-ups or small emerging companies
- Private capital invests in existing companies
- Buyout and turnaround funds buy stakes in both profitable and troubled firms

---

At the height of the recent economic expansion, a leading consultant, Russell Investment Group, proposed a model portfolio of 45% equity, 25% fixed income, 20% alternative investments, and 10% "opportunistic" investments.[25] Clearly, Russell made an aggressive statement about breaking away from the traditional split between public equities and bonds. Was it too aggressive?

According to the International Financial Services, London (IFSL), institutional investors in the U.S. allocated, on average, 7% of their portfolios in 2007 to private equity funds. Indeed, U.S. pension funds doubled their investments in private equity deals in the period from 2005 to 2007. And, institutional investors increased their share of assets under management in hedge funds from 2% in 2000 to 50% by 2007 (see Chapter Four).[26] However, as investment scholars have discovered, while it's true that the returns of the top performers in private equity are stellar, many averaging above 25% in good years, it is also true that many others have had lackluster returns. So caution must be the watchword. It is not a given that all firms will yield the same stratospheric results.[27]

The Role of Private Equity in a Trust Portfolio

Private equity and venture capital funds are considered "alternative" investments, as they are a residual category separate from stocks and bonds. It is common practice for pension funds and other institutional investors to include these types of funds in a well-diversified portfolio. Such investment activity carries the promise of more reward, or so it's thought, but also higher risk.

In essence, pension funds invest both directly and indirectly (for instance, through fund managers) in private equity. Pension funds that invest directly in firms require a specific professional infrastructure—at-scale expertise— to manage that investment. These funds retain their own investment professionals who can provide due diligence and execute, monitor, and manage the investments and the investment "exit." These pension funds tend to be larger, as it is difficult for smaller institutional funds to maintain in-house capacity in all asset classes.

More often, pension funds utilize external professional investment firms. These external firms generally maintain the industry and financial expertise needed to successfully execute and manage investments. Thus, pension funds and institutional investors select private equity and venture fund managers from a universe including funds-of-funds, limited partnerships, pooled vehicles, private placement vehicles, and other syndicated corporations. In indirect investment, the job of pension administrators and stewards is to analyze the track record and professional capacity of fund managers in this field, with the guidance of lawyers and consultants. As explained in the AFL-CIO Investment Product Review, Private Capital 2002, pension stewards would generally retain a qualified professional asset management (QPAM) or investment manager to assemble a diversified portfolio of private equity investment funds.

The challenge for defined benefit pension plan sponsors to maximize returns on plan assets is an old one, of course, but it has taken on new complexities in recent years, as new "alternative investment" vehicles evolved. After the financial market downturn and recession in 2001-2002, many pension funds faced an under-funding crisis. During this time, larger-scale private equity and hedge funds (and other derivative products) that promised higher returns became popular with pension fund managers.

There are added risks, conflicts, and opportunities because Department of Labor rulings[28] and practices made it possible to pursue these more aggressive return scenarios.

What are the risks? In the case of venture investments, while successful investors can hit "home runs," earning large profits, it is also true that a large percentage of start-up companies do not survive. For example, during the "dot-com" failure fallout of the early 2000s, a large number of internet and technology start-ups had inadequate business plans and lacked a market strategy. Small start-up firms also do not have long records of consistently reported information, as compared to public corporations. Growth and buyout funds can typically invest in a range of enterprises, from small firms to large corporations. All things being equal, it is easier to track performance for pre-existing firms, and to construct business plans going forward.

Pension investments in private capital markets can help shape those markets and define the process by which fund managers engage in company governance and obtain information from their portfolio firms, whether start-up, small, medium or large enterprises.[29]

The Impact of Pension Funds in Real Estate Investments

An estimated $100 billion globally in pension funds was invested in real estate as of 2006, according to Barry Vinocur, Realty Stock Review. Pension funds have become a major source of investment in the real estate market. Funds increased their investments in U.S. real estate collectively from $6.9 billion to $29.3 billion over the decade from 1993-2003, according to Institutional Real Estate, which estimated the commercial real estate marketplace in the United States at $4.8 trillion at the time. Russell Investments tracked institutional investments in the U.S. and Canada to $81 billion in 2005 (declining to $68 billion in 2007). Pension funds in the U.S. and Canada own a substantial share of real estate equity funds and are also direct owners of land and structures.

In the real estate market, investors finance, purchase, and develop land or property. Development or redevelopment refers to the financing and construction of new real estate or renovations (e.g. improvements, upgrades, and expansions) to existing stock. Properties and development projects can be either residential (i.e. owner-occupied or rental housing) or non-residential (i.e. commercial, industrial, or retail sites). Investors may also loan money to residential and commercial borrowers who finance and develop their own properties.[30]

Most investors in "core" properties (i.e. high-quality, stable, income-producing office, industrial, multi-family, and retail properties) expect to receive returns approximately equal to equity returns. The appeal of owning both equities and real estate is that when the value of the stock market increases, real estate values are often stagnant; when the stock market falls, however, investors move into real estate and boost returns there. In other words, generally speaking, these two asset classes obtain about the same risk-adjusted return but are often viewed as negatively correlated.

"Opportunistic real estate private equity funds," also known as "value-added" funds and "opportunity" funds, became popular in the 1990s, purchasing property at distressed rates. In these funds, a small percentage of general partners control a large portion of the capital. Most of the larger fund general partners are real estate investing arms of larger private equity groups, whether merchant banking arms of investment banks or stand-alone private equity firms.[31]

Like private equity, the structuring of financing in real estate transactions can often be complex. Depending on the nature of the transaction (e.g. land tracts or properties or development deals) and the potential partnerships or co-investment requirements, a wide range of debt and equity instruments can be utilized, as well as mortgages, mortgage-backed securities, and mortgage loans.

The Role of Real Estate in a Portfolio

As Professors Hamilton and Heinkel pointed out in *The Role of Real Estate in a Pension Portfolio* (1994), an interesting feature of real estate is its relative immobility, meaning that assets such as land, large structures, and other fixtures established on properties (e.g. buildings) are generally permanently rooted in their respective locations. Hence, while the market for direct ownership of real estate is national and international, its operation is uniquely local. Prudent and profitable real estate investing must be based on information that is heavily determined by geography, as regional and community markets are frequently distinct with regard to the nature of properties, supply and demand trends, economic fundamentals, and other area-specific variables. As a consequence, the value in one sub-market may be completely different from that in a neighboring district.

As a private market activity, real estate investments also share these characteristics:

- Long asset life spans or the tendency of real estate properties to last with periodic alterations or improvements;
- Low turnover in real estate ownership (on average, ten years): in other words, these are frequently illiquid investments;
- High capital costs due to generally large scale projects, influenced locally; and,
- Long time horizons in major development and redevelopment initiatives.[32]

As in private equity, pension funds make real estate investments directly and indirectly through fund managers and advisors and pooled real estate funds. Direct investments are more time-consuming, administratively costly, and risky. They require an in-house investment professional or outsourced consultant to provide considerable time and expertise. Direct real estate investments may also expose a fund to decreased liquidity and limited diversification. However, direct investments offer more control, flexibility, and potentially higher returns than passive investments. It's all a matter of capacity, and there are innumerable excellent external fund managers. Pension stewards must consult with real estate investment managers, ERISA, and real estate attorneys, brokers, and accountants to determine whether or not their plan should invest directly or indirectly in real estate and how such transactions should be structured.

CHAPTER TWO

Responsible Investment (RI): A Framework for Considering Long-Term Investment in Alternatives

What Responsible Funds Claim to Do

In February, 2008, UN Secretary-General Ban Ki-moon stood before the Third Investors Summit on Climate Risk at UN Headquarters in New York City and stated: "The shift towards a greener future is still in its infancy and needs nurturing. The ability of the financial community to determine investment flows gives it great influence over the pace of innovation, technological change and adaptation." Some 450 investor, financial, corporate, and labor pension investors, representing $22 trillion in assets, pledged to collectively invest $10 billion in clean technology over the next two years. While the Summit is one of the flagships of responsible investment, the Principles for Responsible Investment are about more than green investing.

Responsible investment is understood as the incorporation of environmental, social, and governance (ESG) analysis into investment decision-making, in addition to the pursuit of risk-adjusted rates of return, according to the *Responsible Investment Handbook*. It is also a growing discipline that offers opportunities for long-term value creation for investors and broader society.

This book focuses on a group of responsible funds that are considered "worker-friendly" (the "S" in ESG). Usually (but not always) capitalized by pension funds, worker-friendly funds have committed, in general, to invest in companies that treat their employees as stakeholders. These funds have also increasingly incorporated environmental impacts, sustainable development concerns, and workers' health and safety into their investment parameters.

These responsible investors claim that there are several pathways to maximizing risk-adjusted financial rates of return, while also achieving positive collateral effects. This should appeal to all investors. Responsible funds claim to be uniquely positioned to find and fill "capital gaps." They argue that many profitable companies and projects may be ignored due to mainstream investor biases (or lack of knowledge) toward small businesses, unionized industries, "green" firms, or green construction. Thankfully, responsible investment is itself becoming more mainstream, as noted in a 2005 global report by the World Economic Forum (WEF).

In addition, some funds claim that investing in worker-friendly firms generates stable profits through increased labor and management productivity, brought forth by improved hours, wages, working conditions, and job security. These firms may enhance and reinforce high levels of employee participation through collective bargaining and employee ownership. In addition, these funds claim that investing in renewable energy, alternative transportation, and environment-technology companies lowers the cost of developing and using the technology, producing the collateral benefit of reducing pollution while maximizing rates of return.

Many argue that these so-called secondary or collateral benefits could so powerfully affect the context in which the company operates that achieving such effects actually becomes the investment fund's dominant strategy to maintain superior risk-adjusted rates of return. Exploring and evaluating that possibility is a primary focus of this book. We compile these funds' philosophies, operating styles, and general performance reporting in Part II.

In crafting their funds' investment strategy, pension trustees must make workers' retirement security their first priority.[1] They must never lose sight of the fact that their first duty is to oversee the investment of plan assets prudently and solely in the interests of plan participants and beneficiaries. They must never jeopardize investment returns in order to promote non-financial goals. At the same time, pension funds are workers' deferred wages, and it makes sense for trustees to invest these funds in ways that advance the interests of beneficiaries more broadly.

Economically-Targeted Investments (ETIs), again, are a methodology of responsible investments for pension trustees and other institutional investors to make investments that benefit workers, communities, and retirees alike. Historically, when pension funds adopted ETI policies, they promoted economic development by investing a portion of their portfolios in real estate projects and privately held companies that face demonstrable biases in ordinary capital markets. ETIs can also target under-capitalized regions.

Investment firms that pay special attention to the quality of labor relations and the number of jobs created or retained (by their investments) have been the strongest proponents of ETI policies. They argue that ETI approaches create a framework for prudent and successful long-term investments by pension funds. While ETIs can encompass a broad array of investment targets, worker-friendly funds have primarily focused on housing and good jobs as supplemental outcomes.

The movement toward larger-scale ETIs began in the mid-1960s, when the AFL-CIO Housing Investment Trust (HIT) was established. Construction union multi-employer pensions began investing systematically to provide both low/middle-income housing and to increase the jobs available to construction union members, while maintaining rates of financial returns that matched or beat standard indexes.[2] Thus, the Building Trades pension funds are the pioneers of ETIs in the U.S.

Meanwhile, large public pension funds like CalPERS, led by Jesse Unruh, the former California State Treasurer, moved toward scale in capitalizing affordable housing investments in the 1980s. And in Canada, construction union pension funds began backing worker-friendly real estate, helping launch Concert Properties in 1986.

In Canada, beginning in the 1980s, a "retail" investment vehicle was launched by Quebec's provincial labor federation. Labour-Sponsored Investment Funds (LSIFs) are capitalized by tax credit savings programs at the provincial and federal levels in Canada. The rapid growth of these funds provided much needed venture capital to Canadian regions and provinces. LSIFs are distinguished from U.S. private equity in that most of their sponsors never claimed to produce the higher rates of return sought by U.S. pension funds.

Also in the 1980s, the United Steelworkers of America (USW), faced with a severe recession and steel industry restructuring, began engaging Wall Street investment banks. They retained labor-friendly bankers to intervene in corporate restructuring through defensive buy-outs, ESOPs, and other tactics to save strategic manufacturers and jobs.[3] They won more balanced terms in some reorganization plans and pushed corporate governance (gaining a seat on some corporate boards) to better protect their members. Other unions such as the Machinists and Pilots followed suit. Two of the investment bankers retained by these unions were Gene Keilin and Ron Bloom, whose advisory firm was a predecessor to the KPS Fund (profiled here). Bloom later joined the Steelworkers to provide corporate strategy advice; today, he is with the U.S. Treasury Department as part of the Auto Crisis Task Force. This history—driven by crisis—would come in handy as the labor movement began to push pension funds to invest in jobs, not just housing.

By the late 1990s, capitalized in whole or in part by multi-employer pension funds, private equity and venture funds began investing in private businesses in a labor-friendly manner. After some initial successes from ULLICO's Separate Account P, union funds such as the Carpenters, UNITE, SEIU, UFCW, etc., were joined by public pension funds in investing in this space.

In the last decade, spurred on by former California State Treasurer Phil Angelides and active trustees, CalPERS backed an increasing number of investment funds to invest in the fields mentioned above and also clean tech, green construction, and other sustainable arenas. CalPERS also invested aggressively in "emerging" urban markets, targeting venture, private equity, development finance, and real estate funds to inner cities.

There has been a recent convergence of Responsible Investment and targeted pension investments in the broader global efforts to address climate risks. In the new decade, for example, many of the active trusts signed the pledge organized by the UN Investor Summit on Climate Risk. Thus, the progress toward responsible investment has been strengthened by a rising tide of progressive workers' capital trustees and their leaders. Guided by farsighted consultants like Jack Marco and Allan Emkin, and trained by pension activism centers set up by the national labor federations in the U.S. and Canada, capital stewards have staked innovative new investment fund managers who have arrived and thrived. Today, many of these investment fund managers claim—and appear to be delivering on the claim—to maximize risk-adjusted returns while pursuing significant targeted effects, such as those that enhance environmental quality, improve workplace and corporate governance, or focus on specific geographical areas or industries.

The interviews with the managers of the "responsible funds" provide insight into their motivations and the analytical frameworks. Stephen Coyle of the labor-backed AFL-CIO Investment Trusts provides some particularly interesting insights, in light of his thirty-year career in urban planning and housing investment. He explains the Trusts' roles (and responsibility) in investing in distressed areas, such as South Los Angeles after the Rodney King race riots, New York City after 9/11, and the Gulf Coast region after Hurricanes Katrina and Rita.

As Lynn Williams, former USW President once said, "The pension savings of American workers should not only guarantee good pensions. They should also guarantee American workers jobs to retire from." Current USW President Leo Gerard views the growth in responsible pension fund investments as an extension of his union's engagement in corporate governance and restructuring, and as a way to promote a preferable vision of the economy—one that is more humane and sustainable.

Best Practice: Responsible Funds

According to the literature of organizational theory, higher performance firms are more productive and yield better jobs for working people. When private equity funds invest in companies that strive toward high performance and that treat their workers fairly, their investment carries the potential for creating significant social and environmental value that otherwise would not exist. Responsible private equity funds also consider environmental impacts, benefits, products and processes, such as:

- Product-focused investments: Funds that invest in the creation,

development and growth of environmentally and/or socially-beneficial
products and services, such as health-care or clean energy firms;
- Economically- and geographically-targeted investments: Funds
  that invest in communities and regions that are underserved; and,
- Process-focused investments: Funds that support entrepreneurs
  and managers who incorporate environmental and social factors
  into their business practices.[4]

Similarly, when real estate funds invest in companies that deploy good
labor relation practices, that investment can yield higher quality construction
outcomes and better jobs. "Responsible" real estate funds also consider
environmental impacts, products, and processes in the course of their
investments. Responsible Property Investment (RPI) is a fast-growing field
with activity across the spectrum of institutional investors, money managers,
real estate funds, and property developers. It can be understood as any real
estate development, management, or investment practice that goes beyond
minimum legal requirements to achieve a positive environmental or social
impact, at a market rate of financial return. RPI encompasses many trends.[5]

All these projects and investment strategies share a number of
characteristics: a focus on the creation of long-term value across the
responsible investment spectrum; the development of tools to measure and
reduce social and environmental impacts; and innovative partnerships and
financing strategies. A recent field report confirmed that investors could
have purchased a portfolio consisting solely of RPI-focused office properties
over the decade and enjoyed performance that was more profitable and less
risky than a portfolio without PRI features.[6]

The United Nations and Responsible Investment

Driving many of the world's capital stewards is a tremendous policy sea-
change created by the release of the United Nations Principles for Responsible
Investment, adopted by some of the largest global institutional investors,
asset managers, and related organizations. This growing coalition, now 580

signatories, including city and state treasurers, pension funds, corporations and unions, and asset managers, etc., represented $19 trillion in assets as of 2009.[7]

RESPONSIBLE PROPERTY INVESTMENTS

- The development of markets and public/private partnerships around the provision of affordable and workforce housing;
- The increasing popularity of green buildings and transit-oriented development;
- The creation of innovative projects that find value in brownfield redevelopment, urban infill, urban revitalization, and land conservation;
- The emergence of responsible investment tools to track and create financial, social, and economic value;
- Engagement with property funds and managers on social and environmental practices.

A 2007 UN report highlighted the socially accountable and responsible investment practices of some of the world's most influential pension funds. *Responsible Investment in Focus: How Leading Public Pension Funds are Meeting the Challenge* was jointly prepared by the United Nations Environment Programme Finance Initiative (UNEP FI) Asset Management Working Group and the UK's Social Investment Forum, UKSIF.[8]

The report includes fifteen case studies on how funds such as CalPERS and Caisse de dépôt in North America and the Netherlands' ABP and Norway's Government Pension Fund internationally approach socially responsible investing (SRI). By presenting examples of the responsible investment practices of the world's largest and most successful pension funds, the UN has made it easier for pension fund trustees and their experts to see how mainstream investment practices use environmental, social, and governance criteria. The funds profiled include:

- ABP (Netherlands)

- AP2 (Sweden)

- ARIA (Australia)

- Caisse de dépôt et placement du Québec (Canada)

- CalPERS (US)

- CIA (Switzerland)

- ERAFP (France)

- Environment Agency Pension Fund (UK)

- Fonds de Réserve pour les Retraites (France)

- Government Pension Fund (Thailand)

- Metallrente (Germany)

- Norges Bank (Norway)

- PGGM (Netherlands)

- PREVI (Brazil)

- TIAA-CREF (US)

When adequate labor, health, safety, and environmental standards, management standards, investment transparency, and labor force consultation are taken into account in the private investment field (as when public corporations adopt "good governance"), the resulting impacts on workers and communities can be huge. Unfortunately, many venture, private, and construction investors have often been indifferent or even hostile to workers' rights. When they join the boards of investee firms, their biases against fair wages and benefits and their impatience with collective bargaining, etc. may sometimes come to the fore. Even when they do not directly participate as members of the board, their attitudes can influence workers' rights, since company managers answer to them and respond to their focus on quarterly profit goals.

But investors of all stripes are being pressed to consider longer-term social and environmental imperatives in their investment practices. Unions are now seizing the initiative, joining the broader RI movements. The European labor movement, in particular, is taking a more political stance towards irresponsible mega-funds. It is calling for the European Union and member nations to regulate private equity and hedge firms. Governments, progressive companies, unions, and NGOs are calling on capital investors to extend the same rules to privately held companies that publicly-traded companies should abide by: good labor relations, transparency, and good corporate governance and sustainability.[9]

THE UN PRINCIPLES OF RESPONSIBLE INVESTMENT

As institutional investors, we have a duty to act in the best long-term interests of our beneficiaries. In this fiduciary role, we believe that environmental, social, and corporate governance (ESG) issues can affect the performance of investment portfolios (to varying degrees across companies, sectors, regions, asset classes, and through time). We also recognize that applying these Principles may better align investors with broader objectives of society. Therefore, where consistent with our fiduciary responsibilities, we commit to the following:

- We will incorporate ESG issues into investment analysis and decision-making processes.
- We will be active owners and incorporate ESG issues into our ownership policies and practices.
- We will seek appropriate disclosure on ESG issues by the entities in which we invest.
- We will promote acceptance and implementation of the Principles within the investment industry.
- We will work together to enhance our effectiveness in implementing the Principles.
- We will each report on our activities and progress towards implementing the Principles.
- The Principles for Responsible Investment were developed by an international group of institutional investors reflecting the increasing relevance of environmental, social and corporate governance issues to investment practices. The process was convened by the United Nations Secretary-General.

CHAPTER THREE

A Short Primer on Economically-Targeted Investments

What are Economically-Targeted Investments (ETIs)?

Responsible, ethical, or targeted investments have historical roots reaching back to ancient religious societies. John Wesley, the 18th century English religious reformer, was a strong advocate of socially responsible investing, which today is known as SRI. The most visible modern example of this, using a negative screen, was the global divestment campaign to end apartheid in South Africa.[1] More recently campaigns have been waged against companies doing business in countries with repressive regimes like Burma, which was said to sanction slave labor.

Capital stewards in many countries also encourage positive targeted pension investments in the "real economy"—in other words, in decent housing, local companies, and small to medium-sized enterprises (SMEs). These types of investments are also known as economically-targeted investments (ETIs). What are ETIs? ETIs are investments that fill capital gaps in alternative asset classes like real estate, venture capital, and private debt placement. ETI policies allow pension funds to promote positive economic development by investing a portion of their portfolios in real estate projects and privately held companies that have trouble getting access to capital. ETIs can also target under-capitalized regions and emerging economies.

ETIs can vary widely. Besides real estate and business investments, typical ETIs might include fixed income, infrastructure, and credit enhancement. And in many cases, pension fund trustees have designed pension investment policies that promote collateral benefits—such as good jobs and affordable housing.

There is a relatively higher degree of risk associated with ETIs, and trustees must not lose sight of their fiduciary duties and potential conflicts of interest. And not every nation has developed clear pension fund guidelines for ETIs. There are some court decisions that appear to block any investment that does not solely maximize return. Because the U.S. has historically provided more legal justification for ETIs, this section will lean on U.S. legal guidance on the issue, as the investment approach is consistent with the fiduciary duties of trustees from other lands.[2]

The first duty of a pension trustee, or "capital steward," is to oversee the investment of plan assets prudently and solely in the interests of plan participants and beneficiaries. In crafting their funds' investment strategy, pension trustees must make workers' retirement security their first priority. Trustees must never jeopardize investment returns in order to promote non-financial goals. But part of a prudent investment strategy is an asset allocation plan, or a plan to diversify investments.

CAPITAL STEWARDSHIP

refers to the actions of pension fund trustees and others concerned about workers' retirement savings to achieve the twin goals of obtaining the best possible risk-adjusted rate of return on investments and promoting the interests of plan participants and beneficiaries.

A critical component of modern portfolio theory and financial planning, asset allocation is the strategy whereby an investor selects investments among various investment classes (e.g., stocks, bonds, etc.). It is by these asset allocation formulas that pension funds make investments in "alternative investment" classes, part of a prudent process to diversify beyond public market investments. Capital stewards should have an interest in exploring these asset classes in ways that advance the interests of beneficiaries and their communities more broadly.

Given a heightened sense of portfolio risk within the framework of fiduciary responsibility, investors are urged to more closely monitor the potential risk and liabilities that might arise from firms or projects that pollute or contribute to global warming. And when investors look to a "high performance" investment framework, rather than investing in lowest-cost or anti-union firms, it is said that they are following a "worker-friendly" investment policy. Some investors claim that investing in these types of firms can generate more stable profits through increased labor productivity or employee participation (often yielding higher quality).

ECONOMICALLY-TARGETED INVESTMENTS

ETIs seek competitive rates of return on invest-ments that also provide collateral benefits. Pension funds that invest in ETIs (directly or indirectly) gain a measure of influence over the employment and labor relations and environmental practices of investee businesses and projects. Trustees can target companies and construction projects that:

- Provide job security.
- Adopt responsible contractor policies.
- Adopt high-performance (or, high-road) workplace practices.
- Follow responsible environmental standards.
- Treat workers with respect and provide for neutrality in labor relations.

ETI Guidelines

According to pension expert Jayne Zanglein, ETIs have been defined by the U.S. Department of Labor (DOL) as "investments selected for the economic benefits they create apart from their investment return to the employee benefit plan."[3] Collateral benefits obtained through ETIs include "expanded employment opportunities, increased housing availability, improved social service facilities, and strengthened infrastructure." ETIs "create new jobs, provide capital to replace loan funds no longer rolling through the bank pipelines, provide startup businesses with access to capital, finance low-cost housing and improve the infrastructure of the nation, all without sacrificing a return on investments or otherwise jeopardizing the pensions of future retirees."[4]

As Zanglein further explained, DOL's landmark Interpretive Bulletin 94-1 clarified that a pension plan may choose an investment that has collateral benefits if the investment has a risk-adjusted market rate of return, which is equal to or superior to alternative investments. The Department has consistently construed ERISA's requirement that a fiduciary act "solely in the interest of," and "for the exclusive purpose of providing benefits to participants and their beneficiaries," as "prohibiting a fiduciary from subordinating the interests of participants and beneficiaries in their retirement income to unrelated objectives."

However, the Department's ETI bulletin states that a fiduciary may invest plan assets in an ETI "if the ETI has an expected rate of return that is commensurate to rates of return of alternative investments with similar risk characteristics that are available to the plan, and if the ETI is otherwise an appropriate investment for the plan in terms of such factors as diversification and the investment policy of the plan."

A related DOL report, "DOL Advisory Council on Pension Welfare and Benefit Plans "(1992), said that prudent investments exist in an inefficient market and remain unfunded due to information gaps and high administrative costs of consummating and monitoring deals: "To the extent that capital markets are judged to be tradition-bound, rigid or incapable of funding all 'worthy' investments, making funds available from the pension investment pool is seen as addressing capital gaps that would otherwise impede local economic development."

The report further stated: "The added costs of acquiring the information needed to make the investment sound must be incorporated in the required rate of return. If the investment can bear these added costs, the ETI strategy may produce additional economic activity in this region. If it isn't able to bear the added costs, the pension fund must: (1) forego the investment, (2) find a third party willing to subsidize some or all of these extra costs, or (3) accept a lower [but still prudent] net return."

THE LANOFF LETTER

DOL's position on collateral benefit investing dates back to at least 1980, when the Department's first ERISA Administrator, Ian Lanoff, stated that while ERISA "does not exclude the provision of incidental benefits to others, the protection of retirement income is, and should continue to be, the overriding social objective governing the investment of plan assets."—**Ian Lanoff**, "The Social Investment of Private Pension Plan Assets: May it Be Done Lawfully Under ERISA?" *Labor Law Journal*, v31, n7, pp. 387, 389 (1980).

ETIs in Practice

Pension funds around the globe are investing in a broad range of ETI strategies, sometimes identified as RI or ESG investments, generating good financial returns and collateral benefits.[5] There are a number of ETI investment vehicles, including some in this report, which might serve as models for pension and institutional fund trustees looking to develop well-rounded and prudent responsible investment policies.[6]

ETIs have been utilized more broadly in the U.S., where surveys found that 18 of the 20 largest public pension funds invested in ETIs, investing from .5% to 8.4% of assets. The California public employees trust (CalPERs) reported in 2003 that approximately $17.2 billon of its assets, though not technically in-state ETIs, are "invested or committed for investment in California." A study of state teachers' funds determined that twenty-two states had ETI language favoring in-state investments.[7]

Types of ETIs

ETI INVESTMENTS IN REAL ESTATE AND BUSINESS

- Real Estate and Fixed Income
- Direct Real Estate Investments
- Private Equity
- Private Placements
- Small and Medium-sized Enterprises (SME's)
- Employee Ownership and Empowerment Transactions
- Specialized Investments

ETI INVESTMENTS TARGETING PLACES AND INDUSTRY SECTORS

Sectoral Targeting:

- Renewable Energy and Clean-tech Investments
- Geographic Targeting: Urban and Rural Revitalization
- Infrastructure and Project Financing
- Micro-Finance and Development Finance

INVESTMENTS IN REAL ESTATE AND BUSINESS

Real Estate and Fixed Income

The use of ETI investments to achieve financial returns and collateral benefits has most often been applied to real estate. Building trades pension trusts have long invested in real estate projects that create housing and jobs for union members and other members of society. Real estate investment vehicles can include pooled funds that make equity and debt investments, mortgage vehicles, and fixed-income funds. Pensions can also invest in fixed income, a debt-based real estate product that can be invested in affordable housing, and in mortgage-backed securities. Trusts can invest in credit enhancements products as well, whereby a pension fund will loan its credit rating to a municipality or state agency for a fee (such as in the case of the AFL-CIO HIT).

Real estate ETIs can fill capital gaps in areas such as low-income housing that would not otherwise be funded—and can seek partnerships with governments and other investors (and try to secure guarantees and other funders to subordinate their positions and lessen risk). Real estate investors finance, purchase, and develop land or property, or redevelop renovations to existing stock. Projects can be residential or non-residential.[8]

Investors and lenders also loan money to residential and commercial borrowers who finance and develop their own properties. Pension trustees who are new to economically-targeted investing may wish to start their ETI programs by investing in well-established pooled real estate funds and/or fixed income projects. These programs are easier to evaluate and also offer competitive returns. Many of the funds cited in this book, such as the AFL-CIO Housing Investment Trust and AFL-CIO Building Investment Trust, Concert Properties, LongView ULTRA, the MEPT Fund, and others invest in real estate. International funds similarly engaged include the Public Investment Corporation (PIC) and Futuregrowth Asset Management in South Africa, Hermes in England, etc.

Direct Real Estate Investments

Many pension funds invest directly in real estate, meaning that they purchase the property directly rather than through a pooled fund. Direct investments are more time-consuming, administratively costly, and risky. They require an in-house or consultant investment manager with a great deal of time and expertise. Direct real estate investments may also expose a fund to decreased liquidity and limited diversification. However, direct investments offer more control, flexibility, and higher potential returns than passive investments. One of the more innovative pension funds directly managing real estate investments is the CIA in Geneva, which has long prioritized low-income housing and sustainable development (Caisse de Prevoyance du Personnel Enseignant de I'Instruction Publique et des Fonctionnaires du Canton of Geneva).

Private Equity

An increasing number of pension funds are making ETI investments in the field of private equity (PE), which involve investments in smaller, non-public companies. Pension funds are attracted to this class of alternative assets due to the potential multiple benefits: good investment returns and good jobs. Private equity funds typically have a measure of control in the management of the companies in which they invest and often bring in new management teams that focus on operating the company more efficiently. Private equity funds in this book include the KPS Fund, GESD, etc., and good international examples include the Industry Fund Service (Australia) and ABP Pension Fund (The Netherlands). PE funds, as we said, can include:

- Venture capital
- Private capital
- Buyout and turnaround funds.[9]

Private Placements

Pension funds also invest in private placements. Private placements are stock or bond issues sold by a corporation directly to an investor without registration under securities regulations (which increases risk). Besides pension funds, private placements are generally made by insurance companies, trusts, private equity funds, etc. The Union Labor Life J for Jobs Fund in this book is one example. The Wisconsin Investment Board invested hundreds of millions in Wisconsin companies over two decades.

SMEs (Small and Medium Enterprises)

According to the OECD, governments worldwide recognize the importance of SMEs and their contribution to economic growth, social cohesion, employment, and local development. It is said that SMEs account for over

95% of enterprises and 60%-70% of employment, and generate a large share of new jobs in OECD economies. SMEs are often the largest provider of new jobs, helping drive research and development, technological innovation, and new products. They are particularly important to emerging countries and can help reduce poverty. However, some banking experts fear that many of the traditional problems facing SMEs—lack of financing, difficulties in exploiting technology, constrained managerial capabilities, low productivity, etc.—become more acute in a globalized environment.

Many private capital funds target small and medium-sized companies. Though smaller, these firms can be part of an important supply chain or strategic to the economy. The Solidarity Fund, GESD, Growth Works and Landmark Growth Capital Partners, among others herein, focus on SMEs. In Chile, the FIDES have increased investments to SMEs starving for capital and R&D.

Employee Ownership and Empowerment Transactions

In the U.S., some investors have structured buyouts so that workers have obtained partial ownership through an Employee Stock Ownership Program (ESOP), an ownership structure provided for under U.S. law that provides tax advantages for worker-owners to purchase firms (and, on a slightly different basis, in Canada). The KPS Funds (profiled later) has provided capital in its buyouts of distressed firms to help a company restructure so that when stock is eventually sold to employees, the firm's financial difficulties have been better addressed. The Yucaipa Companies (U.S.) has also provided capital for a strategy to convert companies to a special employee ownership status (called Sub-chapter S ESOPs, a provision in U.S. tax law that further reduces tax liability). These models offer a unique potential for ETI impacts. More often, though, employee ownership has been viewed as an exit strategy for investment funds.

In British Columbia and Quebec, Growth Works and Solidarity are both structuring investment vehicles that are focused on native populations. These funds are sourced from retail Labour-Sponsored Investment Funds

(LSIFs). In South Africa, Brazil, and other emerging economies, there have been a series of ownership transition initiatives funded by pension funds to share the ownership of in-country corporations (sometimes owned by foreign interests) with historically disadvantaged citizens. "Empowerment Transactions" are meant to increase black ownership and control of targeted companies (as in the case of South Africa). Private equity funds, utilizing workers' pension, have sourced these transactions by partnering with indigenously owned firms to purchase a portion or all of the target company's stock, yielding partial to full control.

Specialized Investments

The Yucaipa Companies made a PIPE investment—private investments in public enterprises—to restructure a large distressed public company (Pathmark). The strategy provided new capital, modernized the company, and stabilized hundreds of union jobs (and provided a good ROI) so that a longer-term strategic buyer could be found.

INVESTMENTS TARGETING PLACES AND INDUSTRY SECTORS

Sectoral Targeting: Clean-tech and Green Building Investments

Increasingly, public pension funds are demanding that investments comply with global climate change compacts, avoid negative environmental impacts, and explore new investments in clean technology and green building. The International Energy Agency (IEA) estimates that $44 billion was spent on new renewable and distributed energy technologies in 2005. As the world diversifies its energy sources from fossil fuels, the level of investments in new energy technologies is expected to quadruple by 2015 (to $167 billion).

For example, as part of the California "Green Wave Initiative," CalPERS engaged two sectors of the economy—transportation and energy—to increase energy efficiency and committed to a 20% improvement in efficiency in its $12 billion dollar real estate portfolio. CalPERs also set aside:

- $500 million for investments in environmentally responsible public firms.
- $200 million to invest in early stage venture capital all the way through to project financing in new clean technologies.

The MEPT Fund won awards for its redevelopment of a long-abandoned, burned-down hospital into a green housing complex (see the Octagon case). The Canadian Workers' Opportunity Fund (WOF) invested in Xantrex Technology, a firm producing inverters and chargers in solar/wind energy systems. The Landmark Fund capitalized a composite company's new windmill fan factory in Iowa. Workers' pension funds or LSIFs in Quebec (Solidarity), the Netherlands, Great Britain, and other counties have targeted huge investments in this field. PKA, the Danish pension fund, made investments in BankInvest's New Energy Solutions fund. In Australia, the IFS owns the largest renewable wind company in the country.

Geographic Targeting

One of the more common pension investment targeting approaches is to commit some proportion of investments within the geographic boundaries of a political entity, such as a nation or province/state. In Quebec, Solidarity has structured regional funds as a fundamental capital decentralization strategy. In the U.S., ERECT manages a state-specific real estate fund, and BUILD has made a commitment to investing some assets in the South. In South Africa, the Public Investment Corporation (PIC) led the capitalization for a Pan-Africa infrastructure fund. By pooling investments, a number of investors can build a more scalable framework to geographic targeting.

Urban Revitalization

Urban targeting by large institutional investors, particularly pension funds, has the potential to revitalize communities and create good jobs, union workplaces, and housing. And it has the ability to have positive environmental impacts, according to pension expert Tessa Hebb. For instance, brownfield redevelopment can lead to inner city urban revitalization. And once an urban area becomes revitalized, businesses can grow or return, leading to job creation.

Pension funds can invest in a range of urban ETI activities, including venture and private capital investments to generate good jobs, affordable housing and commercial improvements, and re-hab/brownfield opportunities. Urban investment strategies have been developed in large urban areas such as New York City (by the city's pension fund, and by HIT and BIT) and Vancouver (Concert Properties). International examples include Hermes, which is investing huge sums to completely revitalize a formerly derelict section of London into a planned community.[10]

Rural Revitalization

Investments can be targeted to rural areas to revitalize the economy and build needed infrastructure, housing and jobs-generating industries. Even in the more mature economies, venture capital tends to congregate in higher growth areas, such as the two coasts of the U.S. and the Toronto-Montreal corridor of Canada. An example of a targeted regional investment strategy in an otherwise mature economy might be in Appalachia in the U.S. or parts of northern and eastern Canada.

In emerging markets, rural areas suffer more emphatically from under-capitalization. The degree of rural de-capitalization—whether the region is growing and exporting along with the national economy, or trading within its region, or is barely surviving—might determine the types and extent of ETI strategies. An example of an international targeted rural investment strategy is that of the PIC in South Africa, which has targeted the Western Cape and townships in other isolated parts of the country.

Infrastructure and Project Financing

A more unconventional pension investment strategy that is growing in both mature and emerging economies alike is infrastructure financing. This field includes traditional transport infrastructure with user fees, such as roads, rail, and airports; regulated infrastructure, such as water, energy and gas distribution, etc. (with a regulated service contract and an availability fee);

and "social" infrastructure, such as schools and hospitals (where governments pay an availability fee over a 20-30 year term).[11] Pension-funded vehicles such as the Futuregrowth Fund and the PIC in South Africa have defined infrastructure in a more expansive way, including churches, health clinics, and other institutions that are part of the social fabric of a community.

Infrastructure has historically been financed by municipal bonds, which often yielded favorable tax treatment. The most prudent approach to this class will always be safe and sound infrastructure bond investment vehicles. More recently, infrastructure funds have been organized as equity-type funds. From the perspective of trade unions and society, there are concerns that workers' pensions may be used to replace the legitimate role of governments, or they may be lured into risky privatization schemes. There has been criticism of some public-private-partnership infrastructure deals due to a lack of appropriate fiduciary oversight and due to post-transaction outcomes (stiff user fee increases, lack of maintenance, anti-union drives, etc.).

Principals interested in infrastructure investment can explore responsible contractor, anti-privatization, opt-out, and other provisions that could be used to protect their investment and the interests of their members. S.A's Futuregrowth applies a social impact test to its investments to ensure a triple bottom-line. According to Tessa Hebb:

> Several public sector pension funds have also adopted Privatization Policies as part of their investment management. [This type of] policy strongly discourages private equity managers from investing in a company or its affiliates, if any have "converted or replaced existing public jobs in schools, public authorities or prisons with institutions staffed by private sector employees, including units such as mailrooms, and food, waste collection, health care, and security guard services. (Hebb, Tessa. Larry Beeferman. 2008. "US Pension Funds' Labour-Friendly Investments," in *The "Social" in Social Security: Market, State and Associations in Retirement Provision*, Mark Hyde and John Dixon eds., Edwin Mellen Press, Lampeter, UK. Forthcoming.)

And related to infrastructure financing is shorter-term project financing: i.e. utility projects. There is a unique opportunity for pension funds to explore energy and transit-related project financings, particularly, for instance, renewable energy projects (windmill and solar project construction, etc.) where financing plans can be structured to ensure expedited labor-outcomes—construction and operating jobs—and a shorter timeline for investment exits. Examples include the Industry Fund Service in Australia, the Boilermakers' Co-Generation Fund in the U.S., and ABP's Ampere Fund in the Netherlands.

Micro-Finance and Development Finance

Community development financial institutions cover a wide range of investment activities, including community lending, community equity investments, micro-loans, etc. While many community-focused investors have historically accepted a lower rate of return, the development finance arena is fielding larger funds that seek more standard risk-adjusted returns. These funds are investing equity whereas the larger field is primarily debt-based. Nonetheless, risks need to be understood, as security collateralization is more difficult.

Micro-finance investments have grown rapidly around the world, especially in emerging markets. But even in more mature markets, these investments are increasing in scale. As noted in such diverse organs as the Financial Times and Social Funds, the UN declaration of 2005 as "International Year of Micro-Credit" focused attention on a wide range of financial services to micro-enterprises across the world. "Although interest in this type of investor is mostly coming from private investors, institutions are now more willing to include that asset class in their portfolios. A good international example is the Dutch pension fund ABP, which made an investment of €5 million in micro-credits." (Financial Times, June 2005) In 2006, TIAA-CREF, the U.S. teachers' retirement fund, announced a $100 million Global Microfinance Investment Program. The Chicago-based Shorebank is an example of a U.S. fund participating in pension-capitalized development finance programs.

CHAPTER FOUR
The Rise of Financialization

Our progress out of the depression is obvious. But that is not what you and I mean by the new order of things. Our pledge was not to do a patchwork job with secondhand materials. By using the new materials of social justice, we have undertaken to erect on the old foundations a more enduring structure for the use of future generations. In that purpose we have been helped by the achievements of mind and spirit. Old truths have been re-learned; untruths have been un-learned.

We have always known that heedless self-interest was bad morals. We know now that it is bad economics...

—**Franklin Delano Roosevelt,** Campaign Speech, Chicago, Illinois, Oct. 13, 1936

The Rush to Short-Term

Historian Kevin Phillips has written often about the growing power of the financial services industry. He points out that in the 1970s, manufacturing led financial services by a two-to-one margin. By 2006, goods production had shrunk to just 12% of GDP while financial services reached "a swollen 20-21% of GDP." He blamed the market crisis of 2007-2009 on the economy's dependence on a burgeoning, unsustainable level of debt.

The field of private finance, especially the mega-buyout and hedge funds operating primarily from Wall Street and London (and some on Bay Street), grew exponentially in the last two decades. In 2006, for the first time, companies in the United States raised more money through private placements ($162 billion) than on the three largest stock exchanges (NYSE, NASDAQ, and the American Stock Exchange). Initial public offerings raised only $154 billion in 2006. Watson Wyatt's Global Alternatives research showed that alternative assets managed on behalf of pension funds by the world's 99 largest investment managers grew by 40% to $822 billion (in 2007) from $586 billion (2006). Pension plans were expected to invest $300 billion in hedge funds in 2008, up from $5 billion in 1998.[1]

ALTERNATIVE INVESTMENTS

Alternative investments include real estate, private equity
and venture capital, commodities, financial derivatives,
hedge strategies (or absolute return strategies), etc. They
are supposed to have a very low correlation with traditional
investment products.

The risk entailed in this business is high. At any given time, higher interest rates, a recession, or regulatory changes could result in big losses for investors. The U.S. Congress began holding hearings in mid-2007 to investigate the effects of private equity and hedge funds on economic growth and taxation. Similar inquiries took place in Europe. One report estimated that the privileged tax treatment provided hedge funds, for instance, might cost the U.S. federal treasury $6 billion per year.[2]

No comprehensive study supports the view that markets thrive on innovative risk-taking by, and rewards to, private equity firms. Many stories, in fact, suggest just the opposite. For instance, in 2005, Ford Motor Company sold its Hertz car rental division in an LBO to three private equity firms for $15 billion (and only $2.3 billion equity). The PE firms "flipped" it as an IPO in 11 months, doubling their investment. But the IPO faltered, according to the International Herald Tribune, due to Hertz's higher debt load, higher interest costs, and lowered profits. The questions are: Did the private equity firms have superior management? Did they have access to cheaper debt? Why couldn't Ford have earned adequate value from the sale and still left

WHAT MEGA-FUNDS DO

- Mega-Buyout Funds: Large leveraged buyout and acquisition funds typically purchase all or part of the assets of the stock or assets of a company. These funds utilize a more significant portion of borrowed capital than traditional private equity firms. Borrowed capital typically consists of some combination of senior and subordinated debt. The investment target may be privately or publicly owned, or a subsidiary or division of the same. According to the IFSL, direct PE investments rose 34.6% to a record $686 billion in 2007, as the buyout category grew to 89% of PE investments.

- Hedge Funds: These are private investment vehicles available primarily to institutional investors and high-net-worth individuals. The underlying assets in which they invest are generally publicly listed securities (stocks and bonds) and their derivative products. Hedge funds can also invest in private companies and real estate, a more recent phenomenon. Hedge funds, in theory, offer investors opportunities to achieve substantial returns and to mitigate against the risk of market downturns— by promising absolute returns and using alternative investments and trading strategies to de-correlate returns from the market (Handbook on Responsible Investment). Hedge funds also typically utilize a larger portion of debt in their transactions. Hedge fund assets increased over ten-fold from 1998 to 2008 (to more than $2 trillion).[4]

Hertz in a stable condition? In any case, profits were rearranged, but the only real change to the company was more debt on its balance sheets. Did this benefit the company and the economy?

To date no definitive study has demonstrated whether the activities of the largest LBO and hedge investors benefit or hurt the economy over the long run. But, some of these firms have recently been accused of using investors' money to hollow out companies. The European press has accused private equity funds of over-leveraging the takeover targets, paying the executives high fees, paying back investors, and leaving the companies "headless chickens."[3] And, as reported in this chapter and earlier, hedge funds may have had questionable roles in the sub-prime bubble collapse and the credit crunch contagion.

Who and What are the "Mega-Funds"?

In terms of the private investment world, the mega-funds—whose managers were dubbed "The New Masters of the Universe" by Tom Wolfe—are generally characterized as large investment vehicles with assets typically in the tens of billions of dollars that specialize in buyouts and hedging activities.

THE TEN LARGEST BUYOUT FUNDS:

The Blackstone Group
Kolberg Kravis Roberts & Co.
The Carlyle Group
Texas Pacific Group
Bain Capital
Providence Equity Partners
Apollo Advisors
Warburg Pincus
Cerebrus
Thomas H. Lee

LBO/buyout funds raised an unprecedented amount of capital in 2006-2007, said a report from CalSTRS (California State Teachers' Retirement System). Private equity funds raised $301 billion, and LBO buyouts amounted to the equivalent to 1/3 of all the leveraged buyouts ever, as cited earlier.

And CFO Magazine recently traced a surge in hostile takeovers as a general proportion of LBOs. Another finance journal warned in February 2005, of the rising impact of mega-private equity fundraising, and how it might impact or crowd-out middle-market funds. While these articles focused on buyout funds, similar concerns have been raised about hedge funds.[5]

By July 2007, the risks to over-levered hedge and private equity funds were becoming better known. As domestic financial debt jumped from about 83% of the GDP in 2000 to 110% in 2007, the potential of a credit contraction held obvious risks for the economy as a whole and was seen as particularly acute for the mega-funds. The spread of hedge funds had grown to encompass more than 1/3 of all U.S. stock trades, and this market peaked at over $2 trillion in assets as of mid-summer 2008, as pensions and other institutional investors continued to pour large sums into firms.[6]

Sadly, as it turns out, hedge funds probably had a role in acerbating the sub-prime mortgage failures. Randall Dodd, a senior financial analyst in the International Monetary Fund (IMF), independently examined the role of hedge funds in the unfolding crisis and noted that because of hedge fund non-transparency, over-leverage, and use of derivative vehicles their "impact in the global credit markets is greater than their assets under management would indicate." Dodd asserted that "there are legitimate concerns that these funds may end up inadvertently exacerbating risk," and noted that the role of hedges "contributed to the market failure that allowed a 3% jump in serious delinquency rates on a subsection of U.S. mortgages to throw a $57 trillion U.S. financial system into turmoil and cause shudders across the globe."[7]

As 2008 ended, the risk-reward continuum turned upside down on many of the most successful alternative investment managers. Analysts predicted that half of the estimated 10,000 hedge funds would disappear. As for mega-buyout funds, the downturn and tightened credit market severely restrained deal flow financings and hampered investment exits, even for LBO managers (like Blackstone, etc.) that had turned to IPOs to bring in new investors. And in the real estate field (beyond real estate sub-prime and bubble damage), PriceWaterhouseCoopers and the Urban Land Institute predicted the U.S. commercial real estate market—another market backed by institutional investments—faced its worst year "since the wrenching 1991-1992 industry recession."[8]

As George Soros explained in a Fall 2008 Congressional hearing on hedge funds, the largest financial interests had become inseparably interconnected as the sub-prime crisis spread. The toll of fallen or wounded dominos was steep and spanned asset classes. They included the investment houses Merrill Lynch, Lehman Brothers, and Bear Sterns; large banks such as Wachovia, Washington Mutual, and IndyMAC; and hedge funds Fortress, Pentagon Capital Management, Ospraie, Amaranth, AQR, Zwirn, Sowood, etc. In Europe and elsewhere, many large investment and banking concerns, often connected with Wall Street interests, similarly failed. In the world of large buyout firms, the Carlyle Group and Apollo Management faced problems due to investments in portfolio firms saddled with exploding debt loads. In the insurance, real estate, and mortgage markets, AIG and quasi-public Fannie Mae and Freddie Mac were bailed out, but Countrywide Financial and Ameriquest Mortgage Company failed.

Special Concerns About Mega-Buyout and Hedge Funds

The 1980s and 1990s saw the rise of corporate raiders, junk bond kings, vulture lenders, and corporate killers like "Chainsaw Al" Dunlap. The mega-LBO and hedge fund managers have been tarred with the same brush, and too often, workers' pensions were their source of capital. Economists and market analysts now have strong reservations about the "New Masters" and the dangers of over-leverage. When the largest buyout/hedge fund managers extract huge profits (and fees and bonuses), the company, workers, and shareholders being replaced often get shortchanged. Hedge funds in particular are notoriously secretive and often only provide sporatic reports to investors.

A May 2007, article in the hedge fund press reported that former SEC chairmen William Donaldson, Arthur Levitt, Harvey Pitt, and David Ruder each criticized the hedge fund industry (during a conference of former SEC chairs). They warned that too little was known about the asset class. The panel also agreed a crisis could take place if the fast-growing industry was not better regulated. Donaldson in particular was fearful of an industry-wide blow-up.

Warren Buffett has been vocal in his distaste for hedge funds: "It's a lopsided system whereby 2% of your principal is paid each year to the manager even if he accomplishes nothing—or, for that matter, loses you a bundle—and, additionally, 20% of your profit is paid to him if he succeeds, even if his success is due simply to a rising tide." In 2002, Buffett made his infamous remarks about the boom in "derivatives" vehicles in general.

WHAT IS "FINANCIALIZATION"?

Financialization refers to both the enhanced importance of financial versus real capital in determining the rhythm and returns expected from investments, and the increased subordination of that investment to the demands of global financial markets. Under these financial imperatives firms in the manufacturing and service sector have essentially become "a bundle of assets to be deployed or redeployed depending on the short-run rates of returns that can be earned." Investors in the manufacturing and non-financial service sectors now demand rates of returns equal to those obtainable in the global financial and stock markets, rates unthinkable even a decade ago.[12]

Warning of the trend toward "financialization" of global markets, labor leaders have decried the increased de-linking of the established relationship between wages and productivity, which in advanced capitalist countries provided the foundation of a growing middle class in the long wave of economic growth after World War II.[9] John Monks, General Secretary of the European Trade Union Federation, used the occasion of the November 2006, Bevan Memorial Lecture to rebuke the rise of mega-private equity and hedge funds as a driver in "the New Capitalism," and asserted that they have become a serious threat in Europe—not only to economic security—but to the progressive social order established in the European Union.[10]

In addition to innumerable alerts by national labor bodies, the International Trade Union Confederation (ITUC) released a report in June 2007, warning union leaders and pension principals about the dangers to their pension funds of investing in the new "Casino Capitalism." The ITUC, the global labor umbrella for 168 million working people, demanded regulatory reforms of these new vehicles.[11] Global Labor called for an end to "financialization," which is described on the previous page.

Financialization was fueled by a worldwide explosion of cash in the mid-2000s, ready to invest in any vehicle, high-risk or not. The sheer volume of demand for financial funds led to a transformation in the way private equity is used: the deals were larger, the number of deals soared, and turnover increased. One consequence of the super-sized amount of liquidity was that the price of debt fell enormously, and banks lost their position as gatekeepers for the credit supply.[13] Some called this development the "shadow" banking system.

There are new demands by international bodies such as the G20, which met in November 2008 and March 2009 in the jaws of the international financial crisis, to regulate hedge funds and derivative products. There are calls for new regulations to protect national economies, indigenous industries, and working populations. Of all the calls, global labor bodies have been the most vociferous, pushing for reforms at the G20, the G8, the European Parliament, and national bodies to investigate the dangers posed by the new investment giants.

In *Working Capital*, authors Dean Baker and Archon Fung examined the ways that pension investment practices damage workers' interests, first focusing on exuberant investments in the dot-com bubble but also offshore entities and unsound mergers. They documented the increasingly short-term focus of pension fund managers. These short-term investment horizons, they argued, led to downsizing, job flight, reduced employee training, and environmental destruction (with Enron becoming, a short time later, the

IN THE REAR-VIEW MIRROR: MEGA-FUNDS AND THE FINANCIAL SHOCK OF OCTOBER 2008

- Hedge Fund Forced Redemptions: The forced selling of hedge funds in the early fall of 2008 may have been a trigger in the global financial market collapse, according to some analysts. Hedge funds borrowed huge amounts of money to buy stock indexes and bought credit default swaps as insurance against potential losses. But for many, that insurance disappeared with the bankruptcy of Lehman Brothers, a counterparty to the swaps. So as the markets declined sharply, hedge funds had to sell $75-$80 billion in stocks in September and October 2008— cash exits that might have been multiplied due to the leverage trap—to pay their debts and pay off investors pulling out of the funds. JP Morgan put the total withdrawal at $400 billion over a longer period of time. The stability of many hedge funds worsened when the U.S. SEC and British FSA banned short-selling temporarily in September 2008.

- Mega-Buyout's Damaging Debt Hangovers: The impact of burgeoning debt on many large and medium-sized firms in the U.S. and Canada is becoming more ominous as a result of the 2008 downturn. The ongoing hangover for purchased companies could cause continuing bankruptcies, asset losses, and mass layoffs for years to come. The crux of the damage to the economy is due to the record dollar volume spent in an LBO buying spree, at inflated asset prices. As The Economist put it, "…Consider the long-term prospects of leveraged buy-outs (LBOs)…In 2006-07, the industry binged, buying companies with an enterprise value of $1.4 trillion…the equivalent of one-third of all the LBOs ever." The fallout will likely be an ongoing drag on the economy (one observer called this scenario the "debt bubble"). Already, in 2008, LBO targets Linens 'n Things, Mervyn's, and Steve and Barry's have filed for bankruptcy, along with others.[14]

flagship for corrupt and bad collateral damage investments). Workers who are hurt by these practices, Baker and Fung demonstrated, may be victims of collateral damage from investments made by their own pension funds. If the authors wrote that piece today, they would most likely agree that the mega-LBOs continued the harmful practices.

As for the business practices of hedge managers, researchers at New York University concluded that when hedge funds get involved, businesses often see their profits drop and debt levels rise. Stock prices tend to increase, even though business prospects falter. Their study found that per share earnings dropped more than 50% and research and development budgets declined over the first year of hedge buyouts.[15]

Perhaps Joseph Stiglitz, a Nobel Prize-winning economist and professor at Columbia University, put it best when summing up the damages wrought by financialization:

> What has happened to the American economy is avoidable. It was not just that those who were entrusted to maintain the economy's safety and soundness failed to do their job. There were also many who benefitted handsomely by ensuring that what needed to be done did not get done. Now we face a choice: whether to let our response to the nation's woes be shaped by those who got us here, or to seize the opportunity for fundamental reforms, striking a new balance between the market and government.

Let's be clear. As Randall Dodd pointed out, not all hedge fund investment strategies are detrimental. But too many are, and this raises serious prudential and public interest concerns in terms of retirement security. And hedge funds didn't cause the financial crash. But they may have provided some of the black powder that quickened the landslide of September/October 2008.[16] The mega-LBO funds didn't cause the downturn and recession. But they have handicapped many of the corporations they bought, loading on debt and weakening firms, heightening the potential for portfolio firms to crater.

Scenarios other than the ones that played out were possible. Instead of being driven by quarterly statements (as are the public stock markets), private fund managers have more leeway to invest and can use long-term sustainable approaches. But many instead exhibited investment traits that caused great harm to our workers, retirees, companies, and communities.

After the crash, the Private Equity Council—the voice of the largest mega-funds on Wall Street—announced, in a surprising development, that it was joining the UN-PRI. Responsible private equity, and venture and real estate firms have shown it is possible to earn real returns while advancing broader social interests. Let's hope these mega-investors embrace not just the spirit but the actual letter of the PRI.

But the die may be cast for the most secretive, risky, and expensive firms, especially the hedge funds (and not just due to proposed regulations). As this book was going to press, some public pension plans had begun to seriously question the exposure, terms, and costs related to hedge funds, and public regulators moved toward greater oversight.

CHAPTER FIVE

Action Steps for Trustees: How to Talk Back to Experts

As a "capital steward," you will be urged to consider how your pension, endowment, or trust fund can be a responsible investor and still earn a competitive risk-adjusted return. You may also be very concerned about ensuring the financial well being of the fund's participants and beneficiaries.

The field of responsible investing has a lot to offer in performing your tasks as a trustee. Responsible investing promises to deliver:

- Competitive risk-adjusted rates of return;
- Collateral benefits that create long-term value for beneficiaries and society;
- Professional management with deep experience in their investment and industry areas.

But there are many pitfalls in investing in alternative investments. In making decisions about what investments to choose, how to evaluate and monitor them, you will have to rely on your carefully chosen experts. You certainly want to hire consultants with good judgment, so they can give you good advice. First and foremost you hire them for their database: the solid information with which they can provide you. Again, they're the professionals. But though they are the experts, you make the final decision. So, a common question among trustees is "How can I tell a pension fund consultant (money manager, staff, lawyer, etc.) what to do when they know so much more than I do?"

Answer: Trustees do not give up their responsibilities because they hire professionals. You, as a trustee, must manage your professionals and use them to give you specialized knowledge. For instance, we know that consultants do not always collect information that trustees need because trustees have not asked for it. Their database is their universe from which they choose the appropriate investment vehicles for your pension, endowment, or trust fund. Many consultants do not routinely put smaller, newer, specialized funds in their database. If you're interested in responsible investing, you may need to demand that your consultants expand their horizons. We suggest writing or speaking to your consultants with language that goes something like this:

I, trustee of XX Fund, understand that several investment vehicles, including Responsible Funds X (see Part Two of this Report), have advertised themselves as favoring investments that yield good returns, along with collateral benefits, or pursue good community development, labor, and environment policies in order to earn competitive market risk-adjusted returns. I want these funds to be included in your research database and considered when we review our investment managers in the relevant asset classes.

The reason for my request is that we are making investment decisions in the context of very challenging circumstances for our employers and communities, the entities that contribute to our pension fund. Without viable employers and communities, the pension fund is at risk. We need to know about investments that can earn high risk-adjusted rates of return over the long run and help sustain our employers and communities over the long-term. We would not fulfill our fiduciary roles if we did not investigate these investments.

Sincerely, You, the trustee

ACTION STEPS TO ENSURE RESPONSIBLE INVESTMENT

1. Understand alternative investments and educate trustees

Alternative investments are complex and fraught with risk. In general, be wary. Real estate managers interviewed here reported that their funds avoided the sub-prime market. And be careful of those "market cowboys" on Wall Street. First, gain an understanding of how the alternative funds operate. If you and your consultants and advisors do not understand what the funds do, don't invest. Second, ask the question: Does the fund management claim to invest in companies to stabilize and/or grow them, and in real estate projects to help communities, or not?

ACTION STEP: Capital stewards need to understand the difference between investing in a general investment portfolio of stocks and bonds, and investing in alternative investments. Trustees can explore responsible and prudent alternative pension investments, but they need to be well educated. And, finally, trustees and capital stewards need to seriously engage the management of any alternative investment funds in which they choose to invest.

2. Should your fund buy more alternative investments?

There are many good reasons for trust funds to invest in alternative investments, since it reflects the principle that trust funds should be diversified. However, most alternative asset classes and strategies are illiquid. If investors need to get their money out of private equity, hedge funds, and real estate, it can sometimes be very difficult. In the recent down market, innumerable investors got caught in a liquidity trap—a situation in which a fund lacks the cash flow from previous investments to make good on other commitments.

Consultants may urge your trust fund to increase its holding in alternative investments. The consultant may argue that these asset classes will boost yields. However much your consultant may be familiar with the field of alternative investments, he/she may be unaware that much of the data available for measuring risk for these investments is incomplete and skewed data; for example, much of the data for returns on hedge funds excludes funds that have failed.

ACTION STEP: Ask your consultant to provide a full investment portfolio rationale as to why your fund needs to increase or begin investing in alternative investments. Also, as alternative investments are designed to spread and diversify risk, ask the consultant to document that private equity returns are not correlated with stocks and bonds.

3. Can you trust reports that alternative investments earn high returns?

A number of studies question the reported high returns of private equity and hedge funds, and the real estate bubble has called into question the returns in property and fixed income investments. Many newer vintage venture/private capital funds have tried to replicate the successes of older established funds (such as those managed for the Harvard Endowments, etc.), but often fail to achieve those results. In some cases, failed funds are not counted when averaging fund class returns (as in the hedge fund arena). Fund managers can manipulate benchmarks and return averages to make their fund appear "top quartile." Can you trust their guarantees?

ACTION STEP: Ask your consultant to independently verify the sources and amount of returns from private equity funds. Be cautious of benchmarks; ask the consultant to disclose cash in/cash out documentation (which can then be compared to a broader index like the S&P 500). Increasingly, the source of private equity returns came from debt: fund owners borrowed against the assets of the newly acquired company to pay themselves capital gains. This meant companies acquired by LBO firms (in particular) may be worse off than they were before they were bought if heavy debts were incurred. Over-leverage factored into the collapse of several hedge funds. Finally, don't forget the over-levered real estate bubble and sub-prime mess.

4. How will future regulation (and/or taxes) affect your alternative fund investments?

The new Administration and Congressional leaders, public regulators, and pension funds are calling for regulations and more transparency for mega-LBO and hedge funds. There are serious doubts about the feasibility of extraordinary fees and levels of secrecy that exist with these alternative fund vehicles. They are asking that funds disclose historical and realized deals, debt levels, etc. Labor unions are demanding that funds negotiate in good faith in advance of final purchase of represented companies (and that new investors respect existing labor agreements). In addition, Congress has been holding hearings on the tax treatment of a number of investment vehicles. These threats of new taxation and regulation could clearly affect potential returns.

ACTION STEP: Urge your consultants and investment managers to research the various proposals for regulating hedge funds and private equity and report to the trustees how each one, if enacted, would affect the risk and return of your holdings.

5. Do quarterly reports penalize long-term sustainable investments?

Many pension and institutional fund trustees receive quarterly performance data on their fund managers. This should not reduce the incentive for capital stewards and money managers to invest in companies that have long-term horizons. Quarterly performance inevitably induces behavior that is focused on short-term results. The demand for short-term performance results by investors and pension trustees has undoubtedly contributed to the fact that the average stock market investment is now held for less than 12 months, compared with seven years in the 1970s.

ACTION STEP: Instruct your consultant to investigate different benchmarks for long-term mandates. Responsible institutional investors need to lead the way to break this short-termist cycle and reward fund managers willing to invest for the long-term.

6. How do you gauge aspects of long-term, ESG investments?

The Enhanced Analytics Initiative (EAI) is an international collaboration between asset owners and asset managers aimed at encouraging better investment research. In particular, this research takes account of the impact of extra-financial issues on long-term investment. Extra-financial issues are best described as fundamentals that have the potential to impact a company's financial performance or reputation in a material way, both positive and negative, yet are generally not part of traditional fundamental analysis.[1] The EAI currently represents total assets under management of €1.8 trillion (c. US$2.4 trillion). In addition, some of the managers of the profiled funds (Part II) have additional ideas about appropriate gauges.

7. How well do your selected private equity and real estate funds understand the businesses in which they invest?

Instruct your consultant or the actual fund managers to report on the labor relations practices of the companies owned by the partnerships in which your fund invests. Ask the managers to quantify, company by company, how many jobs have been created and how many eliminated over the last three years. Ask if funded construction projects are considering the use of green building methods. Ask whether the employees of your portfolio companies are covered by collective bargaining agreements, and if not, why not. If your professional consultants don't know the answers, tell them to investigate and report back to you

8. Request that selected alternative funds adopt a responsible contractor and other worker-friendly policies.

Some pension funds such as CalPERS have adopted "responsible contractor" policies and project labor agreements in their real estate investments. This is to encourage fair wages, benefits, and training for investment projects (like hotels). Some union pension funds, such as Laborers and SEIU, have also adopted such policies. Others pensions have promoted card check neutrality for operating company investments. Similarly, CalPERS and the New York City pension funds have adopted anti-privatization and opt-out policies. These types of policies are now being discussed as an option for investments in private equity funds and infrastructure funds.

ACTION STEP: Push for responsible contractor and worker-friendly policies. By adopting such policies, your pension fund capital stewards can start a productive conversation with your consultant and managers about how your assets are managed and the consequences of private ownership. These policies spell out the standards by which the funds expect their investment managers to evaluate potential real estate projects and acquisitions and to manage those investments. For general guidelines, refer to the AFL-CIO Office of Worker Investment, Change-to-Win, SHARE, or the ILO Standards (International Labour Organization).

9. What are other funds doing to hold their managers accountable?

Talk to trustees at other funds about private equity and real estate. Find out what they do to hold their managers accountable. If they use the same managers as you do, consider organizing a joint meeting to review these issues with the manager. Look at the client list of your managers and reach out to the names you recognize. Ask the trustees of those funds to adopt responsible policies as well. Consider this an optional form of "financial leverage" and put it to work for better investment outcomes.[3]

10. How do I identify opportunities for long-term investments?

Do the consultants describe the performances of alternative investment options on a long-term basis—five, ten years (twenty, if available)—or do they focus on short-term quarterly returns? As we mentioned earlier, rich short-term returns may not stand up over a longer period, especially if the economy changes direction. Do a careful search for fund managers that meet the responsible investor framework. Use ESG Criteria to understand the impacts of the fund's investments on workers, the community, and the environment, and to analyze fund managers.

11. What do I say when the consultants dismiss the Responsible Investment field?

Take the initiative. If responsible capital funds are obtaining returns-on-investment comparable to other investment options, or have respectful results compared to benchmarks, then it will be difficult to dismiss them with ad hoc rationales. Spend time getting to know who the responsible investors are (the ones represented here and others). Check out the websites of umbrella bodies serving the responsible investment community, like UN-PRI, labor and social investment groups. Find out how individual funds' investments are making a difference. And push consultants to disclose the real facts about their favorites (see above). Force disclosure on management fees, as well as transaction and carry fees. Educate your fellow trustees, the principals of the beneficiary groups you represent, pension fund management and consultants, and business, labor, and public leaders.[4]

12. Review the advisories on responsible investments and adopt appropriate policies on investments in alternative asset classes.

ACTION STEP: Read the reports. Many pension fund bodies have adopted thoughtful pension policies on alternative investments in general and responsible investments in particular. You can sometimes find policies on their websites, or you can contact the funds and request copies. In addition, academic centers, policy and governance entities, and global trade unions have issued a number of very important reports and studies on responsible pension policies and alternative investments, including principles and guidelines. SEIU garnered press and sought debate on these issues in "Behind the Buyouts: Inside the World of Private Equity."

Here are some helpful internet resources:

- UN's Principles for Responsible Investment (PRI): www.unpri.org
- Marathon Club Guidance Note on Long-term Investment: www.marathonclub.co.uk

- *Handbook on Responsible Investment Across Asset Classes:*
  http://tinyurl.com/nhuhe8
- Pension Funds and Urban Revitalization Project of the University
  of Oxford, School of Geography and the Environment:
  http://urban.ouce.ox.ac.uk/
- UNI's Report on Pension Fund Investments in Private Equity:
  http://tinyurl.com/ljpoh3

CHAPTER SIX

Dispatches from the Field: Learning Old Truths and Breaking New Ground

Today, as never before, the daily lives of Americans and Canadians are powerfully influenced by Wall Street and Bay Street and international capital markets. Throughout the 1980s and 1990s, badly managed LBOs, M&As, and corporate restructurings downsized our nation's largest employers and closed our plants and factories. In the 2000s, mega-funds and faulty financially engineered schemes destroyed more critical industries and destabilized the housing market. Working people in industrial cities and towns have been hammered by job insecurity, stagnant incomes, heavy debt burdens, and rising inequality. The layoff binge has never let up, and with each recession, it gets worse.

All companies, including North America's biggest corporations, face enormous pressure to meet investors' obsession for higher and quicker profits. This tyranny of the bottom line has diminished the power of communities to influence economic decisions affecting them. It is tragic that pension funds and people's capital at times played a part in this tyranny. A decade after *Equity Analyst* reported that pension funds provided half the capital in the LBOs that drove the market in irrational mergers and acquisitions, these funds doubled-down on the New Masters of the Universe and also heavily invested in the housing bubble and sub-primes.[1]

Up from Wall Street shows that there are more prudent, long-term choices. We surveyed six private equity and seven real estate funds that market to union and public employee pension funds and other institutional investors. Each of these funds emphasizes a particular secondary or collateral benefit that the investment achieves in addition to maximizing risk-adjusted rate of return. The most salient finding is that each fund, whether real estate or private equity, emphasizes its ability to meet standards for traditional financial success while advancing a goal that benefits, rather than harms, working families and communities. There will be a greater benefit to workers, citizens, and regions, as well as to the employer community, if your fund's investments result in positive domestic outcomes, such as the development and diffusion of environmental technology, higher labor standards, or the conservation or creation of well-paid jobs in a region.

In addition to achieving healthy profits, in fact, workers' pension funds around the world have succeeded in achieving positive environmental, social, and governance "returns" from investing in the private economy and local community, promoting more egalitarian growth. In our closing argument, we suggest that these responsible capital fund managers are creating new models of responsible and innovative investment, beyond investing in property or businesses.

Steve Coyle calls these new models an emerging *third wave investment strategy* for pension funds. This third wave often combines and builds on responsible real estate, private equity, and other investment approaches. In summarizing once again, the third wave includes:

- Investing in advanced manufacturing and industrial enterprises, affordable and workforce housing, and commercial real estate, as well as in renewable energy, green construction, and other sustainable products and processes; and,
- Re-investing in urban cities, crafting planned communities and multi-use complexes that are smartly anchored by housing, commercial workplaces, public facilities, and jobs-producing firms, and that are connected to new energy, transportation, and infrastructure hubs; and,
- Building bridges to the broader community and the public sector,

creating training and social services alliances (such as daycare centers, etc.), as part of multi-use developments.

These innovative approaches have been deployed not only in New York, Vancouver, and the U.S. Gulf Coast, as shown in the profiles, but through the work of global pension funds in London, Montreal, South Africa, the Netherlands, and elsewhere.

And capital stewards, through strategic investments, are doing much more. Here's a summary of the specific lessons learned from the profiled funds, highlighting investment-related gains, along with environmental, social, and governance (ESG) advances.

Financial Returns

- *Comparison to Indexes*: Responsible Capital funds report that, in a healthy proportion of funds, they yielded returns that were tracking and often besting their respective indexes, in some cases throwing off top-tier returns. While this book does not claim that all profiled funds accomplished this feat, the reported evidence thus far is impressive.

- *Professional Capacity*: Responsible Capital is managed by innovative investment professionals with advanced degrees and a wealth of experience and knowledge. They are well trained in conventional methods, but they have also pioneered new investment models. They seem to care about the success of their investments and reflect deep concerns about beneficiaries, working families, and their communities. They appear to hold genuine convictions about what constitutes social progress. We have found most of them accessible and open to future collaborations with their colleagues (and across borders).

- *Growing Capital*: Responsible Capital has grown at a respectable rate but could stand additional investment commitments from institutional investors. Some funds have been so successful that they have doubled and quadrupled available capital in successive partnerships. Capital stewards can and should explore pooling their assets into sizable capital funds that are larger in scale and that can invest cross-border.

- *Enhanced Deal Flow*: Responsible Capital has built solid relationships with various constituencies—labor union officials, environmental and community representatives, and business people—who have helped the funds find good deals. Enhanced deal flow is a comparative advantage in the investment field.

- *Close Engagement*: Responsible Capital can closely monitor targeted investment vehicles and their respective investments to ensure, first, profitability, and second, that the long-term interests of beneficiaries are respected. Capital stewards can also provide protection from bad privatization deals and anti-union investments, through "opt-out" and "embarrassment clauses."

Social Returns

- *Good Housing*: Responsible Capital has built and/or rehabilitated thousands of affordable and workforce housing units. Real estate funds have invested in construction projects and mortgage programs to provide homes for, and increasing the jobs available to, construction trades members and other community residents.

- *Commercial and Public Construction*: Responsible Capital has constructed, rehabbed, or provided refinancing for large multi-family housing developments, including apartment and condo buildings, in addition to a wide selection of commercial and public facilities projects, including hotels, clinics, schools, etc. Many earned architectural design awards.

- *Good Jobs*: Responsible Capital has created or saved hundreds of thousands of jobs, many permanent, through investments in construction, jobs-generating industries, energy and domestic infrastructure. Capital stewards are having a growing impact on the jobs front, whether (1) investing in new jobs through venture capital and development finance funds, (2) expanding existing employers through private equity growth funds, (3) stabilizing jobs through special situations funds, (4) generating new industries and occupations through clean-tech funds, or (5) putting construction workers to work every day.

- *Training, Education, Health Care*: Responsible Capital has constructed new apprenticeship, training, and education programs, and consortia, training a smart new generation of workers. Given the preponderance of portfolio firms that have good labor relations, Responsible Capital has also made a practice of investing in firms that, generally, provide a better opportunity for quality health care and pensions.

- *Social and Performance Audits*: Responsible Capital has pioneered new social and performance audit approaches (and ethical and social screens) to ensure their investments fulfill employment commitments, respect workers' health and safety concerns, and support healthy communities.

- *Smart Restructuring*: Responsible Capital has deployed a smart new approach in the difficult field of business restructurings and turnarounds, an approach that minimizes downsizing (avoiding outsourcing and subcontracting) and maximizes smart management and workforce partnerships that yield increased productivity.

- *Broad Industry Investment*: Responsible Capital has invested in diverse, critical strategic industries such as steel and manufacturing, transportation, distribution, communications, and other fields, as well as labor-intensive sectors, including the medical, hotel, restaurant, agriculture, and food processing fields. It has been stabilizing and re-growing seasoned industries, diversifying and modernizing new opportunities in key sectors, and bringing new jobs and improved opportunities to sectors that often paid lower wages.

Environmental Returns

- *Green Construction*: Responsible Capital has fully engaged, in many cases, in green housing and commercial construction, utilizing LEED and other sustainable building products and processes. In some cases, funds are invested in green multi-use real estate and commercial projects that cover multiple city blocks. Some of these projects have won prestigious environmental awards.
- *Clean-Tech and Renewable Investments*: Responsible Capital is capitalizing advanced clean-tech industries, including renewable energy and efficient transit and transportation, and building new solar and wind energy systems that will become part of the renewable grid. They may someday join alliances with workers' pensions in other countries, where pension funds own the largest national renewable energy companies.
- *Waste and Pollution Reduction*: Responsible Capital is modernizing older companies, factories, and offices through equipment, machinery, factory, and process improvements, and waste reduction, reducing pollutants. Funds are also engaged in industrial product recycling on a significant scale. Funds are thus providing safer health conditions for workers and community residents, and a cleaner environment for us all.
- *At-scale Redevelopment:* Responsible Capital is redeveloping blighted regions and urban areas, rehabilitating abandoned and distressed properties, and cleaning up brown-fields. By converting large sections of cities into clean housing, commercial, production, parks, and amenities complexes, these efforts are not only providing good jobs for union members and low-income people but also revitalizing whole communities.
- *Global Environmental and Climate Protection*: Nationally and

internationally, Responsible Capital is investing in initiatives focused on climate change and environmental and clean energy investments.

Governance Returns

- *Responsible Employment Relations*: Responsible Capital has adopted progressive responsible contractor policies, often providing a safe harbor for labor-relations neutrality when workers endeavor to organize collectively. This outcome leads to better labor-management cooperation, a voice on the job, and allows for improved wages, benefits, education, and working conditions (often proxies for improved productivity).

- *Governance Development*: Responsible Capital has developed innovative empowerment strategies in some cases that provide ownership and employment opportunities to working people and historically disadvantaged populations.

- *Workforce Participation and Ownership*: Responsible Capital has invested in new worker-owner partnerships, including employee stock ownership firms (ESOPs) and new Sub-Chapter S ESOP ownership models. They have also supported new workforce participation and labor-management strategies. These approaches can engage workers and labor representatives from the shop floor to the boardroom, leading to new economic ladders, training and education opportunities, and improved productivity.

- *Financial Literacy and Training*: Responsible Capital funds like Quebec's Solidarity Fund are training "knowledge workers," providing extensive financial literacy training to employees of its investee firms. This boosts worker understanding of businesses and the economy, improves labor-management cooperation, and increases job security.

- *Retaining and Increasing Union Density*: Responsible Capital has developed strategic investment platforms to help retain or grow union density in enterprise or real estate markets.

Toward the Third Wave

From the initial findings of this report, it is clear that Responsible Capital provides new tools to engage in the economy at a time when the "gospel of efficient markets" has failed working people and communities. What, then, is the bigger picture emerging from these rich and varied trends and impacts? Some capital stewards, union leaders, fund managers, and entrepreneurs envision a worker-friendly, sustainable marketplace financed by this growing network of responsible funds. Partnering and collaborating with other responsible investors and public/private bodies, pooling and levering resources, capital stewards would explore significant investments that:

- *Co-invest* in renewable energy, green construction, and other clean-tech industries, as well as advanced manufacturing and other essential technology and economic strategies, promoting collaboration across many asset classes;
- *Pool investments across borders* in strategic funds and funds-of-funds along the spectrum of responsible ETIs, including:
    - climate change and clean-tech funds that build new infrastructure and capacity in advanced wind, solar, and efficient transportation technologies,
    - infrastructure bond funds, and
    - defensive buyout and turnaround funds (to hold at bay hostile mega-funds).
- *Link green building projects and complexes* supplying smart, affordable, and workforce housing, as well as safe workplaces for union members and citizens, tied to:
    - green products and resources supply chains to grow the capacity of regional industries to convert to new products and take advantage of this growing market;
    - renewable energy programs and user-friendly utilities, ensuring the installation of solar panels and other green power and conservation methods;

- efficient transportation hubs to re-settle declining urban areas
and reduce sprawl, and to provide non-polluting rail lines to
isolated rural areas.
- *Renovate and retrofit* the millions of substandard homes, offices
and factories in our respective countries, the lowest-hanging fruit
in terms of reducing wasted energy usage, employing renewables
and green building products and processes;
- *Reach across borders* to help re-build cities and regions like New
Orleans and the Gulf (that suffered from a natural disaster)
and Detroit and the U.S./Canadian Great Lakes auto belt (that
has been suffering an economic disaster), as well as guide smart
and sustainable growth for rural areas like Appalachia and the
Canadian North;
- *Partner with international, national, and state/provincial*
governments as well as other stakeholders to invest in the next
generation of innovation platforms, rebuild our communities and
re-new our infrastructure (and build it green), and create green
jobs and educational opportunities for our children.

As we near the end of the first decade of the 2000s, it is important, as a
final caution, to not keep repeating the mistakes of the past. After years of
"dollars searching for deals," our economy will grapple with a lack of access
to venture, growth, expansion, and construction capital and other sources
that could responsibly rebuild the economy. Our capital stewards can and
should re-double their efforts and become early adopters of new responsible
investment approaches.

In conclusion, the stewards of our capital have shown that they can
make responsible, long-term investments that earn a good rate of return
but also yield important collateral benefits. Thus pension and institutional
investors can align investments with the interests of beneficiaries. Capital
stewards can ensure that investment streams are flowing to critical economic
needs and essential opportunities, and doing so profitably. In dramatic

form, capital stewards can invest smartly to re-grow our economy and lay the foundation for the green jobs of the future. In taking these approaches, capital stewards can seize the moment, re-create and renew parts of urban cities, redevelop poor rural areas, and invest in sustainable developments that benefit all of us (beyond borders). And, as the global labor movement and its business and community allies further engage global green initiatives, capital stewards can demand, with their investments, aggressive progress toward climate solutions. Finally, they can create the third wave.

In other words, capital stewards can indeed invest in a responsible future—our future and that of our children—and invest in a vision of the economy that's more humane and sustainable.

PART TWO

A Field Guide
to Responsible Capital

"Responsible" investing does not have to mean inadequate investment returns. Lots of investors have learned how to reach superior risk-adjusted investment returns while at the same time achieving collateral benefits for their beneficiaries, other workers, and communities.

This field guide for this new class of responsible investor contains descriptions of investment funds that are together managing over $30 billion and provides a detailed analyses of some of the firms and projects in which they invest. Please see Appendix 1 for a longer list of portfolio cases.

CHAPTER SEVEN

Responsible Private Equity and Venture Capital Funds

In this chapter we describe six responsible private equity and venture capital funds, displayed below, ranked by alphabet. Then we analyze each fund. We start with an overview of the fund, its structure, capacity, and products. Next we describe the effect of the fund's investments on jobs—labor impacts—and the ways the fund promotes a sustainable environment—environmental and community impacts. This is followed by information on the fund's financial performance, its portfolio, and profiles of principals. Finally, we describe one of the fund's investments in detail.

FUND NAME	ASSETS
GESD Capital Partners (San Francisco	$ 250 million
GrowthWorks (Vancouver, Toronto)	$ 900 million (C)
KPS Capital Partners, LLP (New York)	$ 1.8 billion
Landmark GCP (Simsbury)	$ 78.2 million
Solidarity Fund (Montreal)	$ 7.4 billion (C)
The Yucaipa Companies (Los Angeles)	$ 6.0 billion

GESD Capital Partners (San Francisco)

221 Main Street, Suite 1450
San Francisco, CA 94105
Phone: (415) 477-8200
Fax: (415) 495-8211
Web: www.gesd.net
Contact: Lou Giraudo, Managing Partner
Email: loug@gesd.net

Distinguishing Characteristics:

- Founded: 1998
- Habitat: Based in San Francisco, California
- Range: Invests primarily in U.S.
- Fund Type: Private equity growth and buyout fund
- Fund Structure(s): Limited partnerships
- Capital Partners: Pension and institutional investors, private investors
- Assets: More than $250 million

Overview

GESD Capital Partners (GESD) is a private equity firm based in San Francisco, California. It provides investment capital to middle-market companies. GESD generally invests in companies with revenues between $20 million and $200 million and focuses on manufacturing and service-oriented companies with an emphasis on food manufacturing and consumer product companies. GESD maintains an investment focus in the United States. Total capitalization for the first fund was at $250 million. The firm is currently investing its second fund: GESD Investors II. Current capital assets are over $250 million.

Structure

GESD acts as the general partner of limited partnerships for the benefit of institutional investors. The company deploys eight investment professionals. GESD is typically a "control" investor (i.e. it prefers to invest in companies it can control) but will consider minority positions in certain situations. GESD maintains an advisory board for each of its funds. These boards include labor representatives. There is no specific provision for co-investment opportunities.

Capacity and Products

The GESD principals have substantial experience, having acted as both advisors and principals over the course of their business careers. The principals have participated in transactions with an estimated combined value of more than $10 billion in a wide range of industries. The principals also have more than 20 years of operations experience in various sectors and have had direct management responsibilities as successful entrepreneurs and executives in firms with sales ranging from $3 million to over $500 million.

GESD considers family-owned or owner managed recapitalizations, management buyouts, leveraged buyouts, growth financings, private investments in public equities, bankruptcy reorganizations, and joint ventures. GESD focuses on companies with the following characteristics: significant market share positions, strong growth potential, solid customer relationships, strong brand recognition, and proprietary products and processes. Investments by GESD may be structured in a variety of ways, depending upon the circumstances of a particular transaction.

Labor Impacts

GESD's first goal is to achieve appropriate risk-adjusted returns for their limited partners. As a secondary social policy, GESD encourages good labor relations. GESD believes that considerable growth results when sound business strategies are combined with mutually beneficial employee relationships, including equity-sharing and other performance-based arrangements. GESD further believes that value creation often takes time to develop and, therefore is a "patient" investor, focusing on companies that have a long-term focus.

As GESD Co-Founder Lou Giraudo explains, the first GESD fund made eight investments, yielding 1,000 new union jobs. The fund also saved 700 jobs in one project and thus far has also provided approximately 250,000 hours of union construction work.

Giraudo notes that good labor relations requires work on all sides. His thoughts on the subject of responsible investing: "As a general partner operating in private equity, I have a fiduciary obligation to our investors. But, I also feel an obligation to the workers who produce our high quality products, that they have the right to organize and to an agreement that will give them a fair and decent wage for the work that they do."

Environmental/Community Impacts

In 2002, GESD bought Boudin Bakeries, Inc., the oldest continuing business in San Francisco. Andre-Boudin is a world-class producer of French sourdough bread, pastries, sandwiches, soups, and sourdough pizzas. Andre-Boudin currently operates 21 bakery cafes and 3 wholesale bakeries located in Northern California, Southern California, and the greater Chicago area.

In 2005, the company unveiled a new 26,000 square foot multi-use facility on San Francisco's famed Fisherman's Wharf. The facility features a demonstration bakery, Bakers Hall market, Bistro Boudin (a Boudin Café), a full-service restaurant, and the Boudin Museum & Bakery Tour.

"The history of San Francisco and the story of Boudin Bakery have been intertwined since the Gold Rush," noted Giraudo in a business article at the time. "Boudin at the Wharf is our way of celebrating that connection." Giraudo says the facility is a "fully interactive demonstration bakery with a walkthrough history of San Francisco sourdough."

We visited the new Fisherman's Wharf landmark in the summer of 2006, and it was packed. Visitors can tour the bakery, and a glass-walled catwalk overlooking the operations provides a vantage point from which visitors can watch what is going on below. Museum-like panels with pictures and text narrate Boudin's history. Each tour concludes with a visit to the tasting room, where visitors sample oven-fresh bread. We had lunch in the upstairs restaurant and also purchased sourdough bread from the "food hall," a shop selling Boudin bread and other West Coast goods.

The waterfront has had few unionized employers, but here the BCGTM (Bakery, Confectionery, Tobacco, Workers, and Grain Millers International Union), UFCW (United Food and Commercial Workers), and UNITE/HERE represent a majority of the employees. GESD is also committed to a program of diversity, encouraging participation by minority-owned businesses and locally owned businesses in designing and constructing the improvements. The project utilized an all-union workforce during construction and paid prevailing wages (rate paid to a majority of people engaged in a particular craft, classification, or type of work within a geographic area).

The San Francisco Port Commission announced at the time that "Boudin's proposed development will be a benefit to the Port's assets at Fisherman's Wharf…The proposed redevelopment of the Property will create a new vibrant facility bringing Fisherman's Wharf into the building while exposing the building's interior to Fisherman's Wharf. The building's modern design reflects the historic maritime architecture of the Port. Its location at the entrance to Fisherman's Wharf will create a new and inviting entrance point to San Francisco's most significant tourist attraction." For more info, see www.boudinbakery.com.

Portfolio

GESD has two funds: GESD Investors, LP and GESD Investors II, LP. The first fund, GESD Investors, LP, holds eight companies, six of which are platform holding companies and two of which are stand-alone entities. The eight investments are in the restaurant, baking, food processing, and entertainment industries. Many of these are listed in the appendix.

Performance

As of submission for publication, GESD anticipated future realizations for most of its portfolio.

Challenges

Lou Giraudo often talks about the first time a labor representative asked him, "Can you really make money?" His short answer was yes. The longer answer? He said that the private equity landscape changed quickly in the last few years, with an enormous amount of capital being committed to leveraged buyouts. The task of investing this capital profitably while implementing a secondary social policy is challenging. It is a task that requires an understanding of not only underlying business dynamics but a deep-running knowledge and appreciation of labor issues and concerns, which may at times seem to run counter to company profitability. Moreover, it is a task that requires flexibility and understanding from the entire range of the pension community, including trustees, advisors, consultants, QPAMs, and international and local labor leaders.

Principals

Louis J. Giraudo, Senior Managing Partner and Co-Founder of GESD, has been involved in the bread baking and food industry his entire lifetime. His family ran the original sourdough bread company in San Francisco, and although he took a break to attend law school, practice law, and manage some political campaigns from 1986 to 1993, Giraudo became Chairman and CEO of the Pacific Coast Baking Company and was Chairman of Mother's Cake & Cookie Co., with combined sales of more than $500 million. Mr. Giraudo is a Co-Founder and Principal of GESD Capital Partners, a private equity firm. Prior to GESD, Lou was CEO of Preferred Capital Markets from January 1999 to December 2002.

Lou and his co-founder Sharon Duvall had a previous track record of worker-friendly investment practices, having worked with the Bakery Workers and Teamsters in their expansion of Pacific Coast. And in addition to serving on many of the boards of GESD's companies, Lou has held numerous public service and corporate board positions throughout his career, including Chairman of the Board of Trustees of the University of San Francisco. He currently also serves as the Chairman of the Board of Pabst Brewing Company.

Lou's father, Steven Giraudo, came to San Francisco from Italy in 1935, taking his first job at Boudin and eventually becoming master baker. In 1946, he and a partner bought the business from the Boudin family. By 1993, the Boudin brand was just a small part of a $2.5-billion-per-year Giraudo family food-products business. Specialty Foods of Illinois bought the whole business in 1993. Then, in 2002, GESD Capital Partners bought Boudin back from Specialty, returning it to San Francisco. His business partner, Sharon Duvall, was brought in as CEO. "We regard our ownership of Boudin as a public trust," Giraudo said at the time.

SHARON B. DUVALL, is the other Senior Managing Partner and Co-Founder of GESD. She serves on the board of several portfolio companies, including Forklift Holdings (Boudin, Go Roma), Innobake Brands, Austin's Entertainment LLC, and Milton's Baking Company. Duvall oversees the firm's investment strategy as well as portfolio company relations. Duvall's other responsibilities include investor relations, deal generation, and evaluation.

Prior to GESD, Duvall managed and directed Breadboard Enterprises and Breadboard Investments, which are private equity investment vehicles. She was also a consultant to Preferred Capital Markets, Inc. ("PCM"), and advised PCM on several equity transactions. Prior to her work in private equity investing, Duvall was an executive with the Pacific Coast Baking Company ("PCB") and several of its related entities, where she led PCB's consolidation of regional bakeries and distributors along with Giraudo. She was Chief Financial Officer of PCB, Chairman and CEO of Andre-Boudin Bakeries, Inc., and a member of the board of both PCB and Mother's Cake & Cookie Co. Before her work in the food industry, Duvall, a Certified Public Accountant, worked at Coopers & Lybrand.

Giraudo and Duvall are joined by co-founders and partners MARK L. BRIGGS and DAN STROMBERG, each of who have more than 20 years of professional advisory and investment experience. GESD employs four other investment professionals, including Chief Financial Officer Bill Dozier who joined the firm in 2001.

Project Showcase: Golden Country Foods, Inc.

In December 2002, GESD bought Golden County Foods, Inc., a Wisconsin-based frozen food manufacturer. At the time the company had a small but high quality customer base, a highly skilled manufacturing-oriented management team, one plant, and was focused nearly exclusively on specialty potato products. The 400-person workforce was unorganized and suffered from nearly a 70% turnover rate. Upon acquisition, a two-pronged approach was developed with management: (1) creating a growth strategy focused on utilizing existing manufacturing expertise to expand the product offering and reduce customer concentration while growing revenue and earnings, and (2) stabilizing the work force via better pre-employment screening, extensive cross-training, and an increased focus on employee safety practices.

The company quickly expanded its production capabilities and gained traction with batter-breaded appetizers. Based on a number of large opportunities presented to the company and the need to expand its capabilities and capacity, GESD approved the acquisition and retrofit of a second facility for appetizer products. As with other construction undertaken by GESD's companies, this was completed almost entirely with union labor.

At about this time, the company entered into a Card Check Neutrality Agreement with UFCW Local 73A, resulting in recognition of Local 73A as the bargaining representative. Negotiations were undertaken and concluded on terms acceptable to management and GESD, and the employees then overwhelmingly ratified the contract. Since implementation of the agreement the number of cross-trained employees has increased dramatically and the turnover rate fell to an all time low of 17%. Local 73A officials indicate that it has been pleased in its relationship with this employer.

As of this writing, the company continues to grow rapidly, reporting dramatic year over year increases in revenues and earnings. Appetizers—particularly the company branded product line SNAPPS—have fueled this growth and now represent approximately 40% of the company's revenues. Customer concentration has also been reduced dramatically since acquisition. Giraudo indicates that Golden County is a model of what GESD aims to accomplish—achieving strong, profitable growth within the context of stabilizing a previously strained work environment and ultimately becoming an excellent union employer (for more information, visit www.goldencountyfoods.com).

GrowthWorks (Vancouver and Toronto)

2600-1055 West Georgia Street, P.O. 11170
Royale Center
Vancouver, British Columbia V6E 3R5
Phone: 1-800-268-8244
Fax: 1-866-688-3431
Web: www.growthworks.ca
Contact: David Levi, President, CEO and Director of
GrowthWorks Capital LTD and affiliates
Email: david.levi@growthworks.ca

Distinguishing Characteristics

- Founded: 1991
- Habitat: Main office Vancouver, B.C., but also Toronto,
  Ontario (and affiliate offices)
- Range: Funds invest in B.C., Ontario, Atlantic Provinces, other
  provinces in Canada
- Fund Type: Venture and private capital funds
- Fund Structure(s): "Retail" VC/PE Labor-Sponsored
  Investment Funds (LSIFs)
- Capital Partners: Individual investors capitalize the fund
  through a tax-credit savings program
- Assets: C$ 900 million

Overview

GrowthWorks[1] is a family of worker-friendly funds across Canada. Managed funds include the Working Opportunity Fund (WOF), GrowthWorks Canadian Fund, GrowthWorks Commercialization Fund, and GrowthWorks Atlantic Venture Fund. In all, GW is managing $900 million in assets, with a primary focus on Canada's most promising industry sectors. These funds include national, regional, and specialized funds.

This profile will focus on the most seasoned of GW funds, the Working

Opportunity Fund. The Working Opportunity Fund (EVCC) Ltd. is a venture capital investment fund owned by approximately 50,000 individual British Columbians. The Fund currently has approximately $400 million in assets and has almost half of those assets invested in small and medium-sized B.C. businesses. WOF was incorporated under the Company Act (B.C.) in 1991, and began offering common shares to the public in January 1992. Subsequent to a partnership agreement reached with organized labor in B.C. to help launch the Fund, the Province provided start-up support. Commercialization Shares can be also invested in early-stage, research-oriented companies, and fixed income investments.

WOF is a labour-sponsored investment fund (LSIF) under federal legislation, providing eligibility for RRSP tax credits. It is also an Employee Venture Capital Corporation (EVCC) under the B.C. provincial Employee Investment Act, a statute passed in 1989 to encourage B.C. residents to invest in eligible small and medium-sized businesses in the province, encourage greater employee participation in share ownership and enterprise development, create and protect jobs, and promote growth and diversification of the B.C. economy. Labor Sponsored Investment Funds (LSIFs) were created under federal and provincial statutes designed to promote privately-funded and managed venture capital pools (see also the profile for Solidarity Fund).

WOF's purpose is to provide a competitive long-term return for its shareholders by making equity investments in small to medium-sized innovative, high-growth British Columbia companies. WOF seeks long-term appreciation on investments. The mission of WOF was also to provide capital to diversify the resource-based economy of British Columbia and create or maintain well-paid sustainable jobs. The investors in these labor-sponsored funds are individual investors, most of them middle income earners ($40-60,000) with a bias to union households.

When WOF began, it was managed internally by its own officers and employees. In 1998, WOF's Board and its shareholders approved a restructuring of management so that it would be provided by GrowthWorks

Capital Ltd (GWC). This is more typical of a venture or private equity fund management structure. On January 1, 1999, all WOF employees, including its investment team, started working for GWC.

Structure

GW Funds are organized as LSIFs, and capitalized through "retail" investors. Each of the GW funds has its own board of directors, the majority of whom are appointed by its labor sponsors (see background on LSIFs in appendix). In addition shareholders directly elect directors. Investments made by the funds are reviewed by a business advisory council consisting of highly experienced CEO's who volunteer their time.

WOF's Board of Directors has top-level responsibility for overseeing the management of WOF, subject to the responsibilities delegated to its committees and Manager. Of the thirteen board members, seven are labor leaders or officers. Similar to Quebec's Solidarity Fund, WOF is capitalized by individual B.C. investors who can invest up to $5,000 year and receive a one-time 15% federal and 15% provincial tax credit for their investment.

WOF typically takes a non-controlling equity stake (10-45%) in investee firms. However, WOF can make proportionately larger ownership investments if the investment might result in substantial employee participation in the business, or where a turn-around is required. WOF participates on investee company boards and also provides management expertise, advice and counseling, as well as a network of resources useful to young companies. It does not get involved in the day-to-day activities of a business.

Capacity and Products

GrowthWorks, the fund manager, has a staff of over 90 professionals and support staff with extensive experience in the raising and managing of venture capital as well as back office fund management support. Among all of GW's Funds, the management team has invested more than $600 million in over 400 companies. The funds function initially as an early stage investor but continue to do multiple rounds of investment through to stability.

Therefore their actual weighted invested capital is in companies with rapidly growing revenues that are approaching profitability.

For the GrowthWorks family of funds, preferred investment sectors include new economy (life sciences, medical devices, software, communications and networking, hardware, electronic devices, and internet-related), alternative energy and environmental technologies, and advanced materials and advanced manufacturing. WOF's initial investment targets were information technology, life sciences, and advanced manufacturing. GW also manages a commercialization fund that invests in startups and technology transfers from universities.

Initial investments in any company will normally range from $100,000 to $5 million. WOF investments aim to cover a broad range of businesses in a variety of industries. Patient capital and longer-term (3-6 year) investments are preferred. WOF can partner with other investment companies providing they share the same investment philosophy toward the business.

WOF requires participation on the Board of Directors but does not ordinarily seek control of a business. In most cases, WOF is approached by entrepreneurs to fund their businesses. WOF has an internal review process using outside expertise in specialty areas and seeks an internal hurdle rate of at least 30% annual return on investment.

Labor Impacts

Independent reports have shown that WOF and its network of GWC-managed investment firms have invested over $300 million in more than 100 growth-oriented, entrepreneurial Canadian companies, creating or retaining 10,000 jobs.

All WOF investments are subject to an ethical audit prior and during investments. The audit is quite extensive, and examines both risks and best practices. The audit examines labor practices, health and safety issues, hiring and employment rights, etc., but also business ethics. Labor productivity is a key issue for manufacturing investees. WOF has a growth strategy for all companies and therefore does not use layoffs as a strategy to profitability.

Environmental/Community Impacts

GrowthWorks funds have invested $62.5 million in 14 interesting green technology enterprises over the past decade. GW President/CEO David Levi asserts that green technology companies, or those designing processes to help other companies do their jobs with the least environmental impact, are quickly representing the new innovation frontier and are driving venture capital investment. He maintains that GW began making green investments before the green movement became popular.

WOF has invested in renewable energy firms, specializing in fuel cell, wind, and solar inverters. Xantrex (see showcase) is the largest investment in this category. Angstrom makes micro fuel cells to replace small batteries. Redlen has a novel window-shading technology to reduce HVAC costs. NxtGen is a diesel pollution controls company. Questair is purifying methane gas from garbage dumps.

In 2007, WOF sold one of its stellar "green" investments, Cellex, a company that makes fuel cell-powered lift trucks, to Plug Power, Inc., a stationary fuel cell producer. According to the January 2007, CleanTech News, the Cellex fuel cell-powered lift/pallets were tested in Ohio distribution centers owned by a major retailer. The retailer used Cellex's CX-P150 fuel cell product for four months. Twelve rider pallet trucks worked in continuous operation, logging more than 18,500 hours of active work with over 2,100 indoor fueling occurrences by pallet truck operators. The results of the trials: increased productivity reduced fueling time, safer fueling process, increased operator satisfaction, and quick training ramp-up. Six months later, Plug Power, through Cellex Power Products, announced a purchase order for their GenDrive fuel cell power units, the largest single order to date. The purchase of these fuel cell power units is equivalent to removing approximately 60 cars from the highway in southeastern Ohio in terms of CO_2 and greenhouse gas emissions, according to the retailer (Source: Fuel Cell Today).

In addition, WOF has played a significant role in investing in and providing guidance to the BC Eco Trust, which has worked with Canadian

First Nations and rural communities to protect and steward the natural resources of the province.

The WOF Ethical Audit also screens for a number of environmental and community issues, both in flagging environmental compliance problems and negative community impacts, and in encouraging recycling, energy conservation, and similar best practices.

Portfolio

WOF's investments have focused on information technology, life sciences, and advanced manufacturing, strategic industries viewed as key to jobs growth in British Columbia. Other GW funds have followed this formula but have also targeted such industry sectors as energy and environmental, consumer, entertainment, etc.

Performance

WOF provides the longest venture track record among the GW family of funds. GW reported that WOF recently had a top quartile performance within Canada and had placed in or near top-quartile performance for three-year vintage funds (for U.S. comparable performance). The total returns to investors who have redeemed their shares after holding them for the legal minimum of eight years has varied from 7 to 20% annual compound returns after the tax credit (WOF investors, like those in the Solidarity Fund, benefit from a one-time tax credit payback of up to C$1,500 on a C$5,000 investment). Based on the subscription period, investors can also obtain an EVCC tax credit, as WOF is also organized as a BC Employee Venture Capital Corporation (EVCC).

GW reports that their Canadian Fund has yielded an IRR of 25%, with retail investors receiving an estimated annual compound after tax return of 11% (since GW took over management). The GW Canada Fund won a Lipper Fund Award in 2008. The Lipper Fund Awards program highlights funds that have excelled in delivering consistently strong risk-adjusted performance, relative to peers. GW has also assumed management of LSIFs that have not performed well. With a restructured management and conformance to GW resources and controls, the firm is hopeful for a turnaround in those funds.

Challenges

According to David Levi, founder of GrowthWorks, Canadian venture capital markets continued to rebound in 2007 and to yield solid deal flow. The current up cycle, which coincided with improved economic growth in Canada, resulted in an increase in venture capital investment in Canada during 2007. Unlike some of the other Canadian VC firms, WOF has been well funded and benefited from numerous investment opportunities with attractive valuations during 2007.

Levi echoes a widely-held view that access to venture capital for early stage Canadian companies has historically been scarce and continues to be, prompting the creation of the GW Funds and other LSIF funds. But prior to 2007, Levi witnessed very challenging times for venture capital players in Canada, adding, "The poor returns post-2000 hampered fund raising in Canada. However in the past two years valuations have stabilized and investment has begun increasing. The perennial problems facing the VC community in Canada are first and foremost capable senior executives for our companies. Second, a lack of syndicate partners for larger rounds of investment."

At the same time, Levi believes that progressive groups like labor and its allies are driven by adversity and opportunity. To that end, Levi also created "Working Enterprises," a group fully owned by unions and working people. W.E. has also spun off a number of important institutions to provide capital stewardship training, civic education, and cooperative financing and insurance programs for Canada's union members and citizens.

Levi subscribes to a philosophy of enterprise—whether profit or non-profit—similar to the old Chinese proverb: every enterprise starts with one person.

Principals

DAVID LEVI launched the initial offering of the Working Opportunity Fund in January 1992 and founded GrowthWorks in January 1999. Since that time GrowthWorks has rapidly expanded across Canada, creating new funds and assuming some existing ones. Levi is also President and CEO of Working Enterprises Ltd., a "holding company" for the labor movement. Levi is a founding director of the Columbia Institute and Columbia Foundation as well as Shareholders Association for Research and Education (SHARE). SHARE houses the International Secretariat for Workers' Capital of the International Trade Union Confederation (ITUC). As such, Levi is playing a significant role in the global responsible investment movement among union federations.

In our conversation with David, it is clear that he has had a long background in and commitment to responsible investment, and he sets a high bar: "As an organization we view our investment in high-growth, ethically-screened companies as an opportunity to prove that being a top quartile manager can be done while remaining true to your ideals. It is a rare opportunity to do this work of creating new exciting companies that treat their employees as partners in the business whose products and processes enhance our environment."

Prior to launching WOF, David was chair of VanCity Credit Union. During his tenure at VanCity, he launched the Ethical Growth Fund, Canada's first ethically screened mutual fund and remained as a director until 1996. He began his career as an investment broker for C.M. Oliver in 1981. When he left in 1991, he was Vice President, Broker Services. He was a founding partner of Global Securities in 1991 before leaving to start the Working Opportunity Fund. David currently serves on the boards of two of WOF's investments, Avcorp Industries (past Chair) and Xantrex Technology and chairs Verite, an independent, non-profit social auditing and research organization.

Project Showcase: Xantrex Technology

Xantrex Technology, Inc., is a company that produces inverters, chargers, and accessories in solar and wind energy systems. The company has 500 employees and is headquartered in Vancouver, B.C., with facilities in Arlington, Washington; Livermore, California; Elkhart, Indiana; and Barcelona, Spain. According to Xantrex, its products provide reliable, high-quality "green" electricity as an alternative to centralized power generation or combustion generators. They are smaller and lighter, as well as more efficient, reliable, and intelligent than traditional power conversion equipment. The Xantrex PowerHub is the first backup power system that can be recharged with solar and wind inputs, in addition to a generator or the utility grid. Its use of sustainable energy sources provides consistent sources of power. Xantrex makes on-grid and off-grid power options.

Xantrex operates in high-growth segments of the advanced power electronics market, with well-established products and systems sold to a diverse customer base in the distributed, mobile, and programmable power markets. Their enabling technology converts raw electrical power from any source—central utility, backup power, distributed or renewable generation—into high-quality electricity.

Power applications include:

- Renewable and distributed power including solar, wind, flywheels, micro-turbines, and fuel cells;
- Back up and emergency portable power systems for homes and small businesses during electric grid disruptions;
- Auxiliary electrical power on the move for boats, recreational vehicles, heavy duty trucks, commercial work vehicles, and automobiles; and
- Programmable power to develop, test, and power precision equipment such as semiconductor manufacturing and medical equipment.

Among its other global contracts, Xantrex was selected in March 2007, to develop next generation solar inverters to support the U.S. Department of Energy's (DOE) Solar America Initiative, one of 13 such solar technology development project the DOE has selected for future funding. Xantrex is partnered with consortiums in four of those projects. The solar technology development projects will advance the commercial competitiveness of solar electricity.

Through a rigorous review process, Xantrex and a select group of companies, universities, and researchers will receive funding over three years to develop photovoltaic solutions that achieve a targeted cost of solar electricity, at a level competitive with retail electric rates, by 2010. The current cost of solar electricity, using present photovoltaic system technology, is roughly double the target objectives. For more information, see www.xantrex.com.

KPS CAPITAL PARTNERS, LP (New York)

Manager of the KPS Special Situations Funds
485 Lexington Avenue, 31st Floor
New York, New York 10017
Phone: (212) 338-5100
Fax: (646) 307-7100
Web: www.kpsfund.com
Contact: Michael Psaros, Managing Partner
David Shapiro, Managing Partner
Email: mpsaros@kpsfund.com
dshapiro@kpsfund.com

Distinguishing Characteristics:

- Founded: 1997
- Habitat: New York City, New York
- Range: Invests primarily in U.S., but also in Canada, Europe
- Fund Type: Private equity fund focused on "special situations"
- Fund Structure(s): Limited partnerships
- Capital Partners: Private investors, pension and institutional investors
- Assets Under Management: $1.8 billion

Overview

KPS Capital Partners, LP is the manager of the KPS Special Situations Funds, a family of private equity funds with over $1.8 billion of committed capital focused on constructive investing in restructurings, turnarounds, and other special situations. KPS has created new companies to purchase operating assets out of bankruptcy; established stand-alone entities to operate divested assets; and recapitalized highly leveraged public and private companies. KPS makes controlling equity investments in manufacturing, transportation, and service industries that need to effect immediate and significant change, including turnarounds, bankruptcies, restructurings, and corporate divestitures. KPS targets companies headquartered and with a majority of operations located in the United States and Canada. KPS has also invested in Europe and Asia though its portfolio companies.

The KPS investment strategy targets companies with strong franchises that are experiencing operating and financial problems. Typically, the KPS turnaround plan is accompanied by a financial restructuring of the company's liabilities. Central to the KPS investment strategy is a belief that superior investment returns are achieved primarily by catalyzing the turnaround of the business and operations of underperforming or distressed companies. KPS' turnaround plans are premised on cost reduction, capital investment, capital availability, and in most situations, the introduction of a new management team and business strategy. KPS has implemented successful turnaround plans for companies or assets that had experienced significant and recurrent operating cash losses.

KPS is recognized for its unique ability to see value in underperforming and failed companies, develop turnaround and business plans that address difficult operating and structural problems, and complete complex, multi-constituency transactions, both in and out of bankruptcy. KPS in known to pursue opportunities in which a company's immediate future is troubled or uncertain and the solutions to its operational or financial problems appear too complex.

Structure

The Managing Partners of KPS have worked together since 1991. The KPS investment staff has developed extensive skills and substantial experience in turnarounds, restructurings, bankruptcies, and Special Situation investing. While KPS is always a "control" investor, several portfolio companies have employee representation on boards of directors. KPS has also provided employees with ownership of a company's common stock (via minority employee stock ownership plans, or ESOPs), profit sharing, and gain-sharing programs.

Capacity and Products

KPS focuses on the traditional "special situations" field of investing in financially distressed or underperforming firms. KPS has created new companies to purchase operating assets out of bankruptcy; established stand-alone entities to operate divested assets; and recapitalized highly leveraged public and private companies. KPS's stated goal is to transform the troubled enterprise into a viable, profitable going concern.

KPS has raised three oversubscribed institutional private equity funds in the last decade. Recently, KPS announced the closing of KPS Special Situations Fund III, a $1.2 billion fund. Funds I and II were closed in 1999 and 2002, respectively, at $210 million and $404 million. Investors in the Fund include leading public and private sector pension funds, best-in-class funds of funds, major financial institutions, endowments, foundations, and other investors from North America, Europe, and Asia.

KPS' ultimate objective is to sell the enterprise in which it invests at a profit for its investors. KPS claims to create value for its investors by fixing the business, not by use of financial leverage, changes in capital structures, or "financial engineering."

Labor Impacts

KPS has worked constructively with most of the large industrial and service unions in the U.S. and Canada. KPS sponsors transactions in partnership with unions and seeks to facilitate participatory, communicative, and empowered corporate cultures that encourage employee input and involvement in all levels of decision-making. In addition, KPS has exited one investment by selling most of the company's stock to an ESOP. KPS estimates that its industrial restructuring projects have preserved or created over 15,000 (mainly) union jobs.

Unions regularly provide a significant number of quality "deal flow" investment opportunities to KPS, which has long worked with labor around difficult financial transactions and buyouts. KPS defines "labor-friendliness" as a process that engenders trust and accountability. The firm views "card check" and "neutrality and successorship clauses" as advancing labor-friendliness.

KPS is proud of its high trust-based relationships with many unions around these processes. The firm encourages strong communications with unions and all company stakeholders on operational, financial, and economic conditions of the firm. If there is a serious interest in acquiring the firm, KPS meets with the national and local union and shares its business and turnaround plan with the union, including its views on (i) why the company failed, (ii) what has to be done to turn the company around, (iii) what all the company's stakeholders, including the union, must contribute to the turnaround, and (iv) the financial aspects of the transaction, including KPS's expected investment returns. After the investment goes forward, KPS may also explore, with the union, such issues as corporate governance, participatory operations and sharing in the benefits of the turnaround.

Environmental/Community Impacts

As a result of KPS' successful operating turnarounds, the manufacturing facilities operated by its portfolio companies are commonly modernized and revitalized. They are generally more productive and more energy efficient under its ownership than before, and also renovated to comply with all regulatory environmental standards. KPS' investment strategy prioritizes safe and clean work environments. KPS has invested in the manufacturing of environmental, transportation, and energy products, as well as companies utilizing re-cycled raw materials (such as steel, copper, brass, paper, etc.).

One of KPS' biggest success stories was its purchase of New Flyer Industries, Ltd. New Flyer designs and manufactures transit buses and provides parts and aftermarket sales and services for the North American market; it claims to be the market-share leader in transit bus manufacturing in North America, serving most major municipalities and transit agencies. The company manages manufacturing facilities in Winnipeg, Manitoba, and Crookston and St. Cloud, Minnesota, which employ about 1,800 workers, many represented by the Canadian Auto Workers Union (CAW) and Communications Workers of America (CWA), in addition to ancillary facilities.

In March 2002, after the company suffered major problems during an expansion, KPS completed a change-of-control transaction and recapitalization of New Flyer as part of a multi-stakeholder restructuring of the Company, investing $28 million and gaining control of the firm's common equity structure. KPS principals claim the investment worked because they consulted closely with the firm's unions and workforce, given some organizational changes and jobs reductions essential to the turnaround. Contributing to the deal was the Province of Manitoba, through its Manitoba Development Corporation; New Flyer's key suppliers, customers and lenders; and the Western Economic Development Fund of Canada. KPS exited the investment and sold New Flyer in 2004, and KPS returned more than 7.5 times invested capital in New Flyer to its investors (more than the first fund).

In April 2008, New Flyer was named as one of Canada's most earth-friendly employers by the editors of Canada's Top 100 Employers. John Marinucci, New Flyer's President and CEO, commented that: "Not only do we offer the broadest range of environmentally-friendly vehicles of any heavy-duty transit bus manufacturer in Canada and the U.S., we are committed to building these vehicles in a sustainable manner." Among Flyer's drive systems are those powered by clean diesel, LNG, CNG, hydrogen fuel cell, and electric trolley, as well as energy-efficient gasoline-electric and diesel-electric hybrid vehicles. For more info, see www.newflyer.com.

Portfolio

The portfolio—active and realized—is a diversified one, consisting of industrial and manufacturing companies, including investments in the metals, paper, capital equipment, automotive parts, and transportation industries.

Performance

According to KPS, Fund I was a top-decile performer for a 1999 vintage Fund. KPS II, a 2003 vintage fund, is on track for an even more impressive return.

Challenges

Michael Psaros and David Shapiro, co-founders and Managing Partners of KPS, have long been proponents of worker-friendly investment strategies and are pleased to see the growing interest by union-involved pension funds in investing in private equity. Approximately 15% of KPS Funds' total committed capital is from multi-employer pension plans. They also take great pride that KPS' investment returns have not only been superior but are easily in the funds' top-decile relative to other private equity funds.

Quoted in Fortune in late 2007, Psaros commented on the mounting problems in the capital markets caused by the private equity bubble: "The market is completely out of touch with economic reality." To KPS, the fact that hedge funds have begun invading the same investment space has been another disturbing trend. Whereas KPS has employed an "invest-and-build" strategy in turning around distressed companies, most hedge funds are viewed as primarily securities trading operations that pursue "strip-and-flip" strategies, without ever addressing the core operational problems of the underperforming companies in which they invest.

In a follow-up interview in Mergers and Acquisitions (February 2009), Mike was asked about a forecast he made in 2006 that, due to the economic bubble, there would be no soft landing but instead a financial crash. How did he know? "Basically, the world forgot that there is this concept of risk, and risk metrics were not being applied anywhere, up and down the economy, especially in the credit system." When asked about the future of LBOs, he said: "The 'L' in LBO is dead. But now we get to see how good people are at generating returns through fixing and growing businesses."

Principals

KPS has four partners, MICHAEL PSAROS, DAVID SHAPIRO, RAQUEL VARGAS PALMER, and JAY BERNSTEIN. Mike and Dave are co-Founders and Managing Partners and have worked as a team for over 17 years. Raquel Palmer is one of the few women and minority partners of a large private equity firm.

When KPS began to raise money for their first fund in 1997, multi-employer pension funds were generally not interested in investing in private equity. General Electric Capital Corporation agreed to invest $10 million as an anchor investor. Eventually, KPS I received investments from union pension plans sponsored by the United Mineworkers (UMW) and UNITE. Mike also contends that the early Heartland Network activities benefited the capitalization drive for KPS II, which closed in 2003-04. KPS's third fund increased the level of commitment from union and public pension funds. While KPS's platform investments are North American companies, those platforms have made global acquisitions or joint ventures, giving KPS a world presence.

Mike explained to the editor of Private Equity Week that KPS's relationship with large industrial, transportation and service unions in the U.S. and Canada has contributed 25-33% of KPS's deal flow. When asked if the advertised partnerships with labor are an impediment, Mike countered, "Either you recognize that the union representing employees is critical to your success, or you compromise your ability to succeed…That's why our central thesis when working on turnarounds is transparency." KPS's initial plan was also derided because some investment analysts questioned their investments in established union industries. However, it is common knowledge in the industry that smart investors can succeed at buying and turning around troubled industries.

Project Showcase: Blue Ridge Paper

On May 14, 1999, in the largest union-led buyout in the country since 1994, KPS Special Situations Fund, General Electric Capital Corp.

("GE Capital"), and a minority ESOP formed by employees created a new company to buy a pulp and paper mill, an extruding plant, and five converting plants from Champion International for $200 million. The new company, Blue Ridge Paper Products, was launched with 2,200 new employee owners. Headquartered in Canton, North Carolina, Blue Ridge is a leading integrated manufacturer of liquid packaging, envelope paper, and coated bleach board used in food service packaging. The Company also produces specialty uncoated and extrusion coated papers.

The Company conducted operations in eight manufacturing facilities located in seven states, including the paper mill in Canton, North Carolina, the extruding mill in Waynesville, North Carolina, and in five Dairy Pak converting plants in Georgia, Iowa, Texas, New Jersey, and Olmsted Falls, Ohio. Blue Ridge subsequently acquired another Dairy Pak plant in Richmond, Virginia from MeadWestvaco.

David Shapiro said at this time: "There's been a lot of investment in the mill over the past ten years. By going into partnership with the employees, Blue Ridge Paper has become one of the most cost-competitive mills in the country. We expect Blue Ridge to be a tremendous success."

"This is a real victory for workers," added Boyd Young, then International President of the Paper, Allied-Industrial, Chemical & Energy (PACE) Workers International Union (now part of United Steelworkers).

In October 1997, Champion had put the Canton mill, Waynesville plant, and Dairy Pak plants up for sale as part of its downsizing effort. Though Champion hired Goldman Sachs to sell the facilities, no serious bidders emerged, due to the overcapacity in the paper industry, a declining market for paper cartons for packaging milk and juice, and the checkered environmental history of the Canton mill. In November 1997, an employee buyout effort was initially pursued by PACE Smoky Mountain Local 507, which represented the two North Carolina facilities. It quickly became apparent that if the Canton employees bought the mill, they also needed to buy the converting plants it supplied. Consequently, the buyout became a multi-plant, multi-state project. All the plants but one were organized by PACE, so coordination was relatively easy; the other plant was organized by the United Autoworkers (UAW). The union leadership also recognized the importance of locating an investor with the capital, expertise and bank relationships required to complete a $200 million transaction. PACE's National Headquarters called Michael Psaros at KPS to gauge its interest in the transaction.

The oldest of the Champion converting plants is located in the Cleveland, Ohio suburb of Olmsted Falls. This plant prints coated paper and converts it into liquid packaging cartons for milk or juice. The firm was the largest employer in town and is still a key part of the community's economy, now employing 165 workers. "You never can tell what will happen when a plant like this goes up for sale," Olmsted Falls Mayor Tom Jones commented. "I applaud the employees for having the confidence to purchase it. I'm delighted that the plant will remain here."

The KPS Fund and G.E. Capital provided $35 million of cash equity in a transaction valued at $200 million; the rest of the purchase price was borrowed through a syndicate led by G.E. Capital, Wachovia, PNC Bank, and Bank of Montreal. The consideration to Champion included $170 million of cash proceeds and a $30 million note. KPS and G.E. Capital collectively owned 55% of the Company and was the control investor; the ESOP and senior management owned 45 percent. There was also a profit sharing plan. KPS retained a new CEO and senior management team to run the company according to its investment philosophy.

The Canton mill became a charter member of the EPA National Achievement Track Program in 1999. Due to a $400 million investment in new technology over a decade, the facility is one of the most efficient and environmentally friendly pulp mills in the world.

In July 2007, Blue Ridge was sold to Packaging Holdings Corp. KPS returned approximately 2.5 times its invested capital to its investors, and employee-stockholders had approximately $30 million of cash deposited into their ESOP accounts (for more, go to www.blueridgepaper.com).

Landmark Growth Capital Partners (Simsbury)

10 Mill Pond Lane
Simsbury, CT 06070
Phone: (860) 651-9760
Fax: (860) 651-8890
Web: www.landmarkpartners.com

For Former Fund Manager

C/O 333 Ricciuti Drive, Suite 724
Quincy, MA 02169
Phone: (617) 312-5191
Contact: Patrick Flanagan, Managing Partner
Email:pflanagan@quarry-hillpartners.com

Distinguishing Characteristics:

- Founded: 2002
- Habitat: Simsbury, Connecticut; Boston, Massachusetts
- Range: LGCP invested primarily in U.S.
- Fund Type: Private equity fund growth fund
- Fund Structure(s): Limited partnership
- Capital Partners: Mainly multi-employer pension funds
- Assets Under Management: $78.5 million

Overview

The Landmark Growth Capital Partners Fund was a $78.5 million fund providing growth capital to privately owned, small and mid-size high-performance companies in growing market sectors. It closed in 2002. The fund invested in manufacturing, transportation, media, services, and health care sectors, and financed plant and equipment expansion, new product introduction, strategic acquisitions, and generational change and succession opportunities. The fund completed its investment cycle and is now in the realization stage.

The initial goal of LGCP was to provide capital to privately owned, small and middle-market companies in growing market sectors where labor has a presence and the opportunity exists for long-term value creation. The fund manager expressed a strong preference to target investments in worker-friendly companies. The fund also made a number of investments in portfolio companies that produced green or renewable energy-related products. [The author discloses that he assisted in fund capitalization, and though he endorses the fund manager, experienced a loss of confidence—as did some limited partner principals—in the General Partner.]

Structure

GCP was organized as a limited partnership private equity fund. Landmark Partners, the General Partner, had primarily managed secondary private equity and real estate funds, and had assets in the range of $2 billion. Pat Flanagan was retained as the Fund Manager for GCP, Landmark's first primary fund, and led the initiative to raise capital, closing the fund in the fall of 2002. The nine investors were multi-employer pension funds and one small municipal public pension fund. The fund organized annual limited partnership meetings and a small advisory committee. Within the firms in which GCP invests, it took "control" and "non-control" positions, and insisted upon other positions of influence within the company.

Capacity and Products

Pat Flanagan has a quarter century experience in sourcing, structuring, and closing complex debt and equity transactions, many on behalf of organized labor. GCP provided equity and debt capital to the small middle market that financed a range of growth and succession opportunities. Investments included all levels of the balance sheet (equity and debt with warrants) and ranged from $1 million to a 15% cap (of total fund assets) limit.

Labor Impacts

The Fund expressed a preference for investing in companies with positive labor-management relations, good health and safety and employment practices, strong environmental records, and a commitment to employee education, training, and involvement. The Fund reasoned that an investment philosophy that targets high-performance, worker-friendly firms that practice sustainable production strategies would yield good profits and good collateral benefits. To assist with deal flow and other issues, the Fund convened, on an as-needed basis, an advisory board selected from interested limited partner investors.

GCP invested in fourteen companies, completing deals with five firms where the employees were represented by unions, including the Teamsters, Sheet Metal Workers, Electrical Workers, and Bricklayers. Two firms provided a specific labor-friendly service product to unions and union members. One of the deals led to employment and training opportunities for disadvantaged workers in a southern state, including low-income, partially-disabled, and primarily minority employees.

Environmental/Community Impacts

Landmark GCP invested in a firm that manufactures composite wind-blades for the wind energy industry (and also assembles composite shells for buses and people-movers). Based on a new agreement with two of the world's largest wind companies, the firm will build a large new manufacturing factory in Newton, Iowa, creating hundreds of new jobs. The new plant will expand the firm's capacity to produce blades for some of the most widely used wind turbines in the world.

One portfolio company is a plastics re-manufacturing facility that produces porch deckings, railings, and columns, claimed to be the largest manufacturer in this field in the U.S. Another investment is a post-industrial plastic recycling company. This firm reported it was becoming the largest plastic recycler in the Mid-Atlantic States.

Portfolio

Among its original 14 portfolio investments, the fund invested in companies producing sports helmets, composites, plastics re-manufacturing, signage and building products, and a distribution firm.

Performance

As of submission for publication, LGCF had two realizations and anticipated future realizations for its portfolio, including at least two more this year. Like some other funds profiled, the fund also had a couple of write-downs.

Challenges

Fund Manager Patrick Flanagan left Landmark Partners in 2006 (once GCP was fully invested), to establish a new stand-alone fund. (Thus, the limited partners are reliant on Landmark Partners to manage the wind-down of the investment portfolio and realize the sales.) A Boston-area resident, Flanagan is a seasoned and professional investor, but also a passionate advocate for labor. The core limited partners only decided to invest in LGCP once Flanagan came on board as Fund Manager.

Pat believes that in making investments, the quality of management is crucial. Since the fund is capitalized by pension funds, return on the asset is crucial. But he also values another key asset—the workers. Labor practices are important to his investment process. Pat reasoned that LGCP's focus on high-road, labor-friendly investments will yield both an overall good return-on-investment and positive collateral benefits. His historical perspective was that GCP was launched at an inauspicious time—2002, while the economy was coming out of a recession. He projected that once the economy started recovering, investments would achieve a good ROI.

Pat cautions that the pension community is still wary of private equity, especially worker-friendly strategies. Thus, he is perplexed by the rise of pension investments in the Wall Street mega-hedge funds (doing private equity deals) that have less commitment to long-term investment horizons and questionable records on labor relations.

Principals

We interviewed PATRICK FLANAGAN in a hotel in the Wall Street District. He graciously caught an early-morning commuter train from Boston to facilitate our meeting with him. Pat is one of the more senior practitioners in the investment banking and advisory services field who has collaborated with principals in organized labor. He has completed over 125 financing and M&A advisory transactions in his career, aggregating more than $14 billion in transaction value. He has worked on transactions with over two dozen unions as clients or partners, including high-profile deals such as the Northwest Airlines ESOP. He also has significant plant/corporate management experience. Among the firms that Pat has worked with as partner, vice president, or in other capacities are Drexel Lambert, American Capital Strategies, and Mac-Gray Corp., a NYSE company. He has been a member of eight corporate boards of directors and several nonprofit boards. A graduate of Purdue University with a Bachelor of Science degree in mathematics, Pat has an MBA from Harvard Business School. He served eight years with the U.S. Marine Corps.

Flanagan is a firm proponent that growth investments need to focus on companies with good cash flow, or "cash-flow first." He is also convinced that top-flight management is the first building block to an investment's success.

Project Showcase: Cascade Helmets

Cascade is a sports equipment manufacturer based in Liverpool, New York, a small town near the state's Finger Lakes district. It is the leading manufacturer for lacrosse helmets and eye-ware, and has recently expanded into whitewater sports and hockey helmets. Some of its new lines utilize Cascade's "seven technology," its new lateral displacement technology to "provide the protection of two helmets in one" to prevent concussions. They claim that their helmet protects equally as well against catastrophic hits. Cascade helmets are the "Official Helmet" of the

Major Lacrosse League (MLL) and the helmet worn by 11 of the last 12 champions of the NCAA Division 1. Lacrosse is the fastest growing team sport in the United States. Four years after the investment, LGCP exited and more than tripled its original commitment.

Cascade was founded in 1986 by Bill and Peter Brine, both direct descendents of the Brine sporting goods manufacturing family. As part of the transaction, Bill Brine rolled over a significant portion of his equity, while Peter Brine, who had been inactive in the business, was bought out. Pat was excited about the company because Bill Brine and his team were energetic and talented, and the firm had an estimated 80% market share in a rapidly growing sport.

The firm reports that it chose to produce all of its products in its Liverpool, New York, headquarters (rather than producing offshore) so that its design team can guarantee its corporate vision. It is more expensive for Cascade to produce this way, but when it comes to head and eye protection, total control over production was deemed a necessity.

In 1986, when Bill Brine left his family's company to start Cascade, he and a group of designers from the leading design universities began working on the next generation of lacrosse helmets. Brine strived to be on the leading edge of design and safety, and purportedly devoted substantial resources to research and development. The firm utilizes a NOCSAE test lab on site in its Liverpool headquarters, which ensures that all appropriate helmet design and safety standards are met. In addition, Cascade says it continually works with top-level scientists to fully understand impact attenuation and how it applies to brain and eye injuries. Their design team routinely works in conjunction with eye doctors so that they may design products that offer maximum vision without sacrificing protective integrity. With recent improvements to the production line, the firm now ships all orders within a day or two. For more information, go to www.cascadelacrosse.com.

Solidarity Fund QFL-FTQ (Montreal)

Bureau 200, 545 Boulevard Crémazie
Montreal, Quebec
H2M 2W4
Phone: (514) 942-0553
Fax: (514) 850-4888
Web: www.fondsftq.com
Contact: Yvon Bolduc, Président and CEO, Fonds de
Solidarité FTQ

Distinguishing Characteristics:

- Founded: 1983
- Habitat: Montreal, with regional fund offices throughout Quebec
- Range: Invests primarily in Quebec, but can also invest in North America and globally through subsidiaries and specialized arrangements
- Fund Type: Venture and private capital funds
- Fund Structure(s): "Retail" VC/PE Labor-Sponsored Investment Funds (LSIFs)
- Capital Partners: Individual investors capitalize the fund through a tax-credit savings program
- Assets: C$7.4 billion

Overview:

The original impetus for the Solidarity Fund in Quebec, Canada, came in 1982-83 in the middle of a severe economic downturn in the province. Louis Laberge, then President of the QFL, Québec's largest federation of unions, invited the membership to develop a new union policy in the face of layoffs and plant closures. Leaders of the Fédération de Travailleurs et Travailleuses du Quebec (FTQ, the Quebec Federation of Labour) realized that their members' retirement savings could be put to work building the province's economy and convinced the provincial government to enact enabling legislation. A majority of QFL unions supported Laberge's campaign to launch Solidarity. The legislation was passed permitting the FTQ to sponsor the creation of a regional investment fund. The Québec government showed its support by granting future Fund shareholders valuable tax benefits, a move soon matched by Ottawa.

The Fund's original mission was:

- To invest in Quebec businesses and provide them with services to further their development and to help create, maintain and protect jobs in the province;
- To promote the economic training of workers in order to enhance their contribution to Québec's economic development;
- To stimulate the Québec economy by making strategic investments that will benefit both workers and businesses;
- To make workers aware of the need to save for retirement and to contribute to economic growth by purchasing shares in the Fund.

The legislation originally stipulated that the fund should invest in firms with assets of less than C$50 million in order to create and preserve jobs but also promote workers' economic training to increase their power in shaping the province's economy. The legislation ensured organized labor's control of the fund by establishing a board of directors made up of ten labor representatives and the balance non-labor representatives selected with labor input.

The Solidarity Fund is a labour-sponsored investment fund (LSIF) under federal legislation, providing eligibility for RRSP tax credits. The Solidarity Fund was capitalized by individual worker-investors who can invest up to C$5,000 per year and receive 15% federal and 15% provincial tax credits for their investment. Workers' participation is facilitated by this tax credit. Many workers get additional tax relief for their Solidarity Fund investments by placing them in their individual retirement savings plans, or RRSPs (the Canadian equivalent of an IRA). The Fund has grown dramatically and is mainly capitalized by its 575,000 shareholders. Instead of brokers, the Fund tasks 2-3,000 worker-representatives in the field, in each workplace where the FTQ is represented. These volunteers are trained to promote the fund to new investors and to provide communication between the fund and working people at the local, regional, and provincial levels. They receive no commission. Solidarity celebrated its 25th anniversary in 2008.

Structure:

The Solidarity Fund is organized as an LSIF and capitalized through "retail" investors. The founding legislation required that the Federation of Labour be sole sponsor of the fund within provincial jurisdiction. Thus, the Fund is governed by a Board of Directors composed of seventeen persons, of which twelve are from the FTQ. Michel Arsenault, the current President of the FTQ, is Chairman of the Board of the Solidarity Fund. The other board members represent industrial companies, financial institutions, and socio-economic sectors in Quebec.

While financed quite differently from the pension-capitalized U.S. funds herein, the investment program of the Solidarity Fund operates similarly in some ways. The Fund typically takes a non-controlling equity stake of 10% to 40% in the companies in which it invests. The Fund participates on the investee company's board of directors and helps the company define its strategic vision.

As Tessa Hebb and David Mackenzie pointed out in a chapter in *Working Capital*, Solidarity developed a unique regional investment network in partnership with the Quebec government and other investors: "This network now operates (16) regional funds, each with offices and managers assigned to a local area. Proximity to investment allows for better knowledge in selecting investments and in the subsequent monitoring that is required in this market. Part of the objective of the funds is to play an active role in the education of workers and add expertise to management. The regional network is vital for delivery of these objectives." The investment ceilings of the regional funds are lower than the national fund, allowing for more entrepreneurial risk.

Capacity and Products

The Fund's Management Team is comprised of eight senior investment and management professionals. There are over 150 other professionals working for the Fund.

Fund investments are distributed in all regions and branches of industry. C$2.7 billion is invested directly or through the sixteen regional funds or more than sixty specialized funds (examples: real estate, bio-tech, social housing, native enterprise, etc.). Because it is a worker-financed fund, it has a policy of investing strongly in labor-intensive industry and the services sector. However the Fund also strongly supports the new economy with more than C$1.8 billion investments.

The Solidarity Fund provides unsecured capital for small and medium-sized businesses, unionized and non-unionized, as long as the investment meets the Fund's policy objectives for helping create, maintain, and preserve jobs. The Fund and its subsidiaries can invest at all stages of development, from pre-start-up to IPO, and can make larger investments than originally prescribed:

- The Fund can make a first investment in firms with up to C$100 million in tangible assets or C$50 million in net assets, and a subsequent investment up to C$350 million or C$150 million respectively (so it can continue to support the development of its partner companies).
- The Fund can make a strategic investment in firms with up to C$500 million in tangible assets or C$200 million in net assets.
- The Fund views itself as a long-term partner, with an exit horizon generally of 5 to 7 years. The Fund also provides expertise in turning around businesses in temporary difficulty.

Labor Impacts

The Solidarity Fund and its network have helped create or maintain more than 122,000 jobs and have launched and/or grown nearly 2,100 companies in all sectors of the economy. While assisting in re-investment and revitalization of the manufacturing and industry sectors, the Fund also provides some of the largest sources of capital for new economy sectors. Additionally, the Fund has, through its regional funds, targeted distressed regions of the province, including rural as well as the more urbanized centers.

During a visit to Pittsburgh, Gilles Audette, Director of Partner Worker Relations at Solidarity Fund QFL, explained that, in principle, all of the Fund's investments are in worker-friendly firms. To provide a relative comparison of its investments, the overall unionization rate in Quebec is 42% and in the private sector 29%. The Solidarity Fund is the longest-operating investment fund in North America focused on worker-friendly private equity and venture capital investments. Its social principles and practices include:

- Conducting a "social audit" of each prospective "partner" company.
- Getting agreement that investee companies accept the workers' right to organize.
- Providing "Economic Training" for the workers, including open-book management.

The worker-training program has historically provided "open book management" and financial literacy training for workers of investee companies—examining the firm's financial results on a regular basis—and also economic development training to the staff of the Fund's many regional partners. In comments about the importance of the training, Pierre Gagnon, a union advisor, said: "Economic training gives workers the opportunity to interact with the employer, see the figures and ask questions so they can understand where the company is headed. Employees benefit from such an experience. It's the type of training that sets the record straight."

Environmental/Community Impacts

The social audit program, mentioned above, is the most aggressive component of Solidarity's responsible investment assessment process. This ESG audit, performed by Fund staff, provides an ethical screen around environmental responsibility, product safety standards, positive employee relations, and corporate citizenship.

OVERVIEW OF TARGETED INVESTMENT OPPORTUNITY

CLEAN ENERGY PROJECTS	CLEAN TECHNOLOGIES
New infrastructures (biomass, geothermal energy, solar energy, biofuels, wind energy) Conversion of existing infrastructures.	Energy generation, energy efficiency and carbon reduction (Energy related, air quality, manufacturing, new materials, materials recovery and recycling, and transportation).

In 2004 Solidarity partnered with Fondaction, another leading Quebec labor-sponsored fund, and an environmental NGO to co-launch Cycle Capital, a stand-alone fund dedicated to "green" investments. Cycle Capital's mission is to finance and develop successful businesses that contribute to sustainable development, and its investment strategy is targeted to clean technologies and renewable energy infrastructure projects. Cycle uniquely employs a "life cycle approach" both in the investment process and as a tool to add value to business enterprises. Cycle Capital's approach has been recognized by the International Life Cycle Partnership launched by the United Nations Environment Program, UNEP and the Society for Environmental Toxicology and Chemistry, SETAC. The initiative aims to achieve returns greater than 20%. Cycle's investment philosophy calibrates environmental criteria such as resource usage, waste management, environmental management system and social criteria such as employment creation, labor conditions and relations with stakeholders. As of December 31, 2005, the Fund had made investments in five companies and one renewable energy project, generating an IRR of 21%. In 2005, the founding sponsors doubled their commitments to C$38 million.

Cycle intends to capitalize on the emergence of the low carbon economy, which will create business opportunities in green sectors (showing great potential to counter greenhouse gas) such as renewable energy. The geographic focus is on Canada and on the countries of Central and Eastern Europe and Latin America that are in the best position to benefit from the Kyoto Protocol and other efforts to promote a low carbon economy.

Portfolio

Over a one-year period ending May 31, 2007, the Fund, including its network of regional funds, invested $668 million in 145 companies, making it the foremost source of venture and development capital in Québec. With 74% of its portfolio in industries and services, Solidarity's portfolio includes: industrial technologies, transportation, aerospace, metal products, plastics, tourism, mining, agri-food, culture, wood and furniture, real estate, etc. It also allows for export financing. Some 26% if its portfolio is invested in technology sectors. All in all, Solidarity claims it has invested C$7.2 billion in all these fields, including these critical sectors: C$1.8 billion: new economy; C$415 million: financial services; and, C$161 million: aerospace.

Performance

The Solidarity Fund QFL announced that, as of May 31, 2007, its share price rose to C$25.36, up $1.62 over a one-year period. Net earnings reached C$475 million. Net assets reached C$7.2 billion and the operating expense ratio was said to be at a stable 1.4% of average net assets, positioning the Fund among the best performers in the LSIF industry.

The Fund's overall return was 7.1%. Added to that ROI is a 30% tax credit (which yields, on a one-time basis, up to C$1,500 a year on a C$5,000 investment).

Challenges

Gilles Audette has been Director, Partner Worker Relations at the Solidarity Fund QFL since 1998, and was previously a Relations Development Agent in the same department. Audette is at the helm of an 11-member team charged with maintaining relations with the heads of both unionized and non-unionized companies in which the Fund invests, conducting social audits of companies looking to partner with the Fund, and overseeing the economic training program. This team is also in continual communications with QFL unions and encourages CEOs and union reps in partner companies to work together.

Gilles explained that in the early 1980s, after Quebec fell into a deep recession, Louis Laberge, then President of the QFL, the province's largest federation of unions, invited its membership to develop a new union policy to respond to mass layoffs and plant closures. This is how Solidarity was created. A majority of QFL unions supported Laberge's campaign. The Québec government showed its support by granting future Fund shareholders valuable tax benefits, a move soon matched by Ottawa. Said Audette: "Let me tell you that it was not obvious in these days for a union activist to become a venture capitalist."

Fernand Daoust and Robert Dean, two of the founders of Solidarity, spoke at the Heartland Conference in 1999 about the challenges facing the Solidarity Fund and labor-sponsored funds in general.[2] Daoust, general secretary of the QFL at the time of the Fund's formation and a former Chairman of the Board said, "This collective enterprise is a project inspired by public interest, a real social and economic innovation."

Principals

MICHEL ARSENAULT is Chairman of the Board and of the Executive Committee of the Solidarity Fund QFL. In November 2007, Michel Arsenault was elected president of Québec's umbrella labor body, the Québec Federation of Labour (QFL-FTQ). He is also a member of the Executive Committee of the Canadian Labour Congress (CLC), and the

Executive Bureau of the International Trade Union Confederation (ITUC). In addition, Arsenault serves on the boards of the Commission de la santé et de la sécurité du travail du Québec (CSST) and the Conseil consultatif du travail et de la main-d'œuvre (CCTM). Before becoming president of the QFL, Arsenault was the Québec director of the Steelworkers Union, where he held various positions since 1974, in Sept-Îles, Québec City, Saint-Jean-sur-Richelieu, and Montréal. Arsenault also spent five years as assistant to the Canadian director of the Steelworkers in Toronto, where his responsibilities included overseeing the USW's international affairs.

YVON BOLDUC was appointed President and CEO of the Solidarity Fund QFL in February 2006. Since joining the Fund in 2002 and until his latest appointment, Bolduc was Executive Vice-President, Investments of the Fund, and in this capacity was responsible for the organization's investment activities. Before joining the Fund, Bolduc worked for Canada Post from 2000 to 2002 as Vice-President, Corporate Development, overseeing the company's corporate transactions. From 1990 to 2000, Bolduc was Vice-President, Legal Affairs, at G.T.C. Transcontinental Group, where he played a key role in the company's development. Prior to that, after serving in the Canadian Armed Forces in various officer positions, he worked with the legal firm of Stikeman Elliott in 1985. Bolduc holds a Law degree and an MBA from Ottawa University.

Providing the direct information about the fund was Gilles Audette, a Director of Partner Worker Relations at the Solidarity Fund QFL. His responsibilities are described above. Before joining the Fund, Gilles Audette was a staff representative and then director of the Montréal region of the United Steelworkers from 1979 to 1992. He represented the Canadian Labour Congress and QFL at the Bureau International du Travail à Genève in 1991 and 1992 and was a member of the QFL General Council from 1987 to 1992.

Project Showcase: Glendyne

Glendyne is located in St-Marc-du-Lac-Long in the Temiscouata region near the Maine and New-Brunswick boarders. This region had an unemployment rate in 1996 of more than 20%, so the investment in this firm was projected to have a positive impact on the local economy. Glendyne extracts natural slate and mainly produces roofing slate. Glendyne Slate is also known as La Canadienne, La Québécoise, Glacier, and North Country Slate Unfading Black. Glendyne is the largest operational slate quarry in North America.

When it first invested in the company in 1996, the Fund bought 49% of the company. The plan was to reduce ownership to 30% by the end of 2009. The Fund's two other partners in this company, Dany Dumont and Gilles Fradette (who owned 51% in 1996 and will own 70% by the end of 2008), manage the operation. In 1995, Solidarity invested C$100,000 in capital and C$1.4 million in a non-secured loan. In 2005 Solidarity invested another C$5 million for the acquisition of a distributor in the U.S. and the reimbursement of a loan to another lender. Today the ROI from the investment (for the Fund) is 29%.

When the Fund made its first investment, this enterprise had been in operation for less than a year and went bankrupt. The Fund decided to support the investment because it believed that with a good capitalization the company could succeed. But the main reason it invested is because that project was fundamental for the economic development of the region, and the Fund was the only investor willing to put in money. Due to the quality of the company's slate and strict quality control, Glendyne was able to penetrate world markets within a decade. The two major markets are Europe (90%) and the U.S. (10%).

When the operations started in 1996, there was no union. Initially, a QFL union sought certification in 1998. In the early years, labor relations were strained, leading to a strike in 2001. After that, the parties asked the Fund to help them to improve communications. The Fund set up an economic training program for all the employees and supported the formation of a communication committee involving the union executive and the top management.

While the company only started with 53 jobs, there have been strong investments in technology since the beginning of the partnership. Today there are more than 300 persons working for Glendyne. It is now, by far, the largest employer in a region that has often struggled to find employment. Given the Fund's investments in modernization, and the engagement role of the union, workers have enjoyed improved health and safety conditions, and the firm touts its compliance with environmental regulations.

The Fund has representatives on the Board as part of its corporate governance policies. Through the communication committee, the workers receive regular information related to financial condition, operations and production, and the market, and they participate in efforts to improve the performance of the company. While there is no employee ownership or other forms of profit sharing, workers are encouraged to buy Fund shares. Many have done so, making them indirect shareholders of their company.

The Yucaipa Companies (Los Angeles)

9130 West Sunset Boulevard
Los Angeles, CA 90069
Phone: (310) 789-7200
Contact: Scott Stedman
Jeff Pelletier
Email: scott.stedman@yucaipaco.com
　　　jeff.pelletier@yucaipaco.com

Distinguishing Characteristics:

- Founded: 1986
- Habitat: Los Angeles, California
- Range: Invests primarily in U.S. and Canada
- Fund Type: Private capital buyout and growth investments
- Fund Structure(s): Limited partnerships
- Capital Partners: Multi-employer, public and corporate pension funds, foundations and other institutional investors
- Assets Under Management: $6 billion

Overview

The Yucaipa Companies is an investment management firm specializing in domestic buyout transactions primarily in the distribution/logistics, retail, and manufacturing sectors. Headquartered in Los Angeles and with additional offices in New York City, Washington D.C., and Chicago, Yucaipa represents a family of worker and community-friendly funds with over $6 billion in assets. Founded by Ron Burkle in 1986, Yucaipa highlights its ability to source proprietary investment opportunities, maintain purchasing discipline, and consistently and actively provide value-added guidance to its portfolio companies. Yucaipa has generated annual average returns of approximately 40% on its investments since inception.

Yucaipa primarily targets control transactions in the $200 million to $2 billion range that require $50 million to $300 million of equity. Yucaipa places emphasis on underperforming but promising companies, where the firm has identified specific opportunities to enhance the operations, strategic positioning, and/or financial management of the target company. National in focus, Yucaipa invests primarily in retail, logistics, distribution, and manufacturing industries but has also made real estate and commercial investments including hotels, restaurants, entertainment, and media companies.

Structure

The Yucaipa Companies' investment products are organized as private equity partnerships. Yucaipa is and has always been an activist investor. As a fundamental part of its investment strategy, the firm takes part not only in board meetings and high-level strategy development but also in the development and execution of numerous financial and operating enhancements at its portfolio companies. The Principals believe the firm's hands-on approach has been a critical contributing factor to the more than 20% average EBITDA margin increase at its portfolio companies from time of acquisition to time of sale.

Yucaipa's in-house Operating Partners include several former CEOs, COOs, and CFOs who work closely with the Firm's Transaction Partners in the sourcing, due diligence, and management of portfolio investments. The Operating Partners, through hands-on management and guidance, have been instrumental in the Firm's success virtually since inception and are an integral part of investment operations. The Operating Partners have worked in senior positions at Yucaipa portfolio companies in the past and have experience with the philosophy, approach, strategy, and challenges of managing a private, equity-backed portfolio company.

Yucaipa maintains a dedicated team of labor relations professionals who are active in sourcing deal opportunities directly from the labor community, monitoring and advising portfolio companies on labor relations matters, and advising unions in context of financial transactions even where Yucaipa may not be making an equity investment in the deal. Yucaipa also has a dedicated team of Employee Stock Ownership Plan (ESOP) specialists, who source and structure deal opportunities from among the many companies with existing ESOPs or those seeking to form new ESOPs for their employees.

Capacity and Products

The Yucaipa Companies is comprised of 30 investment professionals, led by founder and managing partner Ron Burkle. The firm highlights the fact that its principals have over 250 years of combined experience. As a "hands-on" investor, Yucaipa aims to work closely with portfolio company management to strategically reposition businesses and implement operational improvements that will result in significant value creation for investors. Yucaipa executed a series of grocery chain mergers and acquisitions involving such companies as Fred Meyer, Ralphs, and Food 4 Less, putting the company on the supermarket map.

Yucaipa has been an active participant in the buyout sector for more than two decades. The principals believe the firm is widely recognized by private market participants, with a reputation as an innovator in (i) early industry consolidations, (ii) the use of operating executives as an integral part of investment operations, (iii) the active maintenance of positive relationships with national labor organizations, (iv) private equity-style investments in public companies, and (v) the distribution/logistics, manufacturing, and retail sectors of the domestic economy.

While not an investor in distressed companies per se, Yucaipa's operating expertise, deep industry knowledge and ability to work effectively with the labor community have allowed the firm to invest and build value in complex situations. The principals believe that these skills provide substantial differentiation for the firm and position Yucaipa to be an active participant in the important evolutionary changes occurring in America's large unionized industries.

Labor Impacts

Yucaipa reports that many of its portfolio companies over the years have operated in unionized industries and have had significant union membership. Yucaipa's philosophy is to treat its employees and their union representatives with respect. The firm has encouraged labor/management cooperation, while seeking to maximize shareholder value. Yucaipa claims that the firm promotes mutual respect, which allows the company to function harmoniously, employees to feel proud and respected, and management to be able to focus on organizational success.

Yucaipa believes that positive relationships with employees and the labor community-at-large have contributed significantly to the firm's success over the years. Positive labor and/or union relations have provided portfolio companies with important benefits. Moreover, Yucaipa says that these relational advantages comprise a sustainable and material competitive edge:

- Pre-acquisition—these relationships provide proprietary deal flow and unique information sourcing which facilitates the assessment and valuation of potential investments.
- Post-acquisition—trust relationships can help mitigate operating risks, enabling Yucaipa to take necessary steps to improve the health of portfolio companies.

Yucaipa's de-leveraging investment in Pathmark (see below) provided much-needed dollars and expertise for a capital investment program designed to enhance the competitiveness of its store base, thereby improving the job security of tens of thousands of union workers. Yucaipa's strategy provided an attractive, creative alternative to a traditional leveraged buyout and/or a sale to buyers focused primarily on the stores' real estate, each of which would likely have jeopardized thousands of jobs. Yucaipa's sale to a strategic buyer in contiguous markets further enhanced job security by keeping Pathmark's store base intact while further expanding the resulting company's geographical footprint.

In another high-profile effort, Yucaipa worked with the International Brotherhood of Teamsters to salvage Allied Holdings, which declared

Chapter 11 in 2005, from threat of liquidation. In 2007, Allied tried to scrap the Collective Bargaining Agreement (CBA), leaving the 3,300 workers without a union and destroying their benefits. After buying up two-thirds of the unsecured claims of Allied Holdings, a large bankrupt car hauler, Yucaipa finessed a deal with the union that reduced by half the annual wage cuts demanded by the company. Yucaipa's successful intervention in the bankruptcy courts prevented a strike and led to a revised CBA and the preservation of pension and health and welfare benefits. The savings negotiated by the investment house, allowing the company to exit bankruptcy in May 2007, were fully allocated to an aggressive capital expenditure program providing for new equipment to be used by Teamster members of Allied, and a new Board of Directors and CEO were appointed (Source: *The Daily Deal*, 2/15/07).

Environmental/Community Impacts

Among other "sustainable" industry investments, Yucaipa invested in Fibertech Polymers, Inc., a manufacturer of fencing, lawn edging, and other products made from 100 percent post-consumer recycled materials, including rejected fiber material from cardboard recycling plants and polymer material from recycled plastic containers. Fibertech's products are sold in Lowe's and other retail outlets. Yucaipa has invested $15 million into Fibertech to fund its growth.

Portfolio

Originally specializing in purchases in the grocery and logistics arenas, the company has built a diverse portfolio of investments in restaurants, marketing, entertainment, manufacturing, retail, distribution, logistics, and other services.

Performance

The principals of Yucaipa report that the Funds have consistently achieved superior returns through periods of economic recession and growth, surpassing both public and private market benchmarks. Since 1986, Yucaipa reports it has transacted over $30 billion in total M&A activity and generated an overall gross annual IRR of 42.6%. According to the CalPERS website, three of the funds have yielded the following returns (dated, as of 9/07):

FUND DESCRIP-TION	VIN-TAGE YEAR	CAPI-TAL COM-MITTED	CASH IN	CASH OUT	CASH OUT & REMAIN-ING VALUE	NET IRR	INVEST-MENT MULTI-PLE
Yucaipa American Alliance Fund I, L.P.	2002	200,000,000	153,375,548	98,311,384	227,082,069	20.2	1.50x
Yucaipa American Special Situations	2002	50,000,000	47,717,460	21,744,427	74,913,556	18.9	1.60x
Yucaipa Corporate Initiative Fund	2001	200,000,000	194,075,989	2,474,693	244,614,156	9.5	1.30x

Challenges

Yucaipa believes that innovation, creativity, and vision are critical elements of successful private equity investing. The firm has displayed a penchant for innovation over the years, including (i) its early pursuit of industry consolidation strategies; (ii) its early utilization of industry executives in the day-to-day execution of the private equity investment business; (iii) its early insistence on strict corporate governance philosophies around reporting, alignment of interests, and management accountability; and (iv) its active maintenance of cooperative relationships with national labor organizations.

Principals

RON BURKLE founded The Yucaipa Companies in 1986 and is widely recognized as one of the pre-eminent investors in the grocery business, as well as retail, manufacturing, and distribution industries. Burkle served as Chairman of the Board and controlling shareholder of numerous companies including Alliance Entertainment, Golden State Foods, Dominick's, Fred Meyer, Ralphs, and Food4Less. He is Co-Chairman of the Burkle Center for International Relations at UCLA and is broadly involved in the community. He is a trustee of the Carter Center, the National Urban League and AIDS Project Los Angeles (APLA). Ron was the Founder and Chairman of the Ralphs/Food4Less Foundation and the Fred Meyer Inc. Foundation. He has received numerous honors and awards including the AFL-CIO's Murray Green Meany Kirkland Community Service Award, the Los Angeles County Federation of Labor Man of the Year, the Los Angeles County Boy Scouts Jimmy Stewart Person of the Year Award, and the APLA Commitment to Life Award.

Project Showcase: Pathmark Stores, Inc.

In 2005, Yucaipa made a unique $150 million investment in Pathmark Stores, Inc., an old-line supermarket chain in the New York, New Jersey, and

Philadelphia metropolitan areas. The investment was structured as a PIPE investment—a private investment in a public enterprise. Pathmark operated 141 supermarkets in fiscal 2005. Yucaipa acquired 48% of Pathmark's shares in 2005. Pathmark generated $4 billion in net sales and employed 27,000 people. The chain is represented by the United Food and Commercial Workers (UFCW), which represents 19,734 Pathmark workers, and the Service Employees union (SEIU), which represents a smaller contingent.

The Yucaipa investment was aimed at helping turn around the company, which was viewed as troubled by the financial markets, due to an earlier leveraged buyout and bankruptcy. Pathmark has used the proceeds from the transaction to upgrade its existing store base and open additional stores, positioning the company for improved top line growth and profitability.

TRANSACTION SUMMARY

DATE OF INVESTMENT	JUNE 2005
Total Enterprise Value at Time of Investment	$875 million
Equity Invested	$150 million
Gross IRR	80.1%
Multiple of Cost	2.9x
Acquisition Multiple (LTM EBITDA)	5.6x
Exit Multiple (LTM EBITDA)	11.0x
Yucaipa Role	Lead
Governance	Management Agreement, 4 Board seats

Pathmark operates large-format, high-volume combination food/drug stores in the New York/New Jersey (112) and Philadelphia (29) metro markets. Pathmark's strategy of geographic clustering in highly populated markets is critical to its high sales volume, brand awareness, and operating efficiency. Its markets have dense populations and have experienced limited penetration by discount competitors like Wal-Mart and Kmart due to the lack of available real estate and community resistance. The Company's entire workforce is substantially unionized.

As an alternative to a proposal from the Pathmark Board of Directors to initiate an auction process to sell the business, Yucaipa proposed a strategic growth investment. Yucaipa approached Pathmark's Board directly with this concept and ultimately negotiated a deal to invest $150 million in Pathmark for a package of securities representing 60% of the equity on a fully diluted basis. The structure was unique in its ability to satisfy key constituencies in the transaction, including labor, management, existing shareholders, and Yucaipa.

UFCW leaders were extremely pleased by the deal. "This is great news for 30,000 Pathmark employees represented by the UFCW," said UFCW International President Joe Hansen. "Yucaipa has a track record of operating successful industry-leading businesses that benefit employees, shareholders and communities. The UFCW members had positive working experiences with Yucaipa when the company ran supermarkets across the country, including Ralph's, Food4Less, Fred Meyer, Smith Food and Drug, and Dominick's. If you asked UFCW members, today, who worked in Yucaipa-operated stores, I'm confident they would say the company was very fair as well as a good place to work." According to the union, Pathmark was once a growing, successful, and highly respected firm in the supermarket industry and then experienced a harmful leveraged buyout in the 1980s. Since then, the company had been saddled with extensive debt, which resulted in burdens on UFCW members.

Yucaipa was attracted to the Pathmark investment opportunity for the following reasons:

- Premier Brand and Market Leader: Pathmark represented a great opportunity to invest in a premier brand and regional market leader.
- Defensible and High Growth Market Locations: Pathmark's store locations are predominantly in dense urban and suburban markets in the Northeast, serving to protect them from aggressive Wal-Mart entrance and position them for growth.
- Opportunity for Significant Post-Transaction Value Creation: Yucaipa believed that additional value could be unlocked by investing in Pathmark's store base, de-leveraging the balance sheet, pursuing leading-edge merchandising strategies, investing in brand expansion, and providing strong leadership.
- Proprietary Structure and Compelling Valuation: Yucaipa's unique proposal and reputation in the sector enabled the firm to participate outside the auction process and ultimately secure an attractive price and compelling terms (management contract, significant warrant position).
- Platform to Catalyze Consolidation: Yucaipa believed that Pathmark could serve as an excellent platform to catalyze the consolidation of the fragmented Northeast supermarket sector. The firm saw this consolidation opportunity as possessing many of the same characteristics that were present in Yucaipa's successful Western U.S. supermarket consolidation in the 1990s.

Working together, management and Yucaipa conceived and executed a store remodeling and re-merchandising program designed to generate future earnings growth and operating efficiencies. Under this program, Yucaipa helped implement other value-enhancing initiatives such as developing a comprehensive labor management strategy and introducing a natural foods initiative in conjunction with Wild Oats Markets (another Yucaipa portfolio company). Yucaipa also played a key role in recruiting seasoned veterans to the CEO and Co-President positions (both individuals had previously led Yucaipa supermarket portfolio companies).

On March 4, 2007, Pathmark signed a definitive agreement to merge with regional grocery chain Great Atlantic & Pacific Tea Company Inc. ("A&P") for $13.10 per Pathmark share. As of March 31, 2007, the Yucaipa's return on the Pathmark investment was an 80.1% gross IRR and a 2.9 times multiple of cost based on the A&P transaction. The transaction was completed in 2008.

CHAPTER EIGHT

Responsible Real Estate/Fixed Income Funds

In this chapter we describe seven responsible real estate funds, displayed in the Table below, ranked by alphabet. As we did for the funds in Chapter Six, we analyze each fund, starting with an overview of the fund, its structure, capacity, and products. Next we describe the effect of the fund's investments on jobs—labor impacts—and the ways the fund promotes a sustainable environment, both in terms of environmental and community impacts. This is followed by information on the fund's overall performance, its portfolio, and profiles of principals. Finally, we describe one of the fund's investments in detail.

FUND NAME	ASSETS
AFL-CIO HIT-BIT (Washington, DC)	$6.7 billion
Amalgamated Bank Long View ULTRA (D.C.)	$1.1 billion
The BUILD Fund of America (Troy)	$228 million
Concert Properties (Vancouver)	C$1.3 billion
The Erect Fund (Pittsburgh)	$200 million
MEPT Fund (Washington, DC)	$7.29 billion
ULLICO, Inc. J for Jobs (Washington, DC)	$2.7 billion

AFL-CIO Housing Investment Trust
(Washington, DC)

2401 Pennsylvania Ave., N.W., Suite 200
Washington, DC 20037
Phone: (202) 331-8055
Fax: (202) 331-8190
Website: www.aflcio-hit.com
Contact: Ted Chandler, Chief Operating Officer
Email: tchandler@aflcio-hit.com

Distinguishing Characteristics:

- Founded: 1965
- Habitat: Washington, D.C.
- Range: Invests primarily in U.S.
- Fund Type: Fixed-income fund specializing in mortgage securities
- Fund Structure: Open-end mutual fund, internally managed
- Capital Partners: Pension funds, institutional investors
- Assets: $3.7 billion

AFL-CIO Building Investment Trust
(Washington, DC)

1425 K Street, NW - Suite 900
Washington, DC 20005
Phone: (202) 898-9190
Fax: (202) 898-9194
Website: www.aflcio-bit.com
Contact: Michael M. Arnold, Secretary-Treasurer and Executive Vice President,
AFL-CIO Investment Trust Corporation
Email: marnold@aflcio-itc.com

Distinguishing Characteristics:

- Founded: 1988
- Habitat: Washington, D.C.
- Range: Invests primarily in U.S.
- Fund Type: Real estate equity fund
- Fund Structure: Bank Collective Trust, with PNC Bank as Fund Trustee and PNC Realty Investors, Inc. (PRI) as investment advisor
- Capital Partners: Pension funds, institutional investors
- Assets: $3 billion

Overview

The AFL-CIO Investment Program is a socially responsible investment program comprised of the AFL-CIO Housing Investment Trust (HIT), the AFL-CIO Building Investment Trust (BIT), and the AFL-CIO Investment Trust Corporation (ITC). The HIT, BIT, and ITC are three separate entities, each with its own investment and business objectives, as described below, but with a shared commitment to enhancing the retirement security of union members while also achieving social and economic objectives important to working people.

HIT: The AFL-CIO Housing Investment Trust is a fixed-income fund specializing in mortgage-backed securities insured or guaranteed by the federal government or government-sponsored enterprises. The HIT is one of the nation's earliest and most experienced, socially-responsible investment funds. Since inception it has made financing commitments of over $5 billion for multifamily housing projects valued at an estimated $6.9 billion. The HIT is proud that it has over 350 investors that include major public and multi-employer pension plans. As of December 2007, the HIT held $3.7 billion in assets. Over four decades, the HIT and its predecessor fund have invested in more than 500 projects with more than 84,000 units of housing.

BIT: The AFL-CIO Building Investment Trust is a $3 billion real estate fund that focuses primarily on equity investing in institutional quality commercial real estate in major U.S. markets, including multi-family housing, office, retail, industrial, hotel, and mixed-use projects. Over 160 union and public pension plans are invested in the BIT. The BIT seeks to deliver competitive risk-adjusted returns to its participants and benchmarks its performance to the National Council of Real Estate Investment Fiduciaries (NCREIF) Property Index. Consistent with its primary performance objectives, the BIT also implements the investment industry's most comprehensive union labor policies, covering all construction on BIT financed projects as well as the operation, repair, and maintenance of properties held by the BIT.

ITC: The AFL-CIO Investment Trust Corporation was formed in 1998 as a taxable non-profit corporation to provide the BIT with assistance in marketing, investor relations, labor relations, and certain non-fiduciary functions such as pre-development assistance; it has raised nearly $1.4 billion in new capital. As the company has grown, it has taken on additional challenges, including the formation of a new fund in 2002, the AFL-CIO Urban Development Fund.

Structure

The HIT is an open-end mutual fund that pioneered labor-sponsored investment vehicles in the U.S., according to Michael Calabrese in *Working Capital*. Inspired by then-President of the AFL-CIO, George Meany, the AFL-CIO's embrace of alternative pension fund strategies began with creation of the Mortgage Investment Trust (MIT) in 1965, the predecessor to the HIT. The AFL-CIO authorized the creation of the HIT in 1981 to build on the work of the MIT and expand investments in housing and mortgages. Part of the HIT's success has been its partnerships with the public sector, including a number of investment initiatives in targeted cities. The HIT invests primarily in mortgages and mortgage-backed securities that are guaranteed by the federal government or government-sponsored enterprises.

The HIT is governed by a Board of Trustees comprised of approximately one-half labor trustees—the executive officers of the AFL-CIO, officers of international and national unions—and one-half management trustees. The Board is chaired by an independent Chairman.

The BIT is structured as a bank collective trust, a structure claimed to offer significant advantages to pension investors under the Employee Retirement Income Security Act of 1974 (ERISA). PNC Bank, National Association, of Pittsburgh serves as fund Trustee and PNC Realty Investors, Inc. (PRI), serves as investment advisor. The Trustee has final fiduciary responsibility for investment decision-making, as advised by the advisor. At the request of the Trustee, the AFL-CIO has appointed an Advisory Board that provides policy guidance and also includes senior union officers of the AFL-CIO and affiliated unions, as well as industry experts and public sector leaders.

Capacity and Products

The HIT specializes in multi-family housing finance, along with focused management of its portfolio of mortgage-backed securities, seeking to provide pension investors with important diversification within the fixed-income sector. Because it originates multi-family investments, the HIT is able to negotiate terms beneficial to its portfolio. The HIT offers financing to meet various needs related to the development, rehabilitation, or preservation of real estate, including construction financing, permanent financing, fixed or floating rate forward commitments, and secured bridge loans. The HIT protects its investors with credit enhancements provided by a variety of sources, including the FHA, Ginnie Mae, Fannie Mae and Freddie Mac. The HIT claims that its financing expertise and its broad-based relationships with public financing, labor, and private partners have made the HIT one of the leading sources of finance for the development of workforce housing.

The BIT invests primarily in equity interests in institutional quality commercial real estate, including multi-family, office, retail, industrial, mixed-use, and hotel properties. For development projects, the BIT generally participates as a joint venture partner with developers. On a selective basis, the BIT also provides participating debt and construction financing. The

BIT's investment strategy focuses on the development and acquisition of high-quality real estate, primarily for long-term ownership.

Through the overall AFL-CIO Investment Program, the HIT and BIT have joined forces in recent years to launch successful community investment initiatives in targeted areas with extraordinary needs for affordable housing, homeownership opportunities, and economic development. The HIT and BIT have worked closely with mayors, housing authorities, developers, and labor leaders to address local housing and building needs. Among the current initiatives are:

- The New York City Community Investment Initiative, established in the wake of the 9/11 tragedy. HIT and BIT invested $560 million in multi-family housing in New York City, generating 3,500 union construction jobs and developing or preserving over 14,000 housing units (84% affordable). An additional $882 million in single-family mortgages have been provided to union members and city employees through the HIT HOME program. Both funds are targeting large investments under "phase two" of the initiative.
- The Chicago Community Investment Plan. The HIT invested $85 million in multifamily housing and BIT $145 million toward longer-term investment goals of $250 million and $250 million, respectively. These investments will generate over 1,700 housing units and 1,100 union construction jobs.
- The AFL-CIO Gulf Coast Revitalization Program. (See Project Showcase.)

Labor Impacts

The HIT estimates that its projects have created 53,000 union jobs over its lifetime, as part of its collateral objective of facilitating employment for union members in construction and related trades, in the process financing more than 84,000 units of housing nationwide. Through its single-family programs, the

HIT has also provided construction financing or home mortgage opportunities for some 15,000 working families. The HIT's labor policy requires 100% union construction on the projects it finances. To ensure the success of these projects, the HIT offers Labor Relations Services to developers, contractors, and unions. It is believed that the HIT's labor requirements:

- Benefit housing developers and contractors by assuring that highly skilled workers build the projects.
- Add value to financed projects through the skills, knowledge, and experience that union workers bring to the job.
- Promote positive labor relations and productivity on financed projects, while also minimizing any possible costs associated with labor-management disputes.

The BIT estimates its projects have created 27,000 union construction jobs, investing in 156 commercial properties across the U.S. The BIT has similar worker-friendly investment parameters and offers assistance through its Labor Relations Services and full-time Labor Relations staff. The BIT also requires various neutrality, card-check, and collective bargaining agreements by investors and contractors in hotel, retail, services, and similar companies. According to BIT, a number of its projects have played a significant role in the revitalization and development of downtown areas, including Gallery Place in Washington, DC, which led the revitalization of the long-neglected East End neighborhood (co-sponsored by two other profiled funds). Another BIT-financed project, the $74 million Hudson Crossing project, was the first residential high-rise to break ground in Manhattan following the 9/11 attack, as well as first multi-family project and first residential construction in Manhattan.

Environmental/Social Impacts

The HIT has invested in housing and mixed-use developments that are helping to transform urban communities and strengthen the economic base of the cities and towns that union members live in. By frequently focusing on high-density urban areas, the HIT seeks to promote "transit-oriented development." One such project is near Boston's Ashmont Peabody Square train station.

The BIT has invested in environmentally friendly buildings including One River Terrace, a $372 million mixed-use project in Battery Park City in Manhattan, with a Gold LEED Certification. Additionally, as part of the Gulf recovery initiative, the ITC has supported the establishment of a panelized housing factory that is exploring green building practices.

As an adjunct to its post-9/11 New York City initiative, the HIT and its investors invested $600 million in a major transformation of abandoned riverfront industrial areas of Hoboken and Jersey City, New Jersey. HIT invested in 13 multi-family projects in these cities, bringing 3,700 housing units and more than $750 million of total development. Nearing completion on the waterfront in Hoboken is The Sovereign, a $72 million apartment building. With $66 million in HIT financing, The Sovereign provides 261 residences at The Shipyard, an award-winning master-planned residential community.

Portfolio

At year-end 2007, the HIT had 743 holdings in 36 states. The investments in its portfolio were distributed across the U.S. as follows: 19% in the East, 5% in the West, 13% in the Midwest, 1% in the South, and 63% in a national pool (figures exclude cash and cash equivalents as well as single family mortgage-backed securities and other securities). In managing the portfolio, the HIT's strategy is to construct an investment portfolio with a higher yield and lower credit risk than its benchmark, the Lehman Brothers Aggregate Bond Index, while maintaining a similar interest rate and prepayment risk profile to its benchmark. To generate current income and minimize credit risk, 98% of the HIT's portfolio was insured or guaranteed by the government or government-sponsored enterprises (as of year-end 2007).

As of June 30, 2008, the BIT owned 93 properties, with a total portfolio of approximately 21 million square feet of space. Occupancy rates were 93% for multifamily and 93% for other commercial properties. The portfolio composition is Multifamily 30%; Office 29%; Industrial 23%; Retail 17%; and Hotel 1%. Geographically, 37% of BIT's investments are in the East, 28% in the West, 15% in the Midwest, and 20% in the South.

Performance

The HIT seeks to provide competitive risk-adjusted returns relative to its benchmark, the Lehman Brothers Aggregate Bond Index, by investing in assets that provide premium income, while maintaining a portfolio risk profile comparable to its benchmark. At year-end 2006, HIT had outperformed this Index for the one-, three-, five- and ten-year periods ending December 31, 2006. At year-end 2007, HIT slightly trailed the one- and five-year return benchmarks, but continued to outperform in the three- and ten-year periods. The HIT ranked third for the one-year period and eighth for the five-year period, as reported in Pensions & Investments, May 14, 2007. At the close of the first quarter of 2008, the HIT was ranked as a "top ten manager" by Morningstar, Inc., which compared the performance of managers of U.S. intermediate duration collective investment trusts for the period.

The BIT benchmarks its performance to the National Council of Real Estate Investment Fiduciaries Property Index (NPI), the accepted industry index of equity interests in institutional quality real estate. As of year-end 2007, the BIT had barely trailed one-, three-, five-, and ten-year benchmarks but outperformed the NPI on a gross basis since fund inception and had never experienced a negative quarterly return.

Challenges

In frank discussions with Steve Coyle in his Washington, D.C. offices, the CEO of HIT and President of the ITC expressed deep concerns about the housing market slow-down that began in 2006, as well as the broader withdrawal of federal funding for affordable housing that had been underway for many years.

Coyle believes that, as a model of socially responsible investing (SRI) focused on patient capital, the AFL–CIO Investment Program has created the conditions for successful community investing. This model has been developed for over 40 years to meet the investment needs of organized labor and pension funds with union beneficiaries. Coyle thinks that this strategy, combined with the experience and size of the HIT and BIT, can yield targeted investments that move SRI to new levels of direct community impact. The HIT and BIT are able to use their relationships with public officials, developers, union leaders, and finance professionals to leverage investment capital from other market participants to target capital gaps identified by local communities (such as financing for affordable housing, and to meet the diverse needs of working families, the elderly, disabled, or homeless).

The Investment Program has used an initiative investing strategy to create the conditions for successful investments in designated markets. In addition to the Investment Program's community investment initiatives, the BIT created its own National Apartment Initiative (NAI) to leverage investments in a sector of the real estate market in which it saw the potential for strong returns. This initiative was able to invest $231 million of BIT equity in projects valued at over $1.6 billion, which financed over 2,000 units of multi-family housing in five major cities across the U.S.

This patient capital model is being put to a stiff test in the AFL–CIO Investment Program's Gulf Coast initiative. In a region largely lacking sufficient infrastructure to move quickly on redevelopment, the ITC is working to create conditions for investment opportunities that will meet the respective investment criteria of the HIT and BIT while addressing the region's urgent rebuilding needs.

Principals

STEPHEN COYLE has served as Chief Executive Officer of the AFL–CIO Housing Investment Trust since 1992 and is also President of the AFL–CIO Investment Trust Corporation, which is a service provider for the

AFL-CIO Building Investment Trust. During that period the HIT's assets have grown from approximately $500 million to $3.7 billion, and in the last decade the BIT has grown from $370 million to approximately $3 billion in assets. Steve provided a detailed overview of the AFL-CIO Investment Program, and of the new community initiatives in the Gulf, New York City, and Chicago. He is proud of the growth of the Program and the considerable social benefits produced for working people.

Steve believes that the AFL-CIO Investment Program is breaking new ground in the pension investment movement—creating a third wave of investment—by combining construction and permanent jobs strategies with a broad community revitalization campaign entailing job training, youth services, community organizing, and economic development. By focusing on providing a market rate of return for HIT's and BIT's investors, while also providing the collateral benefits of union job creation, the construction of affordable housing, and investment in community economic development, the Investment Program is able to meet its "double bottom line."

Coyle has been active in housing production and finance, economic development, and urban planning for more than 35 years. Before coming to the AFL-CIO Investment Program, Coyle served for seven years as the Director of the Boston Redevelopment Authority and was Executive Vice President of a national architectural and planning firm based in San Francisco, from 1981 to 1984. He served the federal government in Washington, D.C., as Deputy Undersecretary of the U.S. Department of HHS and, earlier, as Executive Assistant to the Secretary of the Department of HUD. Coyle earned a Bachelor's Degree from Brandeis University, a Master's degree from the Kennedy School of Government at Harvard University, and a Jurist Doctor degree from Stanford Law School.

Project Showcase: the Gulf Revitalization Project

We took a site visit to the NOLA offices of the AFL-CIO Investment Trust Corporation to meet with the Director of the Gulf Coast Revitalization Program, Tom O'Malley; Michael M. Arnold, Senior Executive Vice

President, AFL-CIO Investment Trust Corporation; and Art Lujan, Executive Director, Gulf Coast Construction Careers Center. In June 2006, AFL-CIO President John Sweeney inaugurated the AFL-CIO Gulf Coast Revitalization Program (GCRP). Besides NOLA, another regional focus is in Jackson, Mississippi.

THE AIMS OF THE GULF INITIATIVE ARE:
- Affordable Housing, $250 million: The project will seek to build or renovate 5,000 to 10,000 housing units in New Orleans and other Gulf Coast communities, leveraging an additional $150 million from other public and private sources. Special emphasis will be given to workforce and special needs housing.
- Health Care and Hospital Facilities, $100 million: In conjunction with other partners, the HIT plans to invest in health care facilities and hospital construction. These investments will help reduce the significant shortage of health care facilities in the region.
- Homeownership, $250 million: The HIT plans to make available home mortgages for union members and public employees throughout the region. This program will include informational workshops with counseling and tools for homeowners who are facing foreclosure or who need to refinance their homes. In addition, the HIT is working with local CDCs to develop innovative homeownership programs for low-income families.
- Economic Development, $100 million: The BIT has targeted equity investments for commercial real estate development and revitalization to create jobs and boost local economies. The BIT's investment is expected to leverage another $150 million from other sources.

The ITC is spearheading the development of a unionized manufactured housing facility in New Orleans. The ITC announced in October 2007, that the facility received an award of $4 million in New Markets Tax Credits, allowing Housing International Gulf Coast, Inc., the new facility, to move forward. Partnering with Housing International Gulf Coast, Inc., are ITC and Telesis Corporation, a D.C.-based non-profit housing corporation. This facility will help fill the region's critical shortage of high-quality, affordable homes while also providing good jobs, training, and other workforce development services for local residents. When at full capacity, this plant is expected to produce up to 2,000 homes and 400 full time union jobs annually. The employees at the plant are represented by the Metal Trades Department, AFL-CIO. The project will also prioritize "green" building processes, utilizing steel-frame and other sustainable building products that are designed to withstand the region's climate. The GCRP is a multi-faceted approach that addresses area residents' needs for housing, healthcare, and good jobs

The HIT and ITC have been laying the foundation for the overall initiative and ITC has been providing technical assistance to help re-build the New Orleans Redevelopment Authority. The HIT and ITC have been working closely with the building trades to help implement a major training program for area residents, to build the skilled workforce necessary for Gulf Coast reconstruction projects. Sponsored by the Building and Construction Trades Department of the AFL-CIO, this Gulf Coast Construction Careers Center had enrolled three classes of pre-apprentice trainees as of August 2007. Among other activities, the group defended public housing tenants in their efforts to prevent demolition of livable homes.

Amalgamated Bank, LongView ULTRA
(New York)

Amalgamated Bank
1825 K Street, N.W.
Washington, DC 20006
Phone: (202) 721-0778
Fax: (202) 721-0779
Web: www.amalgamatedbank.com
Contact: Deborah Nisson, Sr. V.P. & Portfolio Manager
Email: DebbieNisson@AmalgamatedBank.com

Distinguishing Characteristics:

- Founded: 1998
- Habitat: Washington, D.C.
- Range: Invests primarily in U.S.
- Fund Type: Fixed-income fund focused on real estate
- Fund Structure(s): Commingled Trust (managed by Amalgamated Bank)
- Capital Partners: Pension funds, institutional investors
- Assets Under Management: $1.1 b billion (Dec. 2008)

Overview

The LongView ULTRA Construction Loan Investment Fund is a fixed-income fund focused on real estate. It is a product of the Amalgamated Bank, one of the few surviving labor banks founded in the 1920s to service workers once shunned by banking services. The first investors in 1998 were the National Automatic Sprinkler Industry Pension Fund and the Service Employees International Union Pension Plan Master Trust, two unions (among others) keen to secure a good return on pension fund investments and to expand jobs for their members. The principals of LongView ULTRA believe that their fund offers developers a thorough review of the loan request—with a construction and environmental engineer—in a much shorter time than other lenders.

Structure

Amalgamated Bank, with $39.5 billion in total assets, is the trustee of the LongView ULTRA Construction Loan Investment Fund. The Bank is a privately held New York State chartered commercial Bank. The Bank has provided trustee, investment advisory, custodial, and benefit remittance services for multi-employer funds since 1973. The ULTRA Fund is a commingled trust organized under New York State banking laws.

Amalgamated Bank is a full service commercial bank with headquarters in New York and offices in California, New Jersey, Nevada, and Washington, D.C. The Bank is the only bank in the United States that is fully owned by a union (UNITE-HERE). The Bank is registered under the state of New York and is regulated by New York State and federal banking regulators.

Capacity and Products

The Ultra Fund is managed by a small group of professionals with many years experience in real estate finance. The Fund currently has $1.1 billion in committed assets. The Fund provides construction financing for all types of union-built properties, including apartments, condominiums, industrial, retail, hotel, and office buildings nationwide. The Fund's policy requires an exit strategy for all loans. The Fund can consider projects up to $90 million and will consider loans and participation in some cases over that amount. The Fund will act as sole lender, lead lender, or participant and is currently acting in each of these capacities.

It is useful to note that the Fund is part of a larger bank that in itself provides construction loans and mortgages, including mortgages for government-assisted housing and commercial mortgages for multi-family residential buildings, office buildings, as well as mixed-use properties and shopping centers. Thus, the loan review process for the Fund draws on a broad foundation of banking and financing expertise.

Labor Impacts:

LongView's parent corporation, the Amalgamated Bank, was founded by the predecessor unions of UNITE. The bank is active across a wide range of responsible corporate governance and community development issues. Staff is represented by a collective bargaining agreement and all are members of OPEIU Local 153. The Board of Directors of Amalgamated Bank is composed of all union officers and experts who review the loans for their adherence to the union protection clauses.

The LongView Ultra Fund reports that it has created over 24 million hours of union construction labor since 1998. LongView requires that developers use only union labor and that, while ULTRA is a lender on a project, the service workers' be allowed to organize. The construction loans for the Intercontinental Hotel near the O'Hare Airport required a neutrality agreement for the hotel workers union, UNITE-HERE. While it was possible that many of their projects would have been built union anyway, without LongView ULTRA insisting on all union-built construction, investors could not have ensured high labor standards and responsible contractor agreements once the facility was completed.

In at least two cases, the borrowing developers had never built union and were reluctant to do so. Deborah Nisson, one of LongView ULTRA's principals, assured them it would be profitable because union labor, in the end, is "faster, better, cheaper." A condo developer in Boston reportedly was so pleased with working with union labor that he borrowed more money for three subsequent union-built projects. The principals of ULTRA report that every $10 million loan creates, on average, 77,000 job hours, pointing out that these funds are then recycled into new projects rather than a "build or buy and hold" philosophy.

Environmental/Community Impacts

LongView ULTRA has no formal mandate to condition loans on using energy-conserving technologies. However, Nisson is very concerned about using environmentally conscious techniques and materials; she and her consultants do discuss the use of these new technologies with the developers. She has also joined the Responsible Property Investors (RPI) group and is finding common ground among her peers in the green investment and green building fields. LongView worked with a brownfields developer that converted a Beaux Art power station in Chester, Pennsylvania, into Class A office space (see showcase). The developer had never used union labor, though Nisson claimed he has turned out to be "an excellent developer." The brownfield developments have the positive environmental effect of utilizing and renovating brownfield sites, preserving undeveloped land.

Portfolio

As of 2008, the fund had 49 active and committed loans totaling $2.1 billion. The largest approved projects include an $83 million participation in a loan for Carnegie Tower Condominiums in Portsmouth, Rhode Island, a $63 million condo project in Milwaukee, and a $58 million movie studio in Albuquerque, New Mexico. The larger completed projects include the Philadelphia Avenue North, a student housing project for $60 million (yielding 265,000 union labor hours). Investors include thirty-eight construction union pension funds, eight HERE (Hotel Employees) pension funds, one SEIU fund (Service Employees), the AFL-CIO staff pension fund, two public funds, and others.

Performance

The Fund's returns are benchmarked to the Lehman Aggregate, which is, according to pension fund consultants, the best available, widely accepted index (since ULTRA is considered a fixed income investment). ULTRA has outperformed the Lehman for all years since 1998, except one (ULTRA has much shorter duration loans than the Lehman Aggregate, and the Lehman Aggregate indexes corporate bonds). The largest challenge ULTRA faces in its portfolio is to find loans that are diverse by type of loan (condo, hotel, office space, etc.) and geography. The investment management fee is one percent.

Challenges

In terms of strengths, Deborah Nisson claims that the Fund's loans have a greater multiplier than mortgages since the developer, in paying back the loan quickly, makes funds available for new union-built investments. Another apparent strength is the high-quality service the Fund provides to developers, that is, speed of loan processing and ongoing advice and oversight. The Fund also yields profits for unionized contractors; this is important in order to help management trustees and public sector funds identify the ancillary benefits to their investments in ULTRA.

In addition, Nisson believes that pension consultants should be cognizant that many of the investment vehicles being offered today have unique characteristics. Many consultants gather information and evaluate investment opportunities for their clients by issuing RFP's and RFI's. The more sophisticated consultants maintain internet-based databases that investment managers update with product information. The problem is that there is little or no flexibility in any of these methods. It would be nice to have the option to answer a question with "N/A" or "Other" when a question does not apply to the investment vehicle being evaluated. Thus, many responsible pension and other institutional funds are suffering lost opportunities—both good returns but also good collateral benefits—when they only rate worker-friendly real estate vehicles as part of the standard benchmark process.

Principals

DEBORAH NISSON is a Senior Vice President with Amalgamated Bank and one of the Portfolio Managers of Amalgamated Bank's LongView ULTRA I Construction Loan Investment Fund. We met with Nisson in LongView's suites in the bank's offices in Washington, D.C. She was previously employed from 1974 through 1998 by the International Brotherhood of Electrical Workers (IBEW) and served as the Investment Manager for the IBEW Pension Benefit Fund and the IBEW General Fund. She graduated with a B.S. in Business Management from the University of Maryland and received a Master of Science Degree in Real Estate from The Johns Hopkins

University. Her finance and real estate expertise helped the IBEW's pension fund real estate projects and inspired her to start the Amalgamated LongView ULTRA fund (a mutual fund of construction loans) with Roy Dickinson in 1998.

ROY DICKINSON is also a Senior Vice President and Portfolio Manager. Dickinson was previously employed from 1966 through 1998 by the IBEW (one of the earlier unions to involve itself with construction financing and helping the industry create union jobs) and served as the Executive Assistant to the International Secretary for Investments and Employee Benefits from 1985 to 1998. He is a 50-year member of the IBEW. Dickinson graduated from the University of Maryland in 1966 with a B.S. in General Studies specializing in Economics and Business Administration.

As a team, Debbie and Roy designed and implemented the concept of a construction loan fund that would finance projects exclusively using 100% union labor.

Project Showcase: Wharf at Rivertown

The National Trust for Historic Preservation says it best: "What began as a 396,000-square-foot, six-story neoclassical marketing tool in 1918, now is the $60 million centerpiece of the rebirth of Pennsylvania's oldest city, Chester, founded by Swedish settlers in 1642." In 2002, the LongView Fund participated in the revitalization of an abandoned, polluted brownfield site in Chester, Pennsylvania, and in so doing created the Wharf at Rivertown, a clean, modern office complex that has helped re-shape the community and grow additional businesses and jobs. Not only did the project result in an environmental transformation of a dangerous site, it helped create 1,500 new jobs and is playing a role in reviving the Chester area, a part of Greater Philadelphia.

In 2005, the Wharf at Rivertown won the Phoenix Award, presented annually by the non-profit Phoenix Awards Institute recognizing innovative yet practical remediation projects at brownfields sites in the U.S. and abroad.

The Chester Power Station was built by the Philadelphia Electric Co

(PECO Energy) in 1919 to satisfy growing demand for electricity after World War I. It was a working plant until PECO shut it down in 1981. It sat vacant for two decades.

The LongView Ultra Fund provided $23.35 million in a $44.7 million loan participation to renovate the nine-story structure. The building's smokestacks, fourteen boilers, two large coal bins, and five turbines were removed. All salvageable elements were reused, beginning with the sale of 10,000 tons of metal from within the building, and the redeployment of 20,000 tons of brick and concrete, which were used as parking-lot fill. Selected pieces of power plant equipment, such as switch panels, transformers, and water condensers, were systematically included in the interior renovation.

The Wharf at Rivertown has already had a major economic impact on Chester. The construction was 100% unionized, creating about 150,000 hours of union labor on the renovation project. The 1,500 new permanent jobs have provided a boost to the previous jobs base of 5,000, in this community of 40,000. New corporate tenants currently include Wells Fargo Bank and Syngy Inc., a large Conshocken, Pa.-based software firm. The project has also led to seven new development projects in the city and has been an important catalyst for the planned widening of Route 291, which runs parallel to the site.

The National Trust asserted that the project is showing promise for a city that had been languishing since the 1950s with a failing school system, dwindling tax base, and soaring crime rates. Its population fell from 66,000 to 37,000 between 1950 and 2000. "[The renovation] represents the transition from a heavy industrial waterfront economy that dominated the city and county for over 100 years, back to a mixed-use commercial district with restaurants, exhibition space, and a public park," said State Senator Dominic Pileggi, Chester's mayor when plans to develop the Wharf began. Before, he says, the industrial district was "separated from the citizens by barbed wire and walls."

The National Trust made note of the Wharf's 90 acres of riverfront, two marinas, ample parking, and Philadelphia architect John T. Windrim's grandiose design, featuring a 100-foot vaulted ceiling, ornamental skylights, and Corinthian pilasters in a 35,000-square-foot gallery. To provide more incentive, the state sponsored a special 10-year tax-exempt status to foster business in depressed areas and appropriated $2 million to expand the waterfront's access road from two lanes to four. Thus, the project is revitalizing a blighted, urban community, bringing new businesses to the area; preserving an historic building and utilizing sustainable building processes; and, creating good jobs.

The BUILD Fund of America (Troy)

5455 Corporate Drive, Suite 204
Troy, Michigan 48098
Phone: (248) 267-5070
Fax: (248) 267-5074
Web: www.LMFA.com
Contact: Scott Woosley, Managing Director
Email: woosley@lmfa.com

Distinguishing Characteristics:

- Founded: 1999
- Habitat: Troy, Michigan
- Range: Invests primarily in the U.S. in secondary and tertiary markets.
- Fund Type: Open-end commingled real estate funds
- Fund Structure(s): Specialty Bank Collective Trust; Investment Advisors: Labor-Management Fund Advisors; Fund Trustee: Ameriserv Bank
- Capital Partners: Primarily multi-employer pension funds
- Assets Under Management: $204.7 million (in total $278.6 million)

Overview

The BUILD Fund of America is an open-end commingled real estate fund that invests in institutional quality to-be-built or significantly rehabilitated real estate projects that are constructed with 100% union labor. The BUILD Fund of America provides union pension funds—all of their clients are Taft-Hartley funds—the opportunity to spread a single investment across a number of states creating work for signatory contractors and jobs for union members.

The BUILD America Fund claims it has a portfolio of "quality" real estate, and its investment focus is on providing a stable income stream with the potential for capital appreciation. Qualifying pension plans can invest on a quarterly basis with a minimum investment of $250,000. The small size is a distinguishing characteristic of the Fund. As of the end of 2007, the BUILD Fund had committed to fund approximately $284.1 million in projects. At one time there were a total of five BUILD Funds—the BUILD Fund of America and four other state based funds. However, through consolidation of assets the BUILD Fund of America now includes assets from three of the former state based funds. This profile will focus on the BUILD Fund of America.

The distinction of the BUILD Fund of America from the other "responsible" funds is their leveraging and their focus in the Southern U.S. The managers of the BUILD Fund of America target the South because it is growing. They also believe that projects in northern and urban markets have a stronger likelihood of being built by union labor due to prevailing wage rules and customs that favor unionization. They state that they can have a larger impact in the South. The Fund has also spent a lot of time exploring smaller cities in order to invest in often-overlooked secondary and third-tier markets. The Fund puts a relatively small amount of equity in a project, levering adequate debt. The Fund develops close regional bank relationships in order to find local developers who pass all control tests and will build with unionized labor. The local bank typically funds projects at 70-80%. This approach has the risk-lowering advantages of diversification. There is some interest rate risk, which is handled by using only ten-year loans.

Structure

The BUILD Fund is a "Section 584 Group Trust" and the "Specialty Trust Real Estate Committee" has the final authority to make investment decisions. The Fund is managed by Labor-Management Fund Advisors, LLC, and Ameriserv Financial (of Johnstown, Pennsylvania, a bank whose members are affiliated with the United Steelworkers) serves as the Fund Trustee. The BUILD Fund does not have an advisory Board of current or potential clients because of concerns that conflict of interest issues would be created if the Fund was being considered by a pension board of trustees in which one or more members was on such an advisory board. (The Fund is governed by the Employee Retirement Income Security Act of 1974 and the Office of the Comptroller of the Currency.)

Capacity and Products

Labor-Management Fund Advisors, LLC, employs 12 professionals. LMFA's Investment Philosophy is founded on the premise that the Real Estate Investment Market is an inefficient and segmented market that provides the opportunity for "above market returns." LMFA claims it exploits the market's inefficiencies through an extensive due diligence process that selectively targets successful local and regional developers with expertise in specific markets and product types.

LMFA only invests in development or substantial rehabilitation projects that provide significant potential for value creation. They believe that the secondary and tertiary markets provide the best investment opportunities. Through the BUILD Funds, LMFA provides a vehicle for pension plans to diversify their existing stock and bond portfolios with professionally managed institutional quality real estate. The investment focus is on providing a stable income stream with the potential for capital appreciation.

LMFA believes that institutional real estate investors should take advantage of the inherent put-option* provided by the commercial banking system. Therefore, LMFA employs a prudent level of leverage at the property level to capitalize on the less expensive cost of capital provided by the debt markets and to tap the benefits of this put option. This strategy allows LMFA to provide investors with what it considers a more diversified portfolio given a specific capital commitment than is typically provided by other managers. A $50 million investment in the fund can be deployed in

---

* An option contract giving the owner the right, but not the obligation, to sell a specified amount of an underlying security at a specified price within a specified time.

five $10 million projects ($10 million of equity in each) rather than in one
$50 million project.

Portfolio

The BUILD Fund is currently invested in 43 projects around the country.
Additionally, there have been 8 projects that have been paid off.

Performance

Benchmark Construction: Since the portfolio composition of the BUILD
Fund of America (BFA) contains both debt and equity investments, the
Fund created its own benchmark on the advice of several consultants. The
constructed benchmark combines the NCREIF Property Index and the
Lehman Brothers U.S. Aggregate Bond Index. The weighting of the two
indexes reflects the BFA Portfolio composition (debt and equity) at the end
of each quarter. (The NCREIF Property Index is "unleveraged." It includes
various real estate property types, and excludes cash and other non-property
related assets and liabilities, income, and expenses. The Lehman Brothers
U.S. Aggregate Bond Index includes Treasuries—public obligations of
the U.S. Treasury that have remaining maturities of more than one year,
Government Related Issues, and USD Corporates.)

The BUILD Fund of America has sometimes trailed and sometimes
bettered its benchmark (described above). As of March 31, 2007, the returns
were as follows: the 3 month gross return was 2.09% (benchmark 2.39%);
one year gross return was 11.82% (benchmark 10.56%); 3 year gross return
was 10.52% (benchmark 8.40%); and the 5 year gross return was 7.38%
(benchmark 7.29%).

Labor Impacts

One of the unique strategies of the BUILD Fund is to invest in projects in
areas that would otherwise not use union labor. Finding new or significantly
rehabilitated real estate projects that will increase regional construction
market share for union labor, BUILD utilizes signatory contractors and

requires projects to be constructed with union labor. Since the Fund leverages, they are able to maximize the projects in which they require union labor. Principals argue that union construction jobs have industry-financed skill and safety training as well as strong wage and benefit packages. They claim that union-built projects bring value to project owners and the community. Because of the highly skilled craftsmanship of union-certified building trades, projects are built right the first time, on time, and on budget.

LMFA, through the BUILD Fund, focuses on producing market rate returns while increasing market share for union labor and signatory contractors. LMFA and the BUILD Fund typically encourage development partners to sell the asset or refinance BUILD out of the transaction within five to ten years of project completion. This enables LMFA to reallocate funds to new development projects, keeping with its mission to "gain market share for union labor and signatory contractors by investing in to-be-built or significantly rehabilitated real estate projects that earn competitive market driven returns." However, each asset sale is based on the specific market's viability on a case-by-case basis. LMFA calculates the number of jobs each project creates based on the total cost of hard construction.

Environmental/Community Impacts

The BUILD Fund is involved in green buildings and has invested in projects revitalizing brownfields. The Fund managers maintain they will continue to do so as long as it makes economic sense for their clients.

Challenges

The BUILD Fund faces difficulty finding union contractors in the low union density, economically growing parts of the nation. The primary barrier to building with union labor is getting enough competitive union bids in these growing markets. The BUILD Fund uses previous development partners to supply the testimony to prospective contractors. As the marketing director, Tim Nichols said the developers convey the message that "the high cost of union labor means it will come ahead of schedule and below budget." It is a challenge to get developers and contractors to ask each other about their experiences and to ask for references and recommendations.

The BUILD Fund reports that they have contractors that "follow them around the country." As was mentioned before, the BUILD Fund also avoids competing for a project in a large city where most large construction projects are built with unionized contractors regardless of the funding source. Their perspective is that the yields are bid down in those areas and there is no added impact of the union labor requirement. The Fund managers go to places like Findlay, Ohio, for example, where there is little funding outside of local banks.

Principals

SCOTT B. WOOSLEY, CFA, is the Managing Director. Woosley is a Principal and one of the founders of the BUILD Funds and LMFA, LLC. He has more than 20 years of financial and investment experience. Prior to joining LMFA, Woosley was managing director and portfolio manager for a $1+ billion commingled real estate fund that specialized in financing construction and providing permanent take out financing for office, industrial, retail, and residential projects throughout the United States. He has overseen the underwriting and due diligence for more than $1 billion in equity, participating mortgages, and credit enhancement facilities. In addition, Woosley has extensive experience in valuing real estate of all types under ERISA, OCC, GAAP, and NCREIF guidelines. He has significant experience in the operation of ERISA-regulated real estate investments and in the marketing of those investments to institutional clients. Woosley also has provided pension consulting services, including needs analysis, investment management and administration selection, and employee communication to a variety of corporate and non-profit entities. He has published manuscripts on Accounting for Post-retirement Benefits Other than Pensions—FASB 106, Post-retirement Funding Vehicles, and IRS §457 Plans.

Woosley is a Chartered Financial Analyst and a member of the Association for Investment Management and Research, American Real

Estate Society, and the International Foundation of Employee Benefit
Plans. He graduated in 1984 from the George Washington University with
a B.A. in accounting and received his MBA in 1991 from the University of
Michigan.

Project Showcase: Riviera Dunes

The BUILD Fund of America will provide approximately $20 million in
financing for Riviera Dunes, a luxury high-rise condominium development
on the Manatee River in Palmetto, Florida. The development will have sixty-
two condominium units in each of the three fifteen-story towers. Amenities
will include retail shops, three swimming pools, a community center with
a fitness club, tennis courts, a golf practice area, and views of the Gulf of
Mexico and the Manatee River.

Construction on Towers I and II has been completed. Corvus
International was the developer on the project, as well as on other BUILD
Fund projects in the Midwest and Florida. Wolverine Construction, the
Florida subsidiary of Walbridge Aldinger, is the General Contractor on
this project. Walbridge Aldinger has been the General Contractor on other
BUILD Fund projects in the Midwest.

The BUILD Fund's mezzanine loan to this project will generate a 14%
return. The project, with a budget of $170 million for all phases, will generate
approximately $49 million in wages, fringes and benefits for union workers.

Concert Properties, Ltd. (Vancouver)

9th Floor, 1190 Hornby Street
Vancouver, British Columbia
Canada V6Z 2K5
Phone: 604-688-9486
Fax: 604-688-8882
Web: www.concertproperties.com
Contact: Heather Harley, Marketing Manager
E-Mail: HHarley@ConcertProperties.com

Distinguishing Characteristics:

- Founded: 1986
- Habitat: Vancouver, B.C. with offices in Toronto and Edmonton
- Range: Invests primarily in British Columbia, Ontario, Alberta
- Fund Type: Tax-exempt real estate investment fund
- Fund Structure: Tax-exempt real estate corporation
- Capital Partners: Canadian union and management pension funds.
- Assets: C$1.3 billion

Overview:

Concert Properties is a Canadian diversified real estate enterprise. Owned exclusively by union and management pension funds, Concert is involved in developing and acquiring commercial and industrial properties, rental housing, condominium housing, seniors living communities, and resort properties in British Columbia, Alberta, and Ontario.

Concert was started in British Columbia in the late 1980s as a tax-exempt real estate investment fund. Concert has excelled through dedication to building, acquiring, and managing a diverse portfolio of properties suited to the needs of customers and the community. Concert became a leading investor in new rental properties, even in market downturns. It also became recognized for employing unionized contractors, benefiting local union members in construction and related industries.[1]

Concert was founded by labor leaders, with the help of real estate experts, in 1989. From an initial capitalization of $27.3 million, Concert now has assets in excess of $1.3 billion. One of the original goals of Concert was to finance new, affordable rental and other residential properties in the Greater Vancouver region. Aiming to increase affordable housing and stabilize ownership costs and rental rates, the organizers initially established a partnership with the City of Vancouver. They would build and manage rental accommodations on land leased from the City, funding provided by Concert. Limits on rent increases would be established through this partnership to ensure affordability. All units are guaranteed to remain rental for the life of the land lease (80 years) after which ownership of the land and improvements reverts to the City of Vancouver, unless the lease is extended or renewed.

Concert later re-organized as a corporation totally owned by pension funds. Concert was instrumental in the creation of Mortgage Fund One (MFO), a mortgage trust also owned by pension funds, developed to provide debt financing to real estate developments built with union construction forces, including but not limited to Concert developments. MFO was structured to provide stable long term yields to the participating pension funds.

Concert reports that, since 1989, it has completed developments in excess of $1.9 billion, and:

- Built more than 8,000 rental and condominium homes.
- Developed/acquired over 8.1 million square feet of income-producing properties.

Structure

Concert is a tax-exempt real estate corporation owned exclusively by union and management pension plans. Concert is involved in developing and acquiring rental housing, commercial and industrial properties, condominium housing, seniors living communities, resort developments, and hotels in British Columbia, Alberta, and Ontario.

Capacity and Products

Concert has 141 full and part-time employees across Canada. Concert co-ordinates site acquisition and development approvals for itself, clients, and partners; develops master-planned communities, condominiums, rental, and seniors housing, and industrial, office/retail, and resort properties; and provides project management services in B.C., Alberta, and Ontario to institutional investors, government, and non-profit societies.

Labor Impacts

Bill Clark, the former Telecommunications Workers' Union local union president in Vancouver, led the founding of Concert, and was hugely influential in convincing 29 pension funds and 26 private investors to pool over $27 million together to form Concert (initially named VLC). His union, the TWU, was one of the founding pension funds and continues to be the largest single shareholder of the Company. Today Concert is owned exclusively by 19 union and management pension funds in Canada.

Since 1989, Concert has:

- Created more than 16.2 million person-hours of on-site union employment.
- Contributed $70.5 million to affiliated union pension, health and welfare plans.

Most recently, Concert was recognized as one of *BC Business Magazine*'s Top 25 Best Companies to Work for in British Columbia.

Concert prides itself in taking an active part in finding ways to provide opportunities and funds for educating and training the next generation of trades' people. In 1995, Concert established the Concert Properties Ltd. Bursary Endowment Fund for British Columbia Institute of Technology (BCIT) students who enroll in eligible trades and technology programs related to the construction industry. Concert's bursary endowment now exceeds $428,000 and some 140 students have received bursaries, totaling more than $138,000.

In addition, the Concert Properties Founders Endowment in Honor of Bill Clark was established in 2005 at BCIT with a gift of $40,000. This also supports annual bursaries for Tele- and Wireless Communications & Computing students.

Established in 2002 by Concert Properties Ltd., the Concert Properties & Industry Partners Trades Discovery Program provides financial support for students exploring and training for a career in one of approximately 20 different trades programs offered at BCIT. To date, 462 students have received Graduation Grants of $200 towards recovering the cost of enrolment. As incentive for going on to enroll in a specialty Trades Training Program, 198 students have received either $1,000 or $2,000 Trades Discovery Entrance Grants. The 2008 Concert Masters Golf Tournament raised more than $81,000 for this unique BCIT program bringing total contributions from Concert Properties and Industry Partners to over $474,000.

Environmental/Community Impacts

Concert believes in respecting and retaining the inherent value in the development sites it undertakes, whether a heritage preservation or land restoration. Concert has restored many of the historical aspects of buildings it has redeveloped and has also participated in environmental land reclamation in the commercial and industrial properties it has acquired.

Concert also sees itself as a community builder, providing support to Canadian Habitat for Humanity projects and other social causes. Concert built the Cottage Hospice, a 10-bed hospice for the terminally ill, owned and operated by St. James Community Services Society, and donated project management services. Additional community projects are cited in the Collingwood Village showcase.

Portfolio

Concert has led more than $1.9 billion worth of developments, including 8,000 rental and condominium units, and developed/acquired over 9 million square feet of income-producing properties. It has $437 million worth of projects under development. Concert has also embarked on a major partnership with the Ontario Municipal Employees Retirement System (OMERS) to develop $600 million worth of residential rental income properties.

Performance

Concert reports $800 million in shareholder equity and notes that it has distributed $47 million in dividends to its shareholders over the last five years. Concert was recognized in both 2003 and 2004 with the "Grand SAM Award," presented by the Canadian Home Builders' Association and considered the industry's highest national honor.

Challenges

President/CEO David Podmore values the important role of skilled trades union members in ensuring success in the development industry, thus respecting all the more their investments in Concert. Podmore was interviewed by Business Edge, based in British Columbia, in 2007. When asked about Concert's requirement to use union labor, and whether that increases costs and limits profitability, Podmore responded: "Most developers wouldn't say that today. We've been in business for 18 years. We've had a long, long association with the trades and general contractors and, if anything, it's probably an advantage today. We've got good access to very good-quality trades people that have been loyal to us. There is a bit of a differential, certainly, in terms of cost. As you've seen in the last five years, wage rates in the non-union sector, I would gather, are on the same level."

Podmore has also warned that Canada would inevitably be impacted by the sub-prime mortgage crisis that started in 2007 in the U.S. But he believes that, given large-scale infrastructure commitments and resource commitments spanning several years, there will be excellent development opportunities in Western and Central Canada.

Principals

One of the company's founders, JACK W. POOLE, is the company's Chairman. He had extensive development experience prior to founding Concert having co-founded Daon Development Corporation. He is currently Chairman of the Vancouver Organizing Committee for the 2010 Olympic Winter Games. Poole has been honored by appointment to the Order of Canada, Canada's highest honor for lifetime achievement. In addition, Poole serves as a director of several companies and organizations and was Founding Chairman of the Molson Vancouver Indy.

Co-founder DAVID PODMORE is President & Chief Executive Officer of Concert Properties.

Podmore's extensive development career includes serving as Vice President of Planning, Design and Engineering for BC Place Ltd., and President and Chief Executive Officer of the British Columbia Pavilion Corporation for Expo 86. He was also a Vice President with Bell Canada Enterprises Development. Throughout his more than 33 years in the real estate development industry, Podmore has been actively involved in the community, both professionally and personally. He currently serves as the Chair of the Vancouver Convention Centre Expansion Project (VCCEP) and Chair of the BC Pavilion Corporation (PavCo), as a Director of Borealis BC Labs Inc. (formerly MDS Metro Laboratory Services) and as Vice President of the British Columbia Institute of Technology (BCIT) Foundation. He is the first recipient of the Award of Excellence established by The Real Estate Institute of BC, and in 2005 Podmore was awarded an Honorary Doctor of Technology from the British Columbia Institute of Technology.

Podmore re-affirms that Concert is focused on building and acquiring real estate that will have superior value in the long term. He notes that a new Rights Offering, recently approved by the Board of Directors, will raise an additional $250 million in new equity capital and will surge Concert's asset base to over $1.2 billion.

Project Showcase: Collingwood Village

Since 1993, over $400 million (including infrastructure) has been invested in Collingwood Village, a large urban redevelopment project undertaken on 28 acres of industrial brownfields in a lower-income neighborhood of East Vancouver. Through a unique cooperative planning process with the City, Collingwood was envisioned as a "master planned community." It is a model of community-based planning, benefiting local residents who have enjoyed improvements in amenities and services.

The property was acquired in 1990 and construction began in April 1994. The final project includes over 2,900 residential units in 21 residential buildings housing nearly 5,000 residents. An estimated 3.5 million on-site labor hours are attributed to Concert's investments, generating $118 million in wages/benefits and almost $10 million in pensio   A   s Isla Carmichael cites in a book chapter about Concert and Collingwood, a significant range of community amenities have been provided to Collingwood Village residents. The Collingwood Village Neighborhood House is a social and recreational focus for the community with an 8,000 sq. ft. community gymnasium and childcare facilities for 69 children. Concert also donated lands to the Vancouver school board to build a new elementary school that opened in 2002. Collingwood Village was designed to support recreational pursuits, enhance pedestrian connections, and create a variety of landscaped settings for residents to enjoy. Some 7.4 acres were dedicated to public open space, comprising three separate neighborhood parks. There's also a series of landscaped public open spaces and pedestrian routes.

Another innovation at Collingwood Village was the development of a Community Policing Office, a first in Vancouver, in order provide a sense of security for residents. Because of the project's proximity to the SkyTrain Station and bus loop, additional land has been redeveloped for residential and commercial uses.

Concert's Collingwood Village Stakeholders and Considerations

STAKEHOLDER	CONSIDERATIONS
Investors (Pension funds)	Return on investment Collateral benefits
Developer	Attraction and retention of good employees Relationships with other stakeholders Knowledge development
Employees	Quality of work life Training, Safety Work/life balance
Unions	Contributions to health, welfare, pension funds Job creation
Residents	Quality of life Affordable housing Safety, Leisure, Health
Community	Quality of life Safety Use of non-renewable resources Emissions Multiplier effect
Government	Revenue from taxation/permits Impact on the environment Urban sprawl Traffic congestion

As Laurie Mook pointed out, Collingwood Village is a great case study: not only is it financed by pension funds, but as a model ETI, it includes many of the dimensions for a social accounting framework.[2] She summarizes the project as spanning these dimensions: (1) socially-responsible investment, (2) social accounting and reporting, (3) sustainability, and (4) adult education.

The ERECT Funds (Pittsburgh, PA.)

c/o PenTrust Real Estate Advisory Services, Inc.

Rosslyn Commons, Suite 200

333 Baldwin Road

Pittsburgh, PA 15205

Phone: (412) 279-4100

Fax: (412) 279-8199

Web: www.pentrustonline.com/erectfunds

Contact: James Noland, President/Owner

Email: jnoland@pentrustonline.com

Distinguishing Characteristics:

- Founded: 1987
- Fund Type: Commingled real estate funds
- Fund Structure(s): Specialty Bank Collective Trust; Portfolio Manager: PenTrust Real Estate Advisory Services, Inc.; Trust agent: AmeriServ Trust and Financial Services Company
- Capital Partners: Primarily multi-employer and public pension funds
- Habitat: Pittsburgh, Pennsylvania
- Range: Invests primarily in western Pennsylvania, eastern Ohio and West Virginia
- Assets Under Management: $200 million

Overview

The ERECT (Employee Real Estate Construction Trust) Funds are collective investment trusts capitalized by union building trades pension funds, state and county funding sources, and corporate accounts for the construction of real estate projects built with all-union labor. Since their inception in 1987, the mission of The ERECT Funds has been to safeguard investors' capital and deliver competitive investment returns.

The ERECT Funds are managed by PenTrust Real Estate Advisory Services, Inc., which has been the investment manager and project underwriter since 1987, and AmeriServ Trust and Financial Services Company, which has been the trustee to The ERECT Funds since 1993.

The ERECT Funds were started in 1987 by three construction trades unions in the Pittsburgh area. Union leaders from the Carpenters, Iron Workers and Operating Engineers wanted to pool capital to be more strategically invested in Pittsburgh region construction projects. After five years of discussions starting in 1982, the group raised $7 million in 1987, and a local Pittsburgh based bank that later merged with another entity became the ERECT Funds' trustee. Jim Noland and his firm were asked to provide the underwriting services and have been an integral part of The ERECT Funds since their inception.

The ERECT Funds began investing and other union building trades' pension funds joined the effort. In 1993, The ERECT Funds moved to the trust company that later became AmeriServ Trust Financial Services Company. AmeriServ was a smaller local bank with less chance of being bought out, and had a labor agreement in place with the United Steelworkers for its employees. Today, the ERECT Funds' investors include the Commonwealth of Pennsylvania, Allegheny County, Beaver County, and corporate investors, in addition to the primary union pension investors. However, it took seven to eight years to broaden the investment pool so that most of the trusts in the region were willing to invest.

The gross value of projects created with ERECT Funds participation has reached approximately $600 million.

Structure

While The ERECT Funds are managed by PenTrust and AmeriServ Trust and Financial Services Company, ERECT has maintained an advisory committee since its inception. The committee is mainly composed of its labor investment partners but also includes two bank representatives and Noland himself. The purpose of the advisory board is to give advice on the appropriateness of investments made by The ERECT Funds. This enhances the communications between all parties involved in ERECT. The ultimate responsibility of the investments, custody, and accounting always remain with the bank trustee, AmeriServ Trust and Financial Services Company and the fund's professional real estate underwriter, PenTrust Real Estate Advisory Services, Inc.

A Trust Specialty Real Estate Investment Committee, established by The ERECT Funds' trustee, AmeriServ Trust and Financial Services Company, plays an important role in the approval and administration of debt or equity real estate investments being considered as an investment in the funds. They carefully review each potential investment for adherence to the underwriting criteria established for The ERECT Funds, review project documentation, and analyze the geographic and project diversification effects to The ERECT Funds' portfolio. If approved by the committee and trustee, The ERECT Funds proceed with an investment in the project.

Capacity and Products

The ERECT Funds provide debt and equity financing for commercial projects in the western Pennsylvania, eastern Ohio, and West Virginia markets. Projects financed to date include office, retail, industrial, apartments, condominiums, hotels, as well as other special purpose properties. The dual purposes of The ERECT Funds are to provide good investment returns to the investors and help create union construction employment.

PenTrust fields a staff of six professionals. PenTrust identifies and underwrites transactions for The ERECT Funds' consideration. These debt or equity investments are then monitored and serviced by PenTrust as they are approved and funded. Other PenTrust activities include the structuring of complex real estate financial transactions as an independent intermediary and the direct servicing of debt and equity transactions on behalf of other financial institutions. Many of these investments are made in projects that are funded with ERECT Fund dollars and meet their required construction building standards.

Labor Impacts

Based on the spreadsheets provided by PenTrust, the ERECT Funds have created over 6.3 million union job hours and approximately $250 million in wages and benefits, spread across most of the construction trades. This is a considerable impact on jobs for a regional real estate trust fund. The very active advisory committee (primarily comprised of labor investors) is not involved in final deal decisions or structure, but it does engage in discussions or concerns regarding property type or questions generally related to the construction of the projects under consideration.

Environmental/Community Impacts

Jim Noland has been moving The ERECT Funds toward the principles and practices of environmentally friendly green building. His primary contribution in that regard has been the clean-up and rehabilitation of brownfields and abandoned, contaminated buildings and facilities (see the Cork Factory Lofts showcase). One of Jim's most interesting observations is that the large institutional "buyers"—pension funds, real estate investment trusts, universities, insurance companies, private equity, and other players—are increasingly demanding green buildings. As these buyers are a large and active presence in the "after-market"—investing in newly completed or existing properties—the developers, investors, and contractors in real estate have to shift their attention to address this market.

The marketplace initially had qualms about the higher costs of green building and construction. However, Noland notes that the costs are being refined, as new manufacturers of green building products are coming forward with alternative products. The Pittsburgh region, among the top five U.S. cities in terms of total numbers of "green buildings," had recently launched a new network of green building product manufacturers. While there may still be a premium to lease green buildings, Noland referenced academic studies that showed that green buildings were more conducive to employee morale and were generally healthier for occupants.

PenTrust's sister company, Development Capital Investors, Inc. was awarded a special rate sensitive loan from the Commonwealth of Pennsylvania to invest in real estate projects located in traditionally under-served or under-supported areas in southwestern Pennsylvania, and also to promote green building design. Noland recognizes that the small financial incentive put in place by the state—in this case a slightly lower interest rate—will go a long way to fill the financing gap and make proposed and desirable projects possible.

Performance

The ERECT Funds have historically exceeded the corresponding benchmarks of the Lehman Brothers Mortgage Index and the NCREIF Index for its investments.

Challenges

Jim Noland said that many real estate developers question the union labor requirement implicit in most of the worker-friendly real estate funds and express their concerns that this may cause difficulties. He thinks it is more a problem of perception than reality. Noland agrees this approach may lead to a premium in labor costs but notes that union construction quality in his projects has proven to be far superior. Further, he's had few problems with projects that have suffered major construction setbacks as long as the project was built union. He thinks a greater challenge is in determining labor jurisdictional lines but asserts that can be resolved by being involved early in the planning for a project and with the use of pre-construction meetings to ensure clear lines of communication are established up front.

One reason for the quality advantage is that unions train their members, and almost all of the trades own their own training and apprenticeship schools. In addition, union building trades members are drug-tested by their own union, which protects all employees and helps shield contractors from the liability of dangerous on-site accidents. Another advantage that Jim has appreciated is that many of the union leaders are also well positioned on key civic and government boards around the region, thus having a lot of local influence on what works best for the community.

Noland believes that the greatest challenge for labor investors will be to identify the markets of the future. Labor leaders and union members will need to think progressively and can no longer insist on, or settle for, business-as-usual. He thinks that union advocates have to become "entrepreneurs," in a manner of speaking, in order to create their own market opportunities. Thus, labor has to see these challenging changes as opportunities, not obstacles.

He provided an example that rested on the response of one of his local union pension investors. The union was approached by an international corporation that wanted to build a new state-of-the-art research facility in Pittsburgh, but the research firm had building requirements for their "clean/sterile" conditions for research which were new to the marketplace. The company approached the steamfitters and plumbers union, whose leadership agreed to establish a new training program to prepare their members for the new challenge. The company engaged the union in the construction and adopted the union's training program. Noland sees similar challenges—and opportunities—in the environmental and renewable energy fields connected to the real estate markets.

Finally, Jim agreed with many of the investment leaders in this book that union and public pension trustees need more training and education in order to better understand pension investments in alternative investment classifications. He said that too many ill-informed politicians, consultants, and managers would arbitrarily block a pension board from making a prudent investment in worker-friendly investment vehicles. He was especially critical of pension managers who oppose ETI investments when many of the ETI portfolios have exhibited better than average returns on investment.

Portfolio

The ERECT Funds invest in a wide range of projects including retail, office, hotels, light manufacturing, research and development, and multi-residential properties. At the end of 2007, The ERECT Funds had invested more than $250 million in 67 real estate projects throughout the tri-state region.

Principals

I interviewed JAMES E. NOLAND, the President of PenTrust Real Estate Advisory Services, Inc., and the investment underwriter who was instrumental in creating the concept and philosophy of The ERECT Funds. As I spoke with Jim in the lobby of the newly-renovated Cork Factory Loft apartments (for years a dangerous and abandoned building), it was obvious that he and his partners spent a lot of time working with the developer and architect on the re-habilitation plans for the property. Jim believes that it is important that he and The ERECT Funds are involved early on in project planning and development. He thinks ERECT should be prepared to invest prior to full-scale development of a project, so that the issues important to ERECT's investment partners are addressed. He brought together the eventual unions involved in the Cork Factory Lofts for meetings with the developer, architects, contractors, etc. Labor partners have sometimes been able to advise the developer/contractor to modify building and product plans so that the construction plan is more viable, often yielding savings of money and time on the project.

Noland's career began in 1969 at The Equitable Life Assurance Society in Washington, D.C., in the Real Estate Investment Department. He moved to Pittsburgh with The Equitable in 1971 and soon accepted a position as Vice President in the Pittsburgh field office of the Galbreath Mortgage Company, which later became Chemical Mortgage Company. In 1976, Noland and his two partners founded Lane, Noland, Smith & Company, Inc., a highly respected mortgage banking entity headquartered in Pittsburgh. After 24 successful years of operation, Lane, Noland, Smith & Company was sold in 1999 to a large southeastern bank holding company. At that time, Noland became sole principal of PenTrust. Noland has also invested privately in commercial real estate developments and serves as a director on several boards. Noland's 35 years of experience and expertise in real estate finance have enabled him to bring a reliability and quality to PenTrust's investment recommendations that are respected well beyond the Pittsburgh market.

Project Showcase: Cork Factory Lofts

In 2003, The ERECT Funds were approached by a private development group with a project that involved the renovation of the former Armstrong Cork Factory located in the Strip District section of the City of Pittsburgh. Sitting vacant since 1974, the factory had become an eyesore and health hazard for the community. The project called for the renovation of the existing structure, containing approximately 302,000 square feet, into 295 loft apartments and the construction of a three-story, 428-vehicle parking garage with 33,000 square feet of retail space on the first floor. The ERECT Funds participated in the financing of the project with a subordinated bridge loan of $9,720,000 that enabled this project to move forward. The total project costs were $65,000,000. Of that total, an estimated $40,000,000 was used for hard construction costs. The Cork Factory Lofts were officially opened in May 2007, and today are at full capacity.

The effects of this project on union employment were vast. As is a requirement with any ERECT Funds deal, 100% of the construction and ongoing maintenance had to be performed by union contractors and subcontractors. In all, this transaction created estimated union construction work worth $20,145,000 in wages and benefits, and 325,000 union job hours.

Environmentally, the project led to the clean up and remediation of a polluted and dangerous abandoned building, as well as asbestos-removal. Additionally, because the project was a renovation of an existing building, the construction required significantly fewer materials than if newly built.

Further benefits from the project were felt throughout the Strip District neighborhood and the City of Pittsburgh. Soon after opening, the project was immediately accepted by the marketplace with new residents moving in. The Strip District, long considered a small-business market, now had proof that there is also a demand for residential living. In addition, the amenities provided by local small business should provide a more conducive residential environment and encourage future development in the area. For the City of Pittsburgh, in the midst of a campaign to encourage downtown living, this project will help to further brownfield development and the revitalization of other dead buildings. As an abandoned factory and one of the largest buildings in the Strip District, it could be said that the Armstrong Cork Factory was a symbol of the dying industrial economy that once fed the mouths of Pittsburgh. As the new Cork Factory Lofts, it has now become a symbol of an up-and-coming neighborhood and a revitalized city.

Multi-Employer Property Trust (Washington, DC)

Landon Butler & Company
700 13th Street, NW, Suite 925
Washington, DC 20005
Phone: (202) 737-7300
Fax: (202) 737-7604
Web: www.mept.com
Contact: Sarah Stettinius, Managing Director and Senior
Vice President
E-Mail: sarah@lbutler.com

Distinguishing Characteristics:

- Founded: 1982
- Fund Type: Open-end commingled real estate equity fund
- Fund Structure(s): Bank Collective Trust, with following Portfolio Managers:
- Trustee: NewTower Trust Company, Bethesda, MD; Investment Advisor: Kennedy Associates
- Real Estate Counsel, LP, Seattle, WA; Investor Relations: Landon Butler & Company, LP, Washington, DC
- Capital Partners: Pension funds, institutional investors
- Habitat: Washington, D.C.
- Range: Invests primarily in U.S.
- Assets Under Management: $7.29 billion

Overview

The Multi-Employer Property Trust (MEPT) is an open-end commingled core real estate equity fund that invests in a diversified portfolio of institutional-quality real estate assets and 100% union-built new construction properties. MEPT's portfolio consists of over 188 commercial real estate properties in approximately 25 major U.S. metropolitan markets. MEPT's primary investment strategy is to create top-quality, core, income-producing assets through development, rehabilitation, or acquisition of undervalued assets. MEPT's portfolio includes office buildings, industrial warehouse and distribution centers, retail centers, apartment buildings, and hotels. MEPT commenced operations on April 1, 1982, and was co-founded by Kennedy Associates Real Estate Counsel, Inc. and Landon Butler & Company. More than 330 defined benefit plans invest in MEPT.

Structure

MEPT is organized as a bank collective investment trust, which is maintained by NewTower Trust Company. The Fund is managed by three entities: Kennedy Associates Real Estate Counsel, LP, of Seattle, Washington, serves as the real estate investment advisor; Landon Butler & Company, LP, provides investor relations and marketing services to MEPT; and NewTower Trust Company, of Bethesda, Maryland, serves as the trustee and fiduciary of the Fund. Principals of NewTower, Kennedy, and LBC serve together on MEPT's Policy Board, which determines MEPT's strategic direction, including investment policy and portfolio strategy for the Fund. The Policy Board meets at least twice a year to review the performance and management of the Fund.

In 2001, MEPT established an Advisory Board to provide trustees and professionals of participating plans the opportunity to meet annually with MEPT management to discuss overall Fund strategy, direction and objectives, performance, market conditions, governance, fees, personnel changes, and other topical issues. The Board consists of approximately 18 trustees, serving two-year terms. In addition, trustees, administrators, and consultants representing MEPT's participating plans are welcome to attend the annual Advisory Board meetings as observers.

Capacity and Products

MEPT is an open-end fund with $7.29 billion in net assets (as of early 2008) and is one of the largest commingled core real estate equity funds in the United

States. MEPT makes equity investments in institutional-quality commercial real estate properties and typically holds investments for 7-10 years.

MEPT's management team consists of more than 90 professionals. Kennedy, the real estate investment advisor to MEPT, was founded in 1978. LBC was founded in 1981. Together, Kennedy and LBC founded MEPT in 1982, and NewTower assumed the fiduciary and trustee role in June 2005 from MEPT's predecessor trustee. The Trustee of MEPT has the authority to invest in real estate-related investments, including but not limited to direct or indirect interests in improved and unimproved real property, which can be income producing, mortgages, or notes secured by real property.

Labor Impacts

MEPT develops, redevelops, or acquires assets that produce competitive income returns and offer potential for significant capital appreciation, placing significant emphasis on purchasing at or below replacement cost. MEPT's acquisition strategy focuses primarily on new construction opportunities, and by capturing value relatively early in the life of the asset, MEPT believes that its portfolio generates value appreciation in addition to strong and stable current income. MEPT has a responsible contractor policy that requires all on-site construction, including base building, tenant improvements, capital expenditures, and renovations, be performed by signatory contractors and 100% union labor. As a result, job creation for union building trades members and economic activity in local communities are two significant collateral benefits of the MEPT strategy.

A study completed in August 2006 for MEPT by ECONorthwest, Inc., determined that between 1982 and December 2005, MEPT investments generated:

- 27,300 construction jobs from hard cost investments, which paid $1.5 billion in wages and benefits and created 52.7 million hours of work for construction and special trade contractors, and $74.9 million in government revenues in the form of taxes.

- 7,850 jobs for technical and professional service sector employees from soft cost investments, paying $485 million in wages and benefits, and $24.4 million in government revenues in the form of taxes.
- $9.9 billion in total economic activity (or output) to the communities in which MEPT invests, which yielded 83,900 total jobs, 152 million hours of work and $4 billion in personal income, including health care insurance, retirement, and other benefits, and $327.1 million in government revenues in the form of taxes.

MEPT believes that its commitment to union labor ensures that its newly-constructed projects are built with the highest-quality craftsmanship in a given market, since training for most union workers consists of years of apprenticeship programs, classroom and jobsite training, worksite safety training, and ongoing journeyman training.

For operating properties, MEPT's Responsible Contractor Policy requires signatory janitorial companies, and if not available, employers who pay prevailing wages and benefits. In addition, MEPT requires the management companies of its hotels to execute neutrality agreements and has recently instituted a policy requiring stationary engineers that work on its properties to have the opportunity to be a member of the International Union of Operating Engineers.

Environmental/Community Impacts

MEPT is a leader in Responsible Property Investing (RPI), which is an approach to real estate investment management that takes into consideration the broader social, environmental, and governance ramifications of developing and owning properties. In addition to its 25-years of experience with a Responsible Contractor Policy and the economic benefits created from new construction in a given community, MEPT committed in 2007 to target LEED certification for all development and redevelopment projects going forward. MEPT is also an active participant in the EPA's ENERGY STAR certification benchmarking program.

As of result of its leadership in RPI, MEPT is one of the more active of the pension-capitalized real estate funds in adapting environmental and green building technologies and methods to its acquisitions and asset management practices and strategies. As of March 31, 2008, MEPT had built three LEED-certified buildings, and it has several more development projects in its pipeline—in fact, by year-end 2008, MEPT estimates that it will own, or have in process, approximately $2 billion in LEED-certified projects in its portfolio.

MEPT has also instituted an Energy Star certification and benchmarking program for its portfolio in an effort to improve the energy performance of buildings by managing energy consumption. As of March 31, 2008, MEPT had nearly 90 office buildings and 70 industrial buildings in the Energy Star benchmarking program, and MEPT office properties compose 2% of all Energy Star designated office assets in the United States. According to MEPT, skilled union workers offer a unique advantage to contractors that build green, as they provide the best, most comprehensive, and up-to-date, specialized skills in the construction industry—in emerging technology, systems, and building materials.

Performance

Over its 25-year history, MEPT has structured a portfolio that is diversified by property type and by geographic location, and aims to provide investors with competitive, core real estate returns. MEPT's operating real estate portfolio has outperformed the NCREIF Property Index in 19 out of the last 25 years and has only had one year of negative net returns for its investors. Furthermore, MEPT has always honored withdrawal requests on a quarterly basis and has never had a queue to exit the fund, offering superior liquidity to participating plans. MEPT takes the view that it has consistently delivered competitive and stable returns for its investor base while providing an investment vehicle that offers liquidity, creates jobs, and contributes to overall economic vitality and environmental sustainability in the markets where the Fund invests. Additionally, MEPT projects are routinely completed on-time and within budget, as a result of the skilled and well-trained union labor and experienced contractors responsible for each project. Consequently, MEPT asserts that its assets consistently outperform the competition.

Challenges

Sarah Stettinius of Landon Butler & Company said that the last few years have witnessed a record level of investment in real estate, as the asset class offered relatively strong and attractive returns compared to stocks and bonds, and low interest rates and relatively inexpensive debt created access to capital. During that phase in the market cycle, MEPT believes that the biggest risk investors faced was one of pricing (i.e. not paying significantly over replacement cost). Properties, particularly stabilized assets in coastal markets, were at their highest relative prices since the end of the 1980s real estate boom. MEPT also believes that underlying the substantial transaction volume and high prices were optimistic assumptions made by many investors about rental rates and net operating income growth across most asset classes but especially in the office sector. The challenge, therefore, was to find real estate assets with strong fundamentals that were not overpriced.

Given the current market conditions, good opportunities will often come in the form of new development projects or dislocation in the capital markets as lending institutions restrict the amount of capital available to the marketplace. MEPT believes that trustees of pension plans should consider investing in products that offer multiple benefits, including competitive performance from appreciation and a steady income return for the pension plan, job creation for construction and service workers, and economic activity in the local community, which generate contributions back into pension plans. In addition, projects such as The Octagon (see showcase) provide additional benefits because not only has it yielded high returns and created jobs, but it utilizes state-of-the-art renewable and efficient energy technology and provides quality living space in an underserved area of New York City.

Portfolio

The Fund invests in office buildings, apartments, warehouses, "flex" research and development facilities, retail centers, and hotels. The fund currently owns over 188 assets consisting of approximately 350 buildings. Currently, the Fund's properties are located in 25 U.S. markets, and MEPT has built or owned properties in 24 states.

Principals

We interviewed Sarah Stettinius of Landon Butler & Company on the grounds of MEPT's latest green building success story, The Octagon, on Roosevelt Island in New York City, a 500-unit luxury "green" residential apartment complex. Sarah and the developer, Bruce Becker, took us on a tour of the facility, and we were joined by three local union officers (whose members' pension plans invested in MEPT). These officers expressed pride in the completed project, not only because the historic renovation presented a number of challenges for their members and contractors, but also because they could see first-hand the strong performance of an asset that their pension funds now owned.

As noted above, MEPT is co-managed by three organizations, and many of the founding principals are still active in the management of MEPT. JOHN PARKER is a founding principal of Kennedy Associates and was Director of Acquisitions until March 2007 when he assumed the position of President and CEO. LANDON BUTLER (with an MBA from Harvard School of Business) has a storied career that started in Atlanta in the real estate business and then led to four years as deputy chief of staff for President Jimmy Carter where his duties included serving as the presidential liaison to organized labor. Finally, PAT MAYBERRY, President of NewTower Trust Company, has worked on MEPT since he joined MEPT's predecessor Trustee in 1989. In total, there are over 100 professionals in the three organizations that work on MEPT. In addition, MEPT partners with developers (such as Becker & Becker, developer of The Octagon), property management firms, and leasing and brokerage firms, to execute its strategy.

Project Showcase: the Octagon Apartments

The Octagon, located on New York City's Roosevelt Island, was originally constructed in 1839, and served as a hospital for much of its life. In the 1990s, two major fires destroyed much of the original building. In 2004, MEPT teamed up with Becker & Becker to fashion an award-winning residential development that still retained much of The Octagon's original historic charm, including the interior seven-story "flying" circular staircase, its centerpiece. The current complex has two 13-story high-rise towers on each side, which house 501 residential apartments, 1,300 square feet of commercial space, a 3,850 square-foot child care center, and an underground parking garage. In addition to the residential component, the development has a number of valued community amenities, including public tennis courts and a waterfront ecological park.

The project set a new standard in design by integrating both historic architectural features, as well as the most modern and energy efficient technology. It is estimated that the Octagon consumes 35% less energy than comparable new buildings. It was constructed with locally produced materials and the building has high-efficiency boilers, rooftop solar panels, and Energy Star appliances. The Octagon received LEED Silver certification from the U.S. Green Building Council, as well as the NYC Green Apple Award for leadership in applying sustainable design principles to residential development. An estimated 1.5 million job hours were created for building trades members. The project reached stabilized occupancy in less than half of its projected lease-up time at rents above budget projections.

The Union Labor Life Insurance Company, J for Jobs (Washington, DC)

Separate Account J ("J for Jobs")

The Union Labor Life Insurance Company

1625 Eye Street, NW

Washington, DC 20006

Phone: (202) 682-0900

Web: www.ullico.com

Contact Info: James Kennedy, Sr. Vice President, ULLICO

Market Development Department

E-Mail: jkennedy@ullico.com

Distinguishing Characteristics:

- Founded: 1977
- Habitat: Washington, D.C.
- Range: Invests primarily in U.S.
- Fund Type: Open-ended commingled fixed income insurance company separate account
- Fund Structure(s): Separate account of an insurance company
- Capital Partners: Primarily multi-employer and public pension funds
- Assets Under Management: $3.2 billion

Overview

ULLICO's Separate Account J, popularly known as "J for Jobs" is a commingled fixed-income investment product offered through the Union Labor Life Insurance Company (Union Labor Life), a labor-founded insurance company founded in 1925 and headquartered in Washington, D.C. Union Labor Life is a subsidiary of ULLICO Inc., a holding company. ULLICO Inc. and its family of companies are providers of multi-line insurance, financial services, and administrative products to union organizations, related funds, and members. Among its real estate investment unit's products, J for Jobs is the largest premium product. Designed specifically for multi-employer trust funds to invest in worker-friendly, job-producing construction projects and industries, the J for Jobs account manages roughly $3.2 billion in real estate assets nationwide as of 2007.

The account is an open-ended, commingled, insurance company separate account that invests in high-quality secured mortgages on commercial and residential projects. The portfolio is a diversified one of construction and permanent mortgages, secured by a variety of properties. Investments are primarily in new construction or extensive renovations. A second fund started by Union Labor Life, the USA Realty Fund, buys, develops, owns, and operates commercial real estate properties.

After a well-publicized financial crisis in 2003, the unions overhauled ULLICO, appointing a new board and new executive leadership. With a substantial restructuring and return to core business, ULLICO earned two upgrades from A.M. Best and was turned around, according to a profile in Best's Review (August, 2007), an esteemed insurance industry journal. The Best profile notes ULLICO's return to profitability.

Structure

Founded in 1925 as an affordable and union-owned insurance company for working people, Union Labor Life is governed by officers of the AFL-CIO and Change-To-Win (CtW), and professionally managed. After dramatic changes in the board and reforms of the organization in 2003, Union Labor Life has now fully complied with the governance and transparency requirements of the Sarbanes-Oxley Act.

The Real Estate Investment Group (REIG) of Union Labor Life, a department with more than 20 professionals located in Los Angeles, Chicago, Silver Spring (MD.) and Washington, D.C., is responsible for originating, underwriting, and managing the investments for J for Jobs. Revenue generated by REIG is primarily from fee-based management of the real estate portfolio.

Capacity and Products

J for Jobs investments are spread geographically throughout the U.S. REIG solicits and receives loan proposals from a variety of sources, including developers, brokers, mortgage bankers, other financial institutions, attorneys, and unions. After an extensive due diligence process is completed, the company can write construction loans and forward permanent commitments for $2 million and up. The company, on behalf of Separate Account J, can also participate with other financial institutions and sometimes is the lead lender in loan syndications.

- Permanent loans are generally fixed-rate, amortizing loans, and carry initial terms of 5-10 years with 25-30 years amortization.
- Construction loans are short-term, generally 18-36 months.

Labor Impacts

From 1977 to the end of second quarter 2007, J for Jobs created 215,700 jobs, primarily union construction jobs. J for Jobs invests in construction projects built by construction workers affiliated with the Building and Construction Trades of the AFL-CIO as of January 1, 2001. A borrower must use subcontractors signatory to collective-bargaining agreements with unions affiliated with the AFL-CIO or Change To Win. J for Jobs has developed a cadre of developers and will assist developers in building a relationship with labor. A significant portion of REIG is repeat business.

The properties USA Realty Fund buys, develops, and owns will not only be built union, they will be operated, maintained, and renovated union. Through development, acquisition, and ownership the Fund will create union construction and service jobs and provide opportunities for union contractors and employers. Union Labor Life has also made joint investments with HIT-BIT, complimenting HIT's equity investments with debt.

Environmental/Community Impacts

All things being equal, J for Jobs will consider "green" building projects if the return-on-investment is equal to comparable investments. J for Jobs has engaged in a number of rehabilitation projects and has generally built projects in urban centers.

J for Jobs and the Amalgamated Bank Longview Ultra Fund (providing construction loans) and the AFL-CIO BIT (providing equity) financed the construction of The Gallery Place, the largest urban mixed-use project in modern Washington's history. The project is credited with helping revitalize the East End of the District. Located adjacent to the MCI Center in Chinatown, it is a $250 million multi-faceted development project with approximately 300,000 square feet of retail and entertainment uses, including 14 movie theaters; 275 new condominium housing units; 400,000 square feet of new offices; and 1,000 parking spaces.

Portfolio

By mid-2007, Union Labor Life's J for Jobs had invested $20.3 billion in real estate in 425 projects. From 1995 to Second Quarter 2007, J for Jobs, through its loan syndication program, invested $19.5 billion in 241 projects. Prior to this period, from 1977, J for Jobs invested $776 million in 184 projects. Recent investments include hotels, office buildings, condos and apartment buildings, mixed use, retail, and R&D laboratories.

Performance

J for Jobs claims to have added value during positive fixed-income periods but also has provided value to plan participants in rising rate environments. The returns are benchmarked to the Lehman Aggregate (LA). For the ten-year period ending June 30, 2007, J for Jobs has bettered the LA by 8.02 percent (gross) and 7.21 percent (net). For calendar year 2007, in a lagging fixed income market, J for Jobs claims a return of 53 basis points or 7.49% (net of fees) over the LBAI return of 6.96%.

Challenges

We interviewed Jim Kennedy, one of ULLICO's senior leaders and a long-time principal in the AFL-CIO and labor movement, in Jim's office at ULLICO. Jim, who has been in the labor movement for 50 years, spoke about some of the interesting real estate projects that J for Jobs has undertaken, and from a practitioner level, how challenging some of those projects are to pull together. Given its labor neutrality policies, ULLICO has had to work hard to convince developers that investment partnerships with ULLICO yield superior results. In one difficult construction project, the J for Jobs team learned that the contractor violated the union construction agreement, and ULLICO immediately pulled its investment.

Jim stressed that the investment due diligence for J for Jobs utilizes a conservative approach, protected by high-value collateral, and yields a diversified portfolio well proportioned in different parts of the U.S. He expressed some concern about the current housing bubble, but the company views the primary loan business as solid.

One of the significant changes at the company was the wind-down of a sister private equity fund, Separate Account P, due to losses incurred. While J for Jobs has primarily invested in real estate, one of Union Labor Life's most successful developments was the Newport News shipyard construction projects in the 1990s, in which the now-defunct fund financed double-hull tankers. Separate Account P invested in the construction of five environmentally safe double-hulled oil tankers at a total cost of $280 million. Separate Account P's $10 million equity stake gave it enough leverage to achieve an agreement that the ships would be constructed in the U.S. at one of the nation's few remaining union shipyards, providing work for 12,000 steel workers over a 28-month period. Separate Account P did well on that investment, recovering 100% of invested capital plus an internal rate of return of 20%.

Principals

MARK SINGLETON is CEO of ULLICO Inc., assuming the position in 2006. Singleton joined ULLICO in 2003 as Chief Financial Officer and was part of the turnaround team that stabilized and refocused the company from its former governance and financial troubles. Singleton was instrumental in returning the company to a position of strength, financial stability, and operating profitability. These actions ultimately resulted in several A. M. Best Company rating upgrades. As CEO, Singleton oversees strategic operations of the company's three business units: Life & Health Insurance, Retirement and Investment Services, and Property & Casualty Insurance, as well as all corporate functions.

Prior to joining ULLICO, Singleton was Chief Financial Officer of Inviva, Inc., a New York-based life insurance and annuity holding company he helped found in 2000. Prior to Inviva, he was Chief Financial Officer and Senior Vice President of Finance and Operations of Fidelity & Guaranty Life Insurance Company, a $5 billion life insurance subsidiary of USF&G Corporation in Baltimore that later became the St. Paul Companies. Singleton previously held positions at Legal & General America, the Hay Group, and American Health & Life Insurance Company. A 1983 graduate of the University of Baltimore, Singleton earned his CPA certificate in 1984 and has also earned the FLMI designation from LOMA.

EDWARD M. SMITH became the President of ULLICO Inc. in May 2008. He was formerly appointed Executive Vice President of Market Development in January 2007. He has a lengthy history in the labor movement and has served as Midwest Regional Manager of the Laborers' International Union of North America since 1994, leading more than 50,000 union members. He was elected a vice president of the International Union in 1996 and serves on its General Executive Board. In 2001, Smith was appointed as Assistant to the General President for the International Union. He is the former Chairman of the Illinois State Board of Investment, serves as a member of the Illinois Department of Labor Advisory Board, the Democratic National Committee, and is Chairman of the National Alliance for Fair Contracting.

JIM KENNEDY is Senior Vice President of ULLICO Inc.'s Market Development Department, a position he has held since October 2006. Kennedy joined the Company in February 1994, as Vice President and Assistant Treasurer of ULLICO's subsidiary, ULLICO Investment Advisors, Inc. (formerly Trust Fund Advisors, Inc.) On May 8, 2003, he was elected

Senior Vice President of Government and Public Affairs of ULLICO by the Company's Board of Directors. In April 2004, Kennedy was elected Senior Vice President of Investment Sales, Marketing and Operations. Immediately prior to coming to ULLICO, Kennedy was Senior Vice President for Investments for the Amalgamated Bank of Chicago and AmalgaTrust. Prior to that, he was the founding director of the AFL-CIO Department of Transportation Trades (TTD). Kennedy has served as General Counsel to many unions and was the Executive Assistant to Thomas R. Donahue, Secretary-Treasurer of the AFL-CIO. Kennedy has a Bachelor of Science in Political Theory and Government from Fordham College and a Juris Doctor from the Fordham University School of Law.

HERBERT A. KOLBEN is the Senior Vice President, Real Estate Investment Group of The Union Labor Life Insurance Company and has more than 30 years experience in real estate financing. He joined Union Labor Life in October 1993 with responsibility for mortgage originations on a national basis, including the pooled mortgage separate account J for Jobs. In 1999, he assumed responsibility for the management of the Real Estate Investment Group. From 1977 to 1990, Kolben was with the Real Estate Division of Citibank, N.A. in charge of managing loan production offices throughout the Mid-Atlantic and Southern regions of the United States. In 1989, he became Director of Equities/East with responsibility for equity originations and capital markets interfacing for the Eastern region of the United States. In November 1990, Kolben joined MNC Financial as Senior Vice President for the Washington metropolitan region and was responsible for the administration and workout of a $1.9 billion problem loan portfolio. He is experienced in the structuring and administration of a wide variety of transactions, from single-family ADC loans to larger, complex syndicated transactions. Kolben started his career with First Mortgage Investor's REIT. He holds a Bachelor of Commerce Degree and MBA from Sir George Williams University (now Concordia University), Montreal, Canada.

Project Showcase: Smithsonian Institution

One of the more interesting projects financed by Union Labor Life's J for Jobs is the construction for the Smithsonian Institution Astrophysical Observatory in Cambridge, Massachusetts in 2004. J for Jobs committed to a $40.2 million combined construction loan and forward permanent commitment to finance the development of a 129,000 square foot office/research and development building located that is part of the 450,000 square foot Cambridge Discovery R&D Park.

The Center for Astrophysics combines the resources and research facilities of the Harvard College Observatory and the Smithsonian Astrophysical Observatory under a single director to pursue studies of those basic physical processes that determine the nature and evolution of the universe. The long relationship between the two organizations, which began when the SAO moved its headquarters to Cambridge in 1955, was formalized by the establishment of a joint center in 1973. Today, some 300 Smithsonian and Harvard scientists cooperate in broad programs of astrophysical research supported by Federal appropriations and University funds as well as contracts and grants from government agencies. These scientific investigations, touching on almost all major topics in astronomy, are organized into six divisions.

References

PART I

Introduction

[1] Martin, Jamie. "Civil War widow, final link to old Confederacy, dies," *USA Today*, May 31, 2004. "Last Yankee war widow dies," *BBC News*, January 20, 2003.

[2] For example, see Tonello, Matteo. 2006. "Revisiting Stock Market Short-Termism." The Conference Board Research Report No. R-1386-06-RR; "Breaking the Short-term Cycle: How Corporate Leaders, Asset Managers, Investors and Analysts Can Refocus on Long-term Value." 2006. Center for Financial Market Integrity and Business Roundtable Institute for Corporate Ethics; Simon Zadek. 2005. "Vicious Circle of Short-termism Threatens Pensions." World Economic Forum's Global Corporate Citizenship Initiative, Accountability.

[3] A sign that more attention to these issues will be made is that U.S. investment banks are penalizing utilities with coal plants have haven't taken into account the cost of possible regulation and caps on greenhouse emissions.

[4] Hebb, Tessa. 2008. *No Small Change*. Ithaca, New York: Cornell University Press.

[5] Croft, Thomas. 2008. "Global ETI Report: Helping Workers' Capital Work Harder." Commissioned by Global Union Committee on Workers' Capital (CWC). Nods here to Oliver Rohlfs, former Project Officer, Global Unions CWC; Shannon Rohan of SHARE (Shareholder

Association for Research & Education). Later assists from Amanda Procter, Project Officer, CWC.

[6]"Global Pension Assets Study." 2008. Watson Wyatt Worldwide.

[7]Zweig, Jason. 2008. "The Oracle Speaks." CNNMoney.com, May 2.

[8]Mihm, Steven. 2008. "Dr. Doom." *New York Times*, August 15.

[9]"Bailing Out Financial Capitalism: What Governments Must Demand in Return." 2008. Trade Union Advisory Committee (TUAC) of the Organization for Economic Co-operation and Development (OECD).

[10]McFadden, Ken. 2009. "Brass Tacks." *Mergers and Acquisitions*, the official publication of the Association for Corporate Growth, February 2009.

[11]Samuelson, Robert. 2007. "The Enigma of Private Equity." *Newsweek/ MSNBC*, March 19.

[12]"Understanding the Turmoil in Financial Markets." 2008. *Capital Matters*, the newsletter of the Pensions and Capital Stewardship Project, Harvard Law School, April.

[13]Dooling, Richard. 2008. "The Rise of the Machines." *New York Times*, October 12.

[14]Chan, Nicholas, Mila Getmansky, Shane M. Haas, Andrew W. Lo. 2005. "Systemic Risk and Hedge Funds." NBER Working Paper No. 11200; March. Re-printed as a special inquiry into hedge fund risk by Federal Reserve Bank of Atlanta, *Economic Review*, Volume 91, Number 4, Fourth Qtr. 2006.

[15]Blount, Ed. 2008. 2008. "The Bear Market Posse, or Counterparty Risk Management during the Recent Turmoil." *The RMA Journal*. September.

[16]An observation by Dr. Teresa Ghilarducci, but repeated by many of the readers of this book.

[17]Stack, James, John Balbach, Bob Epstein, Teryn Hanggi. 2007. "Cleantech Venture Capital: How Public Policy Has Stimulated Private Investment." A paper for Cleantech Venture Network, LLC, May.

Chapter One

[1]Hawley, James P., Andrew Williams. 2000. *The Rise of Fiduciary Capitalism:*

How Institutional Investors Can Make Corporate America More Democratic. Philadelphia: University of Pennsylvania Press. Introduction, Page X1; Also helpful, William Lazonick, Mary O'Sullivan. 2000. "American Corporate Finance: From Organizational to Market Control." In Candace Howes and Ajit Singh, eds., *Competitiveness Matters: Industry and Economic Performance in the US*. Ann Arbor: University of Michigan Press. 106-24.

[2]Federal Reserve Statistical Release, Z.1, Flow of Funds Accounts of the United States; Release Date: June 7, 2007 L.213-214.

[3]Federal Reserve Statistical Release, Z.1, Flow of Funds Accounts of the United States; Release Date: June 7, 2007 Tables l.118-19.

[4]Hebb, Tessa, Larry Beeferman. 2008. "US Pension Funds' Labour-Friendly Investments," in *The "Social" in Social Security: Market, State and Associations in Retirement Provision*. Mark Hyde, John Dixon, eds. Lampeter, U.K.: Edwin Mellen Press, forthcoming.

[5]"Global Pension Assets Study." 2007. Watson Wyatt Worldwide.

[6]Guha, Krishna, James Politi. 2008. "Widespread job losses in cards, warns unions." *Financial Times*, November 14, 2008.

[7]Greider, William. 2003. "The Soul of Capitalism." *Nation Magazine*, September 29. This article is adapted from *The Soul of Capitalism*, New York: Simon & Schuster.

[8]Clark, Gordon L., Tess Hebb. 2004. "Pension Fund Corporate Engagement." *Industrial Relations*, Vol. 59, No. 1, pp. 142-171.

[9]"Russell Pension Report." 2007. Russell Investment Group. Tacoma, Washington, (www.russell.com/pensionreport).

[10]Blake, David. 1992. *Issues in Pension Funding*. London: Routledge. Page 90.

[11]Hawley and Williams. Page 3.

[12]"Canadian VC Activity: An Analysis of Trends and Gaps, 1996-2002." SME Financing Data Initiative, Government of Canada. www.ic.gc.ca/epic/site/sme_fdi- prf_pme.nsf/en/01185e.html; Mark Cassell. 2006. "Is There a Capital Gap? An Assessment of Credit and Financing Among Small and Medium-Sized Manufacturing Firms in Northeast Ohio." Kent State University, Kent State, Ohio.

[13]Baker, Dean, Archon Fung. 2001. "Collateral Damage: Do Pension Fund Investments Hurt Workers?" From Fung, Hebb, Rogers, eds., 2001. *Working Capital: The Power of Labor's Pensions.* Ithaca, NY: Cornell University Press; Richard Minns. 2003. "Collateral Damage: The International Consequences of Pension Funds," from *Money on the Line: Workers' Capital in Canada*, Isla Carmichael, Jack Quarter, eds., Canadian Centre for Policy Alternatives, Ottawa.

[14]Wood, David, Belinda Hoff, 2008. *Handbook on Responsible Investment Across Asset Classes.* Institute for Responsible Investment, Boston College Center for Corporate Citizenship. An excellent book that examines responsible investment in all asset classes.

[15]This report does not attempt to resolve the longstanding debate between the "finance model" of the firm (that shareholders are the sole residual claimants of the public corporation and corporate managers, accordingly, ought to focus only on maximizing long-run share value) and the "stakeholder" view of the firm (that managers ought to consider the interests of employees, bondholders, consumers, and other corporate "stakeholders," as well).

[16]Hagerman, Lisa, Gordon Clark, Tessa Hebb. 2005. "New York Case Study: Competitive Returns and a Revitalized New York City." Pension Funds and Urban Revitalization Project, Oxford University Centre for the Environment; Pensions and Capital Stewardship Project, Harvard Law School.

[17]CalPERS website, www.calpers.ca.gov.

[18]Pensions and Investments, 2008.

[19]Pensions and Investments, 2007.

[20]Pensions and Investments, 2007.

[21]Jacobius, Arleen. 2007. "Acting on faith; Institutional investors are leaping into the realms of alternative investments, but lack the tools to properly assess the risks." *Pensions and Investments*, Feb. 1, p. 15.

[22]Galante, Steven P. 2002-2003. "An Overview of the Venture Capital

Industry & Emerging Changes." *The Private Equity Analyst*, www. vcinstitute.org/materials/galante.html.

[23]Angel investing is another method of early stage investment. For more information, see Amis, David, Howard Stevenson. 2001. *Winning Angels: The Seven Fundamentals of Early Stage Investing.* London: Pearson Education Limited.

[24]Pension funds also source investment partnerships that provide debt financing and variations of debt. Senior term debt is the second most common form of financing for a small and mid-sized company. Senior term debt is typically lent against the collateral value of property, plant, and equipment. Senior term debt comes in many varieties and there are many sources of this type of financing. It is typically the second most expensive form of financing.

Subordinated debt financing typically includes both debt and equity. Subordinated debt is substantially riskier than senior debt since the lender generally has less right over collateral and cash flow than the senior lender. As a result, subordinated debt is more expensive financing than either revolving lines of credit or term debt. Lenders usually require equity, generally in the form of warrants, to augment what they earn in interest income.

[25]The Russell Pension Report. 2007.

[26]Bawden, Tom. 2007. "Pension funds seek a direct line to the private equity bonanza." *The Times* Online, January 6.

[27]Lerner, Josh, Antoinette Schoar, Wan Wongsunwai. 2007. "Smart Institutions, Foolish Choices: The Limited Partner Performance Puzzle." *The Journal of Finance*, Vol. 62, Issue 2, pp. 731-764.

[28]For ETIs, DOL Interpretive Letter 94-1, published in Federal Register, June 23, 1994. For the permissibility of private capital, see 29 C.F.R. §2510.3-101, 51 Fed. Reg. 41262, November 13, 1986. The citation allows for pension funds to invest in qualified Venture Capital Operating Companies (VCOC) that meet certain tests. The VCOC exception

is limited to those companies that have demonstrated a "substantial, ongoing commitment to the venture capital business."

[29]Falconer, Kirk. 1999. "Prudence, Patience and Jobs: Pension Investment in a Changing Canadian Economy." Canadian Labour Market and Productivity Centre, Ottawa, Page 23. A very helpful background that was cited frequently in the private equity and real estate sections.

[30]Falconer.

[31]Reiss, Dale Ann, Deborah Levinson and Sanford Presant. 2002. "Opportunistic Investing and Real Estate Private Equity Funds." Zell/Lurie Center Working Papers. Wharton School Samuel Zell and Robert Lurie Real Estate Center, University of Pennsylvania.

[32]Falconer, Kirk. 1999.

Chapter Two

[1]Ghilarducci, Teresa. 1992. *Labor's Capital: The Economics and Politics of Private Pensions*. Boston: MIT Press.

[2]Logue, John, Steve Clem. 2006. "Putting Labor's Capital to Work: Capital Strategies for Ohio Employees." Prepared for seminar organized by the Ohio Employee Ownership Center, Columbus, Ohio. June 6, 2006; See also Michael Calebrese, "Building on Success: Labor-Friendly Investment Vehicles and the Power of Private Equity," Chapter 5 in Fung, Hebb, Rogers.

[3]Wysocki, Bernard, Kris Maher, Paul Glader. 2007. "A Labor Union's Power: Blocking Takeover Bids." *Wall Street Journal*, May 9.

[4]Wood.

[5]Ibid. See also Blank, Stephen. 2006. "Responsible Property Investing." Urban Land Institute; Gary Pivo. 2005. "Is There a Future for Socially Responsible Property Investments." *Real Estate Issues*. Fall issue. More generally, the "triple bottom line" in real estate investments has been reported on by Hermes, CalPERS and the Social Investment Forum.

[6]Pivo, Gary and Jeffrey D. Fisher. 2009. "Investment Returns from Responsible Property Investments: Energy Efficient, Transit-oriented

and Urban Regeneration Office Properties in the U.S. from 1998-2008." Working Paper of the RPI Center, Boston College and University of Arizona. Benecki Center for Real Estate Studies, Indiana University.

[7]Generally, see http://www.unpri.org/. For this citation, http://www.unpri. org/files/Call_For_Papers_Copenhagen_2010_150909.pdf.

[8]"Responsible Investment in Focus: How public pension funds are meeting the challenge," 2007. United Nations Environment Programme Finance Initiative (UNEP FI), Asset Management Working Group, and U.K.'s Social Investment Forum. www.uksif.org/cmsfiles/281411/ Responsiblepercent20Investmentpercent20inpercent20Focus percent20(April percent202007).pdf.

[9]"International Labour Sets Its Sights on Private Equity." 2007. Association for Research and Education.

Chapter Three

[1]Leeds, Zachary. 2004. "Taking its Rightful Place: Social Investing and the Role of Politics in Public Pension Fund Investment Decisions." A paper printed for the "Capital That Matters Conference," 2004, Harvard University.

[2]Carmichael, Isla and Jack Quarter, editors, 2003. *Money on the Line: Workers' Capital in Canada*, p. 91. Canadian Centre for Policy Alternatives, Ottawa.

[3]DOL Interpretive Letter 94-1 (published in U.S. Federal Register, June 23, 1994).

[4]Zanglein, Jayne. 2001. "Overcoming Institutional Barriers on the Economically-targeted Investment Highway," Chapter 8 in Fung, Hebb, Rogers.

[5]"Responsible Investment in Focus: How Leading Public Pension Funds are Meeting the Challenge." 2007. United Nations Environment Programme Finance Initiative (UNEP FI) Asset Management Working Group (AMWG) and the United Kingdom Social Investment Forum (UKSIF) Sustainable Pensions Project (SPP).

[6]Sources for these sections: Hebb, Tessa, et al, *Working Capital, and Croft*, "Global ETI Report." Also, *Croft and Heartland E-Journal*.

[7]Leeds. In addition, according to author Gar Alperovitz (in *America Beyond Capitalism*, Wiley & Sons, 2005), a 2001 study of forty state and local pension investment systems found that 27 percent had ETI plans or included "collateral benefits" when considering investment decisions. Citing Nicholas Greifer, "Pension Investment Policies: The State of the Art," *Governance Finance Review* (February 2002).

[8]Falconer.

[9]Thanks to Falconer and also the "AFL-CIO Investment Product Review: Private Capital." 2002.

[10]Hagerman, Clark, Hebb.

[11]Torrance, Morag I. 2007. "The Power of Governance in Financial Relationships: Governing Tensions in Exotic Infrastructure Territory." *Growth and Change*, the journal of Gatton College of Business and Economics, University of Kentucky.

Chapter Four

[1]Atlas, Riva D., Mary Williams Walsh. 2005. "Pension Officers Putting Billions Into Hedge Funds." *New York Times*, Nov. 27. p.1.

[2]Dodd, Randall. 2007. "Tax breaks for billionaires: Loophole for hedge fund managers costs billions in tax revenue." EPI Policy Memo #120, July 24, 2007.

[3]Smith, Peter, Gillian Tett. 2006. "Buy-outs create 'headless chickens'— Market specialist says high debt could hurt private equity's image." *Financial Times*, November 15.

[4]Statistics from "The Securities Industry in New York City." 2008. New York State Comptroller, November.

[5]Friedlander, Josh. 2005. "How the Emergence of Megafunds Could Impact Middle-Market Private Equity." *Investment Dealers' Digest*, re-posted

in CapitalEyes, Bank of America, February 2005; Avital Louria Hahn. 2008. "Hostiles Take Over." *CFO Magazine*, October 2008. "Loan Rangers." 2008. *The Economist*. August 28.

[6]Oxford Analytica. 2007. "'Credit contraction' is key risk to hedge funds, private equity firms." TheHill.Com, July 18; "Risk Management Watch: Hedge Funds Focus on Risk as Assets Grow." 2008. A.E. Feldman Blog. July 1.

[7]Dodd, Randall. 2007. "Role of Hedge Funds in Subprime Crisis Examined." Republished in *F&D*, December 21.

[8]For this section, for instance, see Story, Louise. 2008. "Hedge Fund Glory Days Fading Fast." *New York Times*, September 12; Christina Williamson. 2008. "Bloodbath Ahead." *PI Online*, September 9, 2008; Christopher Holt. 2008. "How Much of the Hedge Fund Industry is About to Get Chopped?" *FINAlternatives*, October, 2008; "Weak Vintage May Leave Vinegar Taste." 2008. *PI Online*, August 18, 2008; "GLS's Roman, NYU's Roubini Predict Hedge Fund Failures." 2008. Bloomberg.com, October 23; Douglas Kass. 2008. "Private Equity is the Next Shoe to Drop." 2008. *The Street*, October 30; Andrew Ross Sorkin, Michael J. de la Merced. 2008. "Debt Linked to Buyouts Tighten Economic Vise." *New York Times*, November 3; "Emerging Trends in Real Estate. 2009 Report." 2008. Urban Land Institute (ULI) and PricewaterhouseCoopers LLP; Dana Hedgpeth. 2008. "Up in the Air... Economic Downdraft is Blowing through Commercial Real Estate." *Washington Post*, November 5, 2008.

[9]Levy, Frank, Peter Temin. 2007. "Inequality and Institutions in 20th Century America." MIT Department of Economics Working Paper No. 07-17.

[10]John Monks, General Secretary of the European Trade Union Confederation. 2006. "The Challenge of the New Capitalism." The Bevan Memorial Lecture.

[11]ITUC Report, 2007. "Where the house always wins: Private Equity, Hedge

Funds and The New Casino Capitalism." (International Trade Union Confederation).

[12]Rossman, Peter, Gerard Greenfield. 2006. "Financialization: New Routes to Profit, New Challenges for Trade Unions." A paper for ICFTU Workers' Capital Secretariat (now ITUC).

[13]Berman, Dennis L. 2007. "For Private Equity, No More Easy Deals in 2007." *The Wall Street Journal*, January 2. Page C2.

[14]Sources include: Ydstie, John. 2008. "Recession Fears Drive Stocks Down Globally." NPR's *All Things Considered*, October 24; Joe Nocera. 2008. "A Day (Gasp) Like Any Other." October 7; "Loan Rangers." 2008. *The Economist*, August 28; "Is Private Equity Riding a Debt Bubble." 2007. *New York Times*, DealBook Blog, May 1, 2007. Kass; Jacobius; Sorkin and de la Merced; Bloomsburg.

[15]Beck, Rachel. 2006. "All Business: Hedge Fund Hinderance." *New York Times*. October 31.

[16]Bogoslaw, David. 2008. "Funds Big Test: The Great Redemption Rush." *Business Week*, November 24; Nouriel Roubini. 2008. "Hedge Funds' Derivatives Exposure and Margin Calls Driving Stock Market Crash." RGEmonitor.com, October 15.

Chapter Five

[1]See www.enhanced-analytics.com.

[2]We are grateful to Marty Tarbox for this point and discussion.

[3]We are grateful to Marty Tarbox for this point and discussion.

[4]We are grateful to David Wood for this point and discussion.

Chapter Six

[1]Thanks to Tom Schlesinger for passages from the *Heartland Journal*. Fall 1998. Thanks as well to Michael Steed for ideas for this chapter.

PART II

Unless otherwise indicated, the sources for Part Two include, primarily, the Heinz Survey to fund principals and managers, and subsequent personal and phone conversations, general reports, documents, and email exchanges, and information gleaned from fund websites, annual and quarterly reports, previous Heartland Network reports, Heartland and other workers' capital conferences and meetings, and similar citations. Likewise, information on portfolio investments are derived from, in addition to the funds, direct communications with firm/project principals, and firm/project reports and websites, etc.

Chapter Seven

[1]GrowthWorks refers to affiliates of GrowthWorks Ltd. and includes: GrowthWorks Capital Ltd, manager of the Working Opportunity Fund (EVCC) Ltd.; GrowthWorks WV Management Ltd., manager of GrowthWorks Canadian Fund Ltd. and GrowthWorks Commercialization Fund Ltd.; GrowthWorks Atlantic Ltd., manager of GrowthWorks Atlantic Venture Fund Ltd. and ENSIS Management Inc., manager of ENSIS Growth Fund Inc. GrowthWorks is a registered trademark of GrowthWorks Capital Ltd. ENSIS is a registered trademark of ENSIS Capital Corporation.

[2]As pointed out in a Canadian book about workers' capital, there is a problem in the way that some provinces wrote the original provincial legislation for Labour-Sponsored Funds (LSIF) after the formation of Solidarity in Quebec. In the case of Ontario, the legislation did not vest control in the central labour federation as the primary sponsor. Thus, "rent-a-union" funds were formed by investment interests that used labour associations as fronts. This process was a detrimental design flaw in Ontario's LSIFs, meaning that a multitude of funds formed that could not achieve scale in capital formation. See Isla Carmichael, Isla, Jack Quarter, eds., 2003. *Money on the Line: Workers' Capital in Canada.* Canadian Centre for

Policy Alternatives, Ottawa, and the Canadian Labour and Business Center. Page 17, etc.

Chapter Eight

[1]Sources include Carmichael, Quarter, Money on the Line. Also Carmichael. 2005. *Pension Power: Unions, Pension Funds and Social Investment in Canada.* Toronto: University of Toronto Press.

[2]Mook, Laurie. 2004. Presentation to Pensions at Work Conference, Winnipeg, Canada.

APPENDIX I
From Field Observations: A Catalog of Selected Responsible Investments

Here we feature five projects from most of our profiled funds to highlight the strengths of responsible investing, when (1) Financial Profitability, (2) Sustainability, and (3) Worker Friendly Standards have been met in practice. These investments are located all over North America, in various sectors.

Private Equity/Venture Funds

GESD Capital Partners

Go Roma Italian Kitchen® is a fast casual Italian restaurant which features soups, salads, handmade pizzas, and other fresh Italian specialties. The CEO of Go Roma was formerly a co-founder as well as the President of Corner Bakery, a bakery café chain with over 85 units. Go Roma is in the greater Chicago area with plans to open several Go Roma restaurants in the next few years.

Artisan Bakers is a Sonoma, California-based specialty bakery that produces premium-quality, handcrafted artisan breads and pastry products for sale to retail and wholesale customers in the San Francisco Bay Area. The company is led by an internationally renowned baker who won the Coupe du Monde de la Boulangerie (World Cup of Baking) in Paris in 1996 as a member representing the American Baking Team and secured the Gold Medal as a coach in 1999.

Dobake Bakeries, Inc., is an Oakland, California-based sweet goods bakery with national distribution to grocery stores, convenience stores, and vending customers. Products manufactured by the company include fresh doughnuts, gourmet muffins, and loaf cakes.

Socal Bakeries, Inc., is a Santa Ana, California-based manufacturer of San Francisco-style sourdough bread products. Products manufactured by the company include sourdough loafs, hearth-baked and crusty rolls, pan bread, and other specialty bread products. The company distributes its products to the grocery, club, and foodservice channels and sells products under private label and co-pack arrangements.

Milton's Fine Foods, Inc., is a leading branded food company that markets a diverse offering of premium "better-for-you" bread, snack, and frozen food products made from the highest quality natural and organic ingredients, including whole-grain and multi-grains. GESD's second fund acquired Milton, its first portfolio company, in July 2007. Milton's products, including its flagship multi-grain bread, are distributed through the club, grocery, mass merchant, and specialty stores channels throughout the United States, Canada, Mexico, and in the United Kingdom.

Growth Works/Working Opportunity Fund

Avcorp is a leading supplier of engineering design and manufacture of parts, sub assemblies, and complex major assemblies for aircraft manufacturers. Established in 1986, Avcorp is a Canadian public company with over 40 years experience, a highly skilled workforce of approximately 400, and a state-of-the art 300,000 square foot manufacturing facility in Delta, B.C., near Vancouver. Major customers include Boeing, Bombardier, and Cessna. Products range from simple aluminum brackets, high-strength interior panels, and fuel tanks to structural wing components, as well as fully integrated vertical and horizontal stabilizers.

KPS Capital Partners

Wire Rope Corporation of America, Inc. (WRCA), based in St. Joseph, Missouri, is the nation's leading producer of high-carbon wire and wire rope products and is the largest domestic supplier of wire rope products to the mining, oil and gas, construction, and steel industries. In addition to wire rope for cranes, WRCA produces a specialty pre-stressed concrete strand that is in wide use in the South. With the Steelworkers representing most of the over 900 employees, WRCA operates four manufacturing facilities and seven distribution centers across the country. As a result of the transaction, workers in a smaller facility agreed to join the union.

AmeriCast Technologies has facilities in Kansas, Missouri, etc. AmeriCast is a world leader in the design, manufacture, and supply of highly engineered steel and iron sand castings, machined components, and assemblies. Caterpillar Tractor buys critical components from AmeriCast. AmeriCast casts large and difficult-to-manufacture parts and is a critical supplier to Fortune 50 manufacturers in the locomotive, mass transit, mining, agricultural equipment, construction, energy, and heavy-duty truck industries. Unions, including the Steelworkers, represent the 1,000 workers.

Blue Heron Paper Company, headquartered in Oregon City, Oregon, is a manufacturer of newsprint, rebrite, and other groundwood paper products. The employees of Blue Heron own 35 percent of the company through an ESOP. The Association of Western Pulp and Paper Workers (AWPPW) represent the hourly employees of the company.

United Road Services, Inc., headquartered in Albany, New York, is a leading national provider of a broad array of motor vehicle transport, towing, and recovery services. United Road conducts operations through a network of 40 divisions located in 20 states.

Genesis Worldwide II, Inc. (GII), headquartered in Callery, Pennsylvania, was the result of a consolidation of two distressed firms. GII engineers and manufactures high quality metal coil processing and roll coating, and electrostatic oiling equipment in the U.S. The hourly employees at Genesis II are represented by the United Steelworkers (USW) and the International Association of Machinists and Aerospace Workers (IAMAW). KPS recently successfully exited GII.

Landmark GCP

Sign Company is an upscale fabricator/installer of commercial signage, including interactive casino signs. It employs 56 union members, including sheet metal workers and electrical workers. The company provides design development, engineering and technical support, prototyping, permit research, manufacturing, installation, and maintenance.

Specialty Millwork Firm is a leading manufacturer of synthetic and wood specialty millwork, consisting primarily of exterior and interior columns, as well as exterior posts and rails for porch and deck applications. The firm participates in two areas of the U.S. building products industry: the column segment and the synthetic lumber market. Most of the 750 workers at the main plant in the South are minority workers.

Solidarity Fund QFL

FINTAXI: The Solidarity Fund QFL invested $50 million (Canadian) in FINTAXI s.e.c. The goals of the innovative new corporation were to offer taxi drivers a viable alternative to the financing currently available from existing lending institutions, to better structure the financing of taxi licenses, and to promote greater transparency by eventually setting up a license-trading entity that would make transaction values public. Michel Arsenault, former Quebec Director of the United Steelworkers and now president of the Quebec Federation of Labour, added that the creation of FINTAXI addresses one of the main concerns identified by taxi drivers from the moment the union became involved in with the industry. "This service," he said, "will be offered to taxi drivers, with whom we have enjoyed a permanent relationship for nearly 15 years. This is one of the services they need, and we plan on offering others."

LPB Industries: The Solidarity Fund joined with Investissement Québec and invested C$4.8 million in LPB Industries, a producer of wood poles and partner of the Fund since 1999. This financing will allow LPB Industries to acquire IPB International, a company also operating in the wood preservation industry. Founded in 1974, LPB Industries converts Red and

Jack Pine into utility poles. The Solidarity Fund became a partner in 1999 to allow management to purchase the company from Bell Canada. LPB was the first producer in North America to obtain ISO 9002 certification and enjoys an enviable reputation thanks to the quality of its products and services. The company has some 40 employees with 25 unionized workers; IPB International employs some 90 persons, 53 of whom are unionized. LPB's president reported that "This transaction...seeks to increase our exports, enhance our penetration of the Canadian market, develop recycled products from recuperated wood poles, expand our wood treatment services to third parties and reduce our costs."

Van Houtte, Inc., is an integrated gourmet coffee distributor in North America. The Company was founded in 1919 in Montreal and now operates manufacturing and marketing and coffee services divisions with more than 1,900 employees in Canada and the U.S., the majority in Quebec. VH claims it operates the largest coffee services network in North America. Through its subsidiary, VKI Technologies Inc. it also designs, manufactures, and markets hopper-based, single-cup coffeemakers. The Solidarity Fund QFL made a $75 million (Canadian) investment in the company as a minority shareholder in the firm, helping keep its headquarters in Montreal.

Les Meubles Poitras, Inc., is a Québec manufacturer of contemporary ash furniture for the residential market. The Solidarity Fund invested C$2 million in the company, enabling it to finance part of its growth by increasing sales over the next two years. Gaétan Morin, Executive Vice-President, Investments, Solidarity Fund, noted that, while furniture manufacturers face many challenges, Les Meubles Poitras Inc. has enjoyed success over the years thanks to its quality products, niche positioning, and competitive pricing.

Corporation Développement Knowlton, Inc.: In an unusually large investment partnership, the Solidarity Fund, Desjardins Capital Régional et Coopératif, and Fondaction, the CSN's development fund for cooperation and employment, made investments of $23.2 million, $14.5 million and $8.6 million in CDK in early 2007. The funds were used to finance a merger between LEK Inc., owned by Corporation Développement Knowlton, and

Tri-Tech Laboratories Inc., both manufacturers of personal care products for the North-American market. Under the merger, a new company will be formed comprising Tri-Tech's factory in Lynchburg, Virginia, and LEK's two factories in Knowlton and Toronto. The transaction will increase employment to 1,300, including more than 700 jobs in Québec.

Mecachrome International, Inc., is a group of companies specialized in the machining and assembly of parts for the aeronautics and automobile industries. In January 2007, the Solidarity Fund QFL announced a $35 million investment to promote faster growth for the company in Québec and, at the same time, develop the company's position as an integrator in the North American aerospace industry. The Fund pointed out that the Québec aerospace industry needs integrators like Mecachrome if it is to meet the needs of large OEMs, which require that their suppliers play a significant role in the financing of new aircraft construction (Solidarity has invested a total of $50 million in Mecachrome since 2005). The firm could potentially help some 240 SMEs, the industrial fibre of the Québec aerospace industry. Mecachrome has already created 147 jobs in Québec and expects to create another 100 in the next year. The USW represents the workers.

The Yucaipa Companies

AmeriCold Logistics, based in Atlanta, Georgia, handles more than 60 billion pounds of product annually. AmeriCold is the largest provider of temperature-controlled food distribution services in the United States. It has more than 100 facilities in 38 states and employs over 6,000 people. The company has a significant union presence, with bargaining units represented by the United Food and Commercial Workers, Teamsters, and Operating Engineers, among others.

Wild Oats Markets, Inc., is the second largest chain of natural and organic food markets in the U.S., with more than 100 stores across the U.S. and Canada. Wild Oats has a commitment to provide customers with the best selection of natural foods and health care products in a friendly, informative setting. Wild Oats supports the local economy as much as possible by offering locally produced and manufactured products including organic and locally grown produce.

TDS Logistics provides logistics services to the automotive industry. This involves a wide variety of services including, but not limited to, assembly of vehicle modules, supply chain management, parts distribution, and export packaging. The majority of the company's facilities are located in the U.S. and Canada and virtually all of the hourly employees are covered by union contracts. The company recently opened a new facility in Detroit, Michigan, where they expect to employ as many as 1,100 people. Yucaipa made a control investment of $85 million.

Real Estate Funds

AFL-CIO Investment Trusts

West Village Houses, New York, NY: In 2002, tenants of West Village Houses in Manhattan were offered the opportunity to convert their 420-unit rental complex into a tenant-owned cooperative that would preserve affordability and allow residents to stay in their homes. The AFL-CIO Housing Investment Trust stepped in with $40 million in financing for the acquisition and restructuring of the property. HIT staff met regularly with the tenants' association to address their questions about the conversion and also arranged for homebuyer education through the HIT HOME single-family mortgage program. As a result, the complex was successfully converted, and tenants were able to achieve homeownership in Manhattan at below-market costs. Those who preferred not to buy were able to continue renting at rates well below market. The project is part of the HIT's New York City Community Investment Initiative, launched in 2002 and designed to expand housing opportunities for the City's working families. The HIT has since invested nearly $300 million in multifamily housing in New York City, leveraging almost $1 billion in financing and creating or preserving over 13,000 housing units—more than 90% of which are affordable for low- and moderate-income families.

The New York initiative is also responsible for creating hundreds of union construction jobs.

Rollins Square, Boston, MA: To support the City of Boston's urban redevelopment plans for the diverse but deteriorating South End neighborhood while simultaneously addressing the affordable housing needs of local residents, the AFL-CIO Housing Investment Trust was instrumental in putting together financing for the development of Rollins Square—a $43.9 million, 184-unit, mixed-income condominium and rental apartment complex that includes 37 low-income tenants. In 2002, the HIT provided $27 million in construction financing and later invested $2.9 million. Fifteen of the low-income units were rented to formerly homeless individuals. With the HIT's requirement for all-union construction, the project created 194 family-supporting union jobs. Designed to blend with the historic character of the surrounding neighborhood, Rollins Square has been recognized nationally as a model for mixed-income development and for socially responsible urban housing.

Heinz Lofts, Pittsburgh, PA: In 2003, the HIT provided $35 million in financing for the substantial rehabilitation of a Heinz manufacturing plant in Pittsburgh. The plant was converted into 267 rental units, 20 percent of which are reserved for lower-income residents. The rehabilitation of the $67.8 million project created 300 union jobs. Projects such as Heinz Lofts illustrate how former industrial sites can be transformed into valuable housing resources that allow residents to live closer to work, transportation, and recreational and cultural activities.

Umoja Apartments: Investing in housing for the homeless is one of the ways that the AFL-CIO Housing Investment Trust is helping those who desperately need shelter. Projects like the Umoja Apartments in South Central Los Angeles help communities provide supportive services that make a measurable difference in residents' quality of life. In the wake of the 1992 civil disturbances in that impoverished Los Angeles neighborhood, the HIT worked with non-profit housing developers to provide financing for Umoja, an innovative, service-enriched affordable housing development that serves tenants who were previously homeless, at-risk, or living in substandard or overcrowded housing. The building consists of 30 one-, two-, three-, and four-bedroom units, and residents are offered a range of on-site supportive services. The HIT financed over $1 million in permanent loans toward the project's total development cost of $4,760,884. The City of Los Angeles Housing Department and Fannie Mae provided other permanent financing for the project. Construction of Umoja created more than two-dozen full-time equivalent union jobs.

North Town Village: The AFL-CIO Housing Investment Trust helps cities such as Chicago replace run-down and outmoded public housing projects with new, revitalized developments under HUD's HOPE VI program. North Town Village is one such project, designed as part of the City of Chicago's Near North Redevelopment Initiative whose goal was to bring new life to a neighborhood dominated by the Chicago Housing Authority's Cabrini-Green public housing project. The new development, close to the Cabrini-Green tract, includes attractive low-rise rental apartment buildings for mixed-income families, together with market rate homes for purchase, all designed to create a vibrant new community. The HIT helped finance a portion of North Town Village that consists of 116 newly constructed units in five residential buildings. The $23.2 million project created 78 affordable rental units and 38 market rate units, ranging in size from one- to four-bedrooms. One third of the units are set aside for public housing residents, primarily former Cabrini-Green residents. Continuing a successful relationship with the Illinois Housing Development Authority, the HIT purchased a Participation Certificate in the amount of $2.6 million under the FHA Risk Sharing Program for this project. Because of its competitive interest rates and flexible loan terms, the HIT participated in both the construction and permanent financing. North Town Village supports the Chicago Housing Authority's plan to replace high density, high-rise public housing projects with an economically integrated community of attractive low-rise buildings and green spaces. The construction work generated approximately 100 jobs for union members.

Columbus Tower, Jersey City, NJ: With investments of more than $600 million in northern New Jersey, the HIT is helping bring new life to the New Jersey waterfront district, a decaying industrial area that was experiencing economic decline and an exodus of jobs and residents. Now a vigorous renewal is underway, bringing development, commerce, jobs, and housing to waterfront communities. The HIT has played an important role in this renewal, having invested in 13 multifamily projects representing over 3,600 units of housing. The HIT's most recent project is $75 million in financing for the $92 million Columbus Tower apartment building in downtown Jersey City not far from the waterfront. The 392-unit building offers working families housing opportunities conveniently adjacent to public transportation facilities such as on-site access to the new Grove Street PATH train station. In addition, work on this project is creating over 400 union jobs.

Amalgamated Bank, LongView ULTRA

Intercontinental Hotel, Rosemont, Illinois: ULTRA Fund is the lead construction lender in a loan facility that financed the acquisition of the property and construction of a 15-story hotel containing 571 guest rooms, a 780-space parking garage, 35,000 square feet of meeting and banquet space, indoor pool, fitness center, and business center on approximately four acres of land located at the southwest corner of River Road and Berwyn Avenue in Rosemont, Illinois. Total project costs are over $150 million. The project is being built with 100% union labor and the hotel operator signed a neutrality/card check agreement for the hotel and restaurant workers.

Albuquerque Studios, Albuquerque New Mexico: ULTRA Fund financed the construction of a full service motion picture & television production facility that includes eight stages of 168,000 square feet, production offices of 164,000 square feet, and support/mill space of 150,000 square feet. The Albuquerque Studios is a state-of-the-art digitally enabled facility that supports the production of feature films, commercials, television and cable series, and industrials. The studio will provide large soundstages, office space, warehouse and set construction areas, training facilities for local skill development and enhancement, screening rooms, commissary and production services in a campus like setting. This $74 million facility was built using 100% union labor creating over 300,000 worker hours for a union-friendly industry whose workers are organized by AFTRA, IATSE, and SAG to name a few.

Avenue North, Philadelphia Pennsylvania: ULTRA Fund financed the construction of a 12 story, 200 quad unit residential development adjacent to Temple University. The facility houses up to 1,200 students and includes 10,000 square feet of ground floor commercial space. This $64 million project created more than 265,000 hours of union labor. Located at 1600 North Broad Street on property assembled by the Philadelphia Redevelopment Authority, this project has contributed greatly to the revitalization of the neighborhood.

Gallery Place, Washington, DC: ULTRA Fund was the co-lender with Union Labor Life's J for Jobs on the construction loan and the AFL-CIO BIT was an equity investor for this 11-story, one million square foot project containing four major components, including (1) an office component, (2) a Retail/Food Service/General component, (3) a Multifamily component, and (4) a Parking Garage. The 10-story office area is 181,512 square feet. The Retail/Food Service/General component encompasses over 250,000-sq. ft. on three levels, including one below grade, as well as a 65,198 square foot, 12-screen theater and more than 192,000 square feet of upscale destination retail and restaurant space. The upper nine floors contain upscale residential condominiums arranged in a single loaded corridor configuration covering 219,000 square feet. An underground parking garage with 685 spaces is situated on five levels below grade covering 308,000 square feet. Gallery Place received Tax Increment Financing (TIF) from the District of Columbia for $60 million. Located in the Penn Quarter neighborhood at 7th and H Streets, NW, Gallery Place and the adjacent Verizon Center have been the catalysts to the revival of this neighborhood that incorporates D.C.'s own Chinatown. A project labor agreement was employed to ensure the use of union labor creating 765,000 worker hours and to incorporate local minority contractors. Today this project is valued at over $200 million.

Carriage City, Rahway New Jersey: ULTRA Fund provided the $55.2 million construction loan for a 15-story, 360,000 square foot mixed-use condominiums with residential, hotel, and retail components at 80 E. Milton Avenue in Rahway New Jersey. Rahway is a designated New Jersey Transit Village with direct train access to Manhattan. In addition to creating more than 300,000 union labor hours, a neutrality agreement was executed in connection with the hotel portion of the project, which will be an Indigo Hotel.

MEPT Fund

Brewery Block 2, Portland, OR: Brewery Block is a five-block, mixed-use, reconstruction project located in the Pearl District of Portland, Oregon. The project was originally constructed in 1908 as a brewhouse for Bleitz-Weinhard. In 2002, MEPT completed development of Brewery Block 2, one component of the larger Brewery Block development, and built a ten-story, Class A office tower and renovated two historic structures from the original 1908 brewery. In total, Brewery Block 2 contains a total of 219,965 square feet comprised of office space, a restaurant, retail space, and parking. The project is used as the LEED-CS case study by the US Green Building Council. About 90% of waste was recycled during demolition and new construction. It uses nearly 30% less energy than state code with specified resource-efficient building materials. Brewery Block 2 utilized a number of high efficiency features in the building design including high efficiency HVAC, occupancy sensors in common areas, a highly efficient district chilled water plant, operable windows in office towers, and high efficiency glazing, lighting systems, and controls. In addition, over 680,000 job hours were created for building trades members.

Patriots Plaza I, II, and III, Washington, DC: The Patriots Plaza office complex is comprised of three high-rise office towers in downtown Washington, D.C. The project was designed to incorporate government facility security measures required in the post-September 11 environment, including enhanced setbacks, progressive collapse avoidance, blast resistant windows, and reinforced structural elements. Phase I, completed in 2005, houses a 12-story, Class A office building, totaling 280,000 square feet. Upon completion and lease-up of Phase I, MEPT began development of two more buildings, Phases II and III, totaling 701,589 square feet. Patriots II will be a 12-story, 321,502-square-foot office building, while Patriots III will be a 380,087 square foot office building. Phase II and III are also being designed to incorporate enhanced security measures while also being built to LEED-CS Silver Design standards. Phase I of the project created over 1.6 million job hours, and it is estimated that more than 2.6 million job hours will be created for building trades members on Phases II and III.

Gates Plaza, Denver, CO: Gates Plaza is part of a 65-acre Planned Unit Development (PUD) in the Central Platte Valley in Denver. The PUD is a mixed-use area which incorporates office, retail, and multi-family housing into a pedestrian-friendly area in the central business district of lower downtown Denver, known as "LoDo." The site has direct access to the "16th Street Mall," as well as easy access to Denver's intermodal transportation facility. Gates Plaza, completed in 2003, is a 285,197 square foot, ten-story, Class A office building. Gates Plaza was the first asset in MEPT's portfolio to receive the Energy Star rating. It is also expected to earn LEED-Certification in 2008. When it was completed, Gates Plaza obtained rents higher than most buildings in the central business district in Denver. More than 950,000 job hours were created for building trades members.

Tanasbourne I, Hillsboro, OR: Tanasbourne I and II are comprised of 183,662 square feet of flex and office space in Hillsboro, Oregon. Tanasbourne I contains 132,606 square feet in two single-story, flex/office buildings that were built in 1986 and one two-story office building that was built in 1995. The two-story office building in Tanasbourne I was one of the first "green" buildings in the nation, built before the creation of LEED-Certification. It serves as the headquarters for the eco-friendly company, Norm Thompson Outfitters. During the construction process, recycled materials and sustainable harvested wood were used. The design elements used in the building include having a southern facing exposure, high ceilings, and reflective surfaces and lighting that maximize solar energy available for heat and daylight, while enhancing setting and view and reducing energy demand. For internal features, the building utilizes fluorescent bulbs, computer-controlled dimmable ballasts to adjust lights in response to daylight levels, and "light sweeps" that turn off all lights at night. Utility bills at the site have been reduced by 40% and the property has received tax credits from the state for green building. Tanasbourne I achieved the Business for an Environmentally Sustainable Tomorrow (BEST) Innovation Award in 1997 for exceptional environmental sustainability and an Earth Smart™ recognition from the Pacific Gas and Electric regional utility corporation. Tanasbourne I created more than 100,000 job hours for building trades members.

1717 Rhode Island Avenue, Washington, DC: 1717 Rhode Island Avenue is a historical rehabilitation development in the central business district in Northwest Washington, D.C. The original structure contained four historic townhouses from the 1800s with frontage on Rhode Island Avenue. The townhouses had been vacant for many years and were in need of significant renovation to become viable space within the surrounding business district. Through a partnership with the neighboring St. Matthew's Cathedral, MEPT redesigned the four structures and added a 157,094 square foot, ten-story, Class A office building. The project was designed to complement the architecture of the historic buildings and the landmark Cathedral and integrated the original facade of the townhouses with the new office structure behind them. Over 1.6 million job hours were created for building trade members in the area.

The BUILD Funds

Android: The Android/GM Facility, located in Flint, Michigan, is a 407,500 square foot industrial building that was sold for $21,500,000 in June 2002. BUILD invested $5,200,000 and received $8,000,000 from the sale. The project produced a 55.73% return in just one year for the fund and created approximately $4.8 million in wages and fringe benefits.

Wabash Landing: A 104-room Hilton Garden Inn in West Lafayette, Indiana, located in the new retail/entertainment development known as Wabash Landing. BUILD invested $2,650,000 in December of 2001 and the asset has since been refinanced and BUILD has been paid down by $1,609,806. The hotel has seen strong appreciation, performs above expectations, and has created approximately $2.8 million in wages and fringe benefits.

Cornerhouse Lofts is a 42-unit high-rise student apartment building located in Ann Arbor, Michigan. The BUILD Fund invested $2,525,000 in February of 2002. Since then BUILD has received excess senior debt refinancing proceeds and excess cash flow distributions. BUILD's equity investment has been reduced to $635,707. It is estimated that the original investment created around $2.9 million in wages and fringe benefits.

Lordstown is a 70,000 square-foot, build-to-suit industrial facility for AutoModular Inc., a tier one supplier to GM, for which the BUILD Fund provided a $4,100,000 construction loan facility during July of 2004. Since then the loan has been converted to a participating mortgage where BUILD receives 50% of excess cash flows. The property is performing as projected and is estimated to have created approximately $1.2 million in wages and fringe benefits for union workers.

Perrysburg Plaza is a retail project located in Perrysburg, Ohio. The BUILD Fund originally invested $2,695,000 in December of 2002 into Phase I, a 8,500-square-foot commercial site. The project is currently undergoing Phase II construction, which will have approximately 150,000 square feet of retail space. The BUILD Fund has a $783,000 equity investment in Perrysburg Plaza as of May 2007. This project has created over $6 million in wages and fringe benefits for union workers.

The ERECT Fund

Bridgeside Point: In April 2000, the ERECT Funds made a $4,655,000 equity investment in Bridgeside Point, a 153,110-square-foot office building in the

Pittsburgh Technology Center, formerly an industrial site, approximately two and one half miles east of the Pittsburgh central business district. Total project costs were $21,405,750. Because of ERECT's investment, the project created an estimated 307,192 job hours and $8,601,375 in wages and benefits for union construction workers. In addition, Bridgeside Point met the demand for biotech research space and brought new economic life to a former steel mill site. The ERECT Fund teamed with the Ferchill Group, the general partner, to supply the needed equity. The building was sold in November 2005.

Lawrenceville Shopping Center: In 1998, the ERECT Funds made a $3,275,000 first mortgage loan for the development of the Lawrenceville Shopping Center. Lawrenceville, approximately 5 miles from the City of Pittsburgh central business district, is an urban neighborhood characterized by mill-style industrial buildings and commercial properties that is currently experiencing revitalization. The shopping center met the demand for convenient retail in the neighborhood and included a much-needed supermarket. The project created 78,800 job hours and $2,125,000 in wages and benefits for building trades union members.

The RAND Building: In April 2004, the ERECT Fund provided a $4,300,000 equity contribution for the construction of an 113,900-square-foot, five-story office building in the Oakland district of Pittsburgh, Pennsylvania. The ERECT Fund partnered with the Elmhurst Group to help develop this building that is now the Pittsburgh home of the RAND Corporation. The RAND Corporation, a global think tank, is considered a great asset to the city, bringing the best and brightest young minds as well as a global corporate presence to the region. The project created an estimated 127,874 job hours and $7,928,202 in wages and benefits to the union building trades.

Stone Quarry Commons: In 2004 and 2005, the ERECT Funds made a series of loans for the site acquisition and development of 76 acres that now encompasses a Target, Best Buy, Kohl's, Aldi's, Marshalls, Ross Dress for Less, and other retailers in Center Township, Beaver County. In all, ERECT loans totaled $12.3 million of total project costs amounting to $21.3 million. The construction created an estimated 117,846 job hours and $7,306,459 in wages and benefits for the local building trades. The project helped Beaver County obtain some major big-box retailers that had previously been absent from the region.

Airside Business Park: In June 1999, the ERECT Fund began to provide equity for the construction of a five-building office and flex-space park adjacent to Pittsburgh International Airport developed by The Elmhurst Group. Airside Business Park was one of the first projects in the Airport Corridor that Allegheny County is seeking to re-develop. Currently, numerous other developments such as the Imperial Business Park and Clinton Industrial Park are following the lead of the Airside Business Park, turning once vacant land surrounding the Pittsburgh International Airport into a powerful office and industrial market. An estimated 525,584 job hours and $16,378,776 in wages and benefits have been created for union building trades as a result of the project. The project is currently 90% leased. The fifth and final building is currently under construction.

ULLICO, Inc: J for Jobs

Gramercy Green Condominiums, New York, NY: J for Jobs approved a $90.5 million dollar participation in a PB Capital-led $181 million facility for the construction of a 21-story, 206,575-square-foot luxury condominium building in the Gramercy Park section of Manhattan, which also will contain 19,083 square feet of leasable space. Gramercy Park is an attractive and desirable residential neighborhood situated along the edge of the Midtown Business District.

Waterfront Square Condominiums, Phase II, Philadelphia, PA: J for Jobs approved up to a $107.5 million participation in a ULLICO led $215 million facility for the construction of the next two towers that will contain a total of 421 units and 9,953 square feet of retail space. The property is located on the Delaware Riverfront, immediately northeast of Center City in the section known as Northern Liberties. The site provides dramatic views of the Delaware River and Center City and is located within minutes of Philadelphia's retail district, business district, airport, and sports complexes. ULLICO was previously repaid on a $95 million construction loan for the first two towers that contain 308 units.

The Residences at MGM Grand-Tower III, Las Vegas, NV: J for Jobs approved up to a $40 million participation in a Bank of America-led $245.5 million facility for the construction of a 38-story third tower at the MGM Grand. The 576 units are being marketed as condominiums, with owners having the option to place their units in the MGM Grand rental program. The site is located on the former site of the MGM Grand Theme Park, and Tower C represents the third tower of a multiphase, high-rise condominium/hotel development. Upon completion of this multiphase development plan, The Residences at MGM Grand will consist of three towers totaling in excess of 1,700 condominium/hotel units.

Renaissance Plaza, Phase II, White Plains, NY: J for Jobs approved a $41,666,667 participation in a $125 million CIBC-led facility for the construction of a 40-story, 206-unit residential rental building with 40,000 square feet of office space, 3,000 square feet of retail space, and a four-level sub-grade parking garage with 500 spaces. Renaissance Square is a 1.1 million square feet, two-phased, mixed-use project located in White Plains, New York.

184 Kent, Brooklyn NY: J for Jobs approved up to $68,265,000 participation in a $205,000,000 facility for the redevelopment of an existing building on the East River in North Williamsburg Brooklyn. The other participating lenders are Helaba Bank and PB Capital. The building will contain approximately 12,500 square feet of ground floor retail space and 394,654 net saleable square feet of condominium space. Three hundred parking spaces will also be provided on the ground floor. The Developer plans to redevelop the building in a fashion that simultaneously incorporates the attributes of the existing historic structure with a contemporary, distinctive rooftop addition.

APPENDIX 2

Glossary*

Alternative investment is a class of investments that excludes publicly traded stocks and bonds, and also cash. Alternative investments can include private equity, venture capital, real estate, and hedge funds. Pension plans, college endowments, and large institutional investors invest in this class usually to diversify their portfolios.

Asset allocation is a strategy used by investors, as part of financial planning, to diversify investments across a spectrum of asset classes, such as stocks, bonds, cash, etc., in order to ensure a broad range of risk exposure.

Asset managing refers to exercising the ownership rights and responsibilities that shareholders acquire along a given regulatory framework. There is a range of practices available to shareholders to assert their influence, including proxy voting and shareholder engagement.

Asset screening describes the application of certain "screens" to the investment process. For example, negative screens could be applied to geographic areas. Divestment during apartheid South Africa is an example of this strategy, as are current investor campaigns against investments in Burma and Sudan. Negative screens could also apply to a product type, such as tobacco and alcohol. Positive screens could include investing where there is a strong record of labor relations or environmental policy.

---

* Thanks to Amanda Procter, Project Officer, Global Union Committee on Workers' Capital (CWC), for help in drafting most of this glossary.

Asset targeting refers to the active targeting of investments, utilizing responsible investment principles and ETI methodologies.

Buyout funds specialize in acquiring a large or controlling stake in more companies, either mature or underperforming ones.

Capital gap is the result of inefficiencies in the financial markets where a potentially profitable undertaking is unable to secure affordable financing. This situation is seen as an information asymmetry that causes uncertainty among investors. Holders of capital overlook opportunities or demand a higher risk premium to offset the perceived uncertainty of the investment. Small firms, minority-owned or employee-owned companies, renewable and alternative energy start-ups, businesses from certain geographic locales, or non-enterprise investments like affordable housing developments are examples of sectors that commonly face the capital gap problem.

Collateral Benefit is the benefit that accrues when an investment generates both a market-based rate of return and a positive impact on one or more of the firm's stakeholders.

Economically-Targeted Investments (ETIs) are investments that seek competitive rates of return but that also provide specific collateral benefits to communities and to society in general.

Empowerment transactions are transition initiatives to share the ownership of in-country corporations with historically disadvantaged citizens.

Fixed-income funds are investments that provide a regular, constant income stream.

Hedge fund is an unregulated private investment fund that can invest and trade, generally, in more risky positions in the market, including taking short, long, leveraged, and derivatives positions. Hedge funds are associated with higher management and performance fees.

Liquidity trap is a situation in which an investor is committed to funding certain alternative investments but lacks the cash flow from previous investments to readily do so.

LBO fund is a fund that purchases another company by using large amounts of borrowed money, or, in some cases, by collateralizing the assets of the firm being acquired.

Mortgage vehicle is a fund engaged in the business of originating and/or funding mortgages for residential or commercial property. A mortgage is a loan collateralized by property.

Pension fund is a type of retirement plan that is established by an employer and employees, often through collective bargaining, in which the employer makes contributions into a common pool for the purposes of providing stable income to individuals upon retirement.

Pooled funds are aggregated funds from many individual investors.

Private capital traditionally invests in existing companies seeking to expand or to add new products. Private capital is generally employed as sizable privately placed debt and equity investments in SMEs in many industries, including manufacturing, transportation, distribution, communications, and technology.

Private equity is an asset class consisting of equity securities in operating companies that are not publicly traded on a stock exchange.

Private placement is a sale of stocks or bonds directly to an investor and not the general public.

Property development is financing for the construction of new buildings and property.

Property re-development is financing for improvements, upgrades, and expansions to existing real-estate stock.

Senior term debt is the second most common form of financing for a small or mid-sized company. Senior term debt is typically lent against the collateral value of property, plant, and equipment. Senior term debt comes in many varieties, and there are many sources of this type of financing. It is typically the second most expensive form of financing.

Subordinated debt financing typically includes both debt and equity. Subordinated debt is substantially riskier than senior debt since the lender generally has less right over collateral and cash flow than the senior lender. As a result, subordinated debt is more expensive financing than either revolving lines of credit or term debt. Lenders usually require equity, generally in the form of warrants, to augment what they earn in interest income.

Special situations funds are a subset of buyout and turnaround funds that target financially distressed firms, even those in bankruptcy.

Venture capital is capital that is made available to companies whose products or projects are still in development and are often made in the fields of technology, renewable energy. and bio-science, among others.

Methodology

General Questions: Heinz-sponsored Survey of Responsible Funds

We gleaned basic information from site visits, direct interviews, and documents provided by the funds, as well as other research. This information included:

1. Name of fund and date of formation;
2. Capitalization level (and number of funds);
3. Contact information, including direct phone number, email address, and web pages.

The goals of each interview were to obtain the following information:

- Overview of fund and general sense of the identity of the investors;
- Summary of fund structure;
- Summary of the fund's capacity (professional staffing, investment process, etc.) and products;
- General sense of the portfolio and performance.

We also aimed to understand the particular point of view of the fund's principals and what they claimed to be their specific impact on the following:

- Labor impacts
- Environmental and community impacts
- Challenges faced
- Personal views on their funds and the field (and economy, etc.) as principals

Private Equity/VC-Related Questions

To achieve our goals we asked the following questions in more or less the same way:

- In general, what challenges are there in the private equity/ VC market, and what challenges are there in capitalizing an investment fund with union/public pensions?
- How do you decide what to invest in?
- How do you document the company's "responsible" aspects?
- How much does labor productivity matter in profitability calculations?

Re: specific investments:

- What is the strategic impact of the investment(s) in general?
- Are there investments in any companies/projects that are involved in any of these special categories: alternative energy or transportation, environmental technology, green buildings or products? (example: a steel firm that supplies windmill industry)
- How many new jobs were created because of the investment?
- How many workers would have been fired or laid off without the investments (this estimation will be self-reported)?
- Number of employees, percent unionized, any card-check agreements?
- Can you more fully describe the impact of this investment in terms of jobs or the environment?
- How do you calculate and incorporate positive collateral benefits?
- What benchmarks does the firm use in performing risk/return analysis on portfolio investments when compared to traditional?
- What kinds of company governance measures are being established, and do they make a difference to the performance of the firm?

- Are workers participating in ownership or in management decisions on the "shop-floor" of the firm?

Real Estate-Related Questions

In general, what challenges are there for the current real estate market and the real estate private equity market?

- What targeted investment screens do you use in choosing projects (union labor, green buildings, etc.)?
- Has the market valuation of green projects acknowledged any increased cost-benefit advantages to green construction?
- What are the barriers in terms of building with union labor or building green?
- What benchmarks does the firm use in performing risk/return analysis on portfolio investments when compared to traditional?
- What socially responsible screening tools does the investment firm utilize to decide whether to lend or take an equity stake in a project?
- What measurement devices, if any, does the investment fund use to determine whether the project manager they invested in has adopted socially responsible and/or high-performance standards?
- What measurement devices, if any, does the investment fund use to determine whether the project manager has achieved productivity improvements?

Index

ABOUT THE HEARTLAND NETWORK

The Heartland Labor/Capital Network has been exploring and promoting practical, jobs-oriented investment strategies since 1995. Heartland has encouraged responsible pension capital investments and helped bring attention to a broader universe of worker-friendly investment strategies, including private equity and real estate funds.

The Network was co-founded by the Steel Valley Authority (SVA) and the United Steelworkers, and was launched by a broad-based working group in the U.S. and Canada. In addition to two national conferences and several regional roundtables, the Network commissioned *Workers' Capital: The Power of Labor's Pensions*, published by Cornell University Press in 2001. The book received widespread notice in the U.S. and Canadian press, media, and blogosphere. With the help of the Heinz Endowments, a new "Heartland Center for Responsible Capital" is under development.

The Network has been operating a "capital strategies" website, www.heartlandnetwork.org, to monitor the economy and track developments in the alternative pension investment field.

To visit the SVA, see www.steelvalley.org.

ABOUT THE AUTHOR

 **Thomas Croft** is an international expert on innovative capital strategies and jobs-oriented economic revitalization policies. He serves as Director of the Heartland Network and Executive Director of the Steel Valley Authority and has authored or commissioned vital new perspectives on alternative pension investment strategies and a fair economy. Tom is currently happily engaged to Patricia Boswell and has two wonderful daughters, Kelsey and Taylor.

COSIMO is a specialty publisher of books and publications that inspire, inform, and engage readers. Our mission is to offer unique books to niche audiences around the world.

COSIMO BOOKS publishes books and publications for innovative authors, nonprofit organizations, and businesses.

COSIMO BOOKS specializes in bringing books back into print, publishing new books quickly and effectively, and making these publications available to readers around the world.

COSIMO CLASSICS offers a collection of distinctive titles by the great authors and thinkers throughout the ages.

At COSIMO CLASSICS timeless works find new life as affordable books, covering a variety of subjects including: Business, Economics, History, Personal Development, Philosophy, Religion & Spirituality, and much more!

COSIMO REPORTS publishes public reports that affect your world, from global trends to the economy, and from health to geopolitics.

FOR MORE INFORMATION CONTACT US AT
INFO@COSIMOBOOKS.COM

➢ if you are a book lover interested in our current catalog of books

➢ if you represent a bookstore, book club, or anyone else interested in special discounts for bulk purchases

➢ if you are an author who wants to get published

➢ if you represent an organization or business seeking to publish books and other publications for your members, donors, or customers.

COSIMO BOOKS ARE ALWAYS
AVAILABLE AT ONLINE BOOKSTORES

VISIT COSIMOBOOKS.COM

—— BE INSPIRED, BE INFORMED ——

Breinigsville, PA USA
25 October 2009

226416BV00001B/3/P